July 1997

IDEOLOGY AND ECONOMIC REFORM UNDER DENG XIAOPING 1978–1993

A PUBLICATION OF THE GRADUATE INSTITUTE
OF INTERNATIONAL STUDIES,
GENEVA

Also published in this series:

The United States and the Politicization of the World Bank
Bartram S. Brown

Trade Negotiations in the OECD
David J. Blair

World Financial Markets after 1992
Hans Genberg and Alexander K. Swoboda

Succession Between International Organisations
Patrick R. Myers

Ten Years of Turbulence: The Chinese Cultural Revolution
Barbara Barnouin and Yu Changgen

The Islamic Movement in Egypt: Perceptions of International Relations 1967–81
Walid M. Abdelnasser

Namibia and Southern Africa: Regional Dynamics of Decolonization 1945–90
Ronald Dreyer

The International Organization of Hunger
Peter Uvin

Citizenship East and West
Edited by André Liebich and Daniel Warner
with Jasna Dragović

Introduction to the Law of Treaties
Paul Reuter

The Imperiled Red Cross and the Palestine–Eretz-Yisrael Conflict 1945–1952
Dominique-D. Junod

IDEOLOGY AND ECONOMIC REFORM UNDER DENG XIAOPING 1978–1993

Wei-Wei Zhang

KEGAN PAUL INTERNATIONAL
London and New York

First published in 1996 by
Kegan Paul International

UK: P.O. Box 256, London WC1B 3SW, England
Tel: (0171) 580 5511 Fax: (0171) 436 0899
E-mail: books@keganpau.demon.co.uk
Internet: http://www.demon.co.uk/keganpaul/
USA: 562 West 113th Street, New York, NY 10025, USA
Tel: (212) 666 1000 Fax: (212) 316 3100

Distributed by
John Wiley & Sons Ltd
Southern Cross Trading Estate
1 Oldlands Way, Bognor Regis
West Sussex, PO22 9SW, England
Tel: (01234) 779 777 Fax: (01234) 820 250

Columbia University Press
562 West 113th Street
New York, NY 10025, USA
Tel: (212) 666 1000 Fax: (212) 316 3100

Phototypeset in Palatino
by Intype, London
Printed in Great Britain by TJ Press, Padstow, Cornwall

ISBN 0–7103–0526–5

British Library Cataloguing in Publication Data
Zhang, Wei-Wei
Ideology and Economic Reform Under Deng Xiaoping,
1978–93. – (Publication of the Graduate
Institute of International Studies,
Geneva)
I. Title II. Series
330.951059

ISBN 0–7103–0526–5

Library of Congress Cataloging-in-Publication Data
Zhang, Wei-Wei 1957–
Ideology and economic reform under Deng Xiaoping, 1978–1993 / Wei-Wei Zhang
250pp. 19cm. — (A publication of the Graduate Institute of
International Studies, Geneva)
Includes bibliographical references and index.
ISBN 0–7103–0526–5
1. Communism—China. 2. Ideology—China. 3. China—Economic
policy—1976– 4. China—Politics and government—1976– 5. Teng,
Hsiao-p' ing, 1904– I. Title. II. Series: Publications de
l'Institut universitaire de hautes études internationales, Genève.
HX418.5.Z48 1996
335.43'45 dc20

95–42692
CIP

To the memory of my mother,
Yi Zunwu,
and to my father,
Zhang Zijia

CONTENTS

ACKNOWLEDGEMENTS

I wish to express my special gratitude to the Graduate Institute of International Studies, University of Geneva, for its decision to publish the study and for its inspiring intellectual environment in which much research for this book has been carried out. My research has benefitted at various times from the seminars and lectures held at the Institute, especially those by Professors Antony Hopkins, Harish Kapur, Curt Gasteyger and Urs Luterbacher.

In preparing this book, I am particularly grateful to Professor Gilbert Etienne of the Institute, Professor Yves Chevrier, Co-Director of the *Centre de Recherches et de Documentation sur la Chine Contemporaine, Ecole des Hautes Etudes en Sciences Sociale*, Paris, and Dr. Peter Nolan, Fellow and Director of Studies in Economics, Jesus College, University of Cambridge for their scholarly advice and constant encouragement.

A special note of thanks goes to my colleagues at the Modern Asia Research Centre, Geneva, in particular, Dr. Philippe Régnier, Director of the Centre, and Mme. Mariejo Duc-Reynaert, who were always supportive of my research efforts.

I also wish to express my appreciation to Professor Robert Cassen and Dr. Graham Clarke of University of Oxford for inviting me to the International Development Centre, Oxford, as a Visiting Fellow in 1991 and engaging me in many of the issues of this study. This inspiring experience has sharpened a number of my arguments.

I am indebted to numerous Chinese scholars, especially, Mr. Wang Xiaoqiang of the Institute for Research on the Restructuring of the Economic System, Professor Wu Jinglian of the State Council, Professor Wang Huning of Fudan University, Dr. Hua

Sheng and Dr. Yang Mo of the Chinese Academy of Social Sciences, and Professor Xu Jingan of the Shenzhen Commission for Restructuring the Economic System, all of whom shared with me their perspectives on many of China's dramatic developments.

I also wish to thank many friends, in particular, Messrs. David Tsui, Li Huijun, Simon T. Liu, David T. Huang, Zhou Shaoping and Zhu Xiaohua, who have helped me in one way or another in the preparation of this book.

My gratitude also goes to the staff of the library of the Institute; the National Library of China, Beijing; the Bodleian Library, Oxford; and the SOAS Library, London; and the East Asian Library of Columbia University, New York, for their invaluable professional assistance.

The author alone, however, bears all responsibility for any shortcomings in this study or in its final conclusions.

Finally, for assistance in publishing this book, I wish to thank Dr. Vera Gowlland, Director of Publications of the Institute, and the Kegan Paul editors and staff, who were most helpful during every phase of publication.

Geneva, 30 January 1995

W.-W.Z.

INTRODUCTION

A Why ideology?

Is ideology still relevant in post-Mao China? Deng Xiaoping's wide-ranging economic reforms have led to declarations that ideology in China is merely a cynical sham or already dead, but a closer look at China seems to suggest a constant conflict of different ideologies associated with the profound transformation of the Chinese society since 1978. Controversy between competing ideologies has evolved to such a degree that Deng had to admit in 1992, after fourteen years of dramatic reforms, that the Left was still the major threat to his reform programme. Many analysts only focus on Deng's practical efforts to solve the problems confronting the Chinese economy. But Deng's pragmatism, which is itself being absorbed into the official ideology, is insufficient in explaining the complexity of China's economic reforms. While pragmatic effort is clearly important for Deng Xiaoping, exclusive attention to practical matters ignores some basic facts about the Chinese political system and its principal actors.

At least four reasons can be given to justify an in-depth discussion on ideology and reform. First, China's top-level decision-makers are by upbringing and training ideological in one way or another, and their ideological orientations do influence their policy preferences. To many individual leaders, ideology is a personal commitment and an important source of their perception of reality. Their experience in the Chinese revolution has cultivated in them a keen sense of a 'correct' or an 'erroneous' path for the Party and China. For instance, Chen

Yun has been a persistent advocate of a moderate Leninist approach to China's economic problems.

Second, there is a well-established institutional commitment to ideology expressed most notably in the form of the Party. Even the most ardent reformer in China does not try to abandon the Party in carrying out the reforms. On the contrary, Chinese reformers and conservatives alike would like to make the Party a leading force in the process of social and economic change. Consequently, ideology has become an important vehicle for communicating regime values to the Party rank and file and to the whole population.

Third, while virtually all political powers involve purpose, strategy, assessment, communication and justification based on certain values, implicit or overt, the Chinese leaders openly declare their normative goals. In this sense, China is largely conditioned by its 'ideological' political system in which all policies require an ideological discourse as justification. For instance, to build consensus and demonstrate the feasibility of a particular policy option, a given leader has to present such policy agenda in a common language and in an acceptable theoretical framework in order to achieve a leadership consensus and communicate it to the Party rank and file.

Fourth, the Chinese traditional political culture strongly favours claims to moral superiority. The legitimacy of the government never solely relies on practical accomplishments but also draws on ethical and moral power. The political elite know well the importance of reinforcing their legitimacy by asserting moral authority. Lucian Pye has described such a cultural commitment to ideology: 'the denial of moral constraints on getting the job done is, of course, the hallmark of pragmatism in all cultures' . . . but Chinese pragmatists are subject to a major constraint because of 'the traditional Chinese imperative that power should always be cloaked in moral or ethical rationalizations.'[1] Chinese reformers might wish to discard many of the orthodox tenets and implement the reform programme, but knowing that the risks for abandoning official conventions are too great, they tend to adopt ideological renovations within a Marxist framework as shown in Zhao Ziyang's 'primary stage of socialism.'

[1]Lucian Pye, 'On Chinese Pragmatism,' *China Quarterly*, No. 106, June 1986, p. 230.

China's economic reform is a complicated political process. An examination of ideological trends and their relationship with economic reform can serve as an important barometer of the policy changes in economic reforms and provide insight into the evolution of post-Mao economic policies and the nature of Chinese politics in general. In fact, general ideological statements are frequently the point of departure for more specific economic strategies and tactics. Stuart Schram has rightly stated:

> the ideological sound and fury of the 1960s and early 1970s (in China) . . . had very little to do with the real problems facing Chinese society, or reflected them in such phantasmagoric fashion that what passed for theory could contribute little to the understanding, or to the effective transformation of reality, . . . (while) the theoretical formulations put forward in China in recent years do bear significant relations to reality.'[2]

This study is therefore an attempt to explore the interactions between major ideological currents and economic reforms. I have three groups of questions in mind: First, what have been the major ideological trends since 1978 and why? In exploring these questions, I shall give special attention to the discursive evolution of Deng Xiaoping's 'socialism with Chinese characteristics,' which is the philosophy of China's economic reform, by tracing and analyzing several persistent themes of Deng's doctrine. Second, how have these ideological trends influenced China's economic reforms and why? My attempt is to study how ideology becomes operative to induce policy changes and how it constrains policy options as well as what tactics have been employed by political actors in the use of ideology for setting policy-agenda over the past 15 years. And third, what conclusions could be reached on Deng's doctrine and on the role of ideology in economic reforms?

My main arguments are as follows:

First, ideological controversy and the political use of ideology to influence decision making by the political elite of various ideological orientations are important features of China's economic reform. Competing ideologies generally operate either as

[2]Stuart R. Schram, *Ideology and Policy in China since the Third Plenum, 1987–1984*, London, Research Notes and Studies, No. 6, School of Oriental and African Studies, University of London, 1984, p. 1.

a stimulus to reforms or as a constraint on them and have thus affected the pace, scope, content and nature of China's economic reforms.

Second, there has been a dynamic process of discursive interactions between Chinese intellectuals and political leaders over the past 15 years of economic reform. While the political leaders are engaged in their efforts for doctrinal renovation or continuity, Chinese intellectuals have endeavoured to interpret and transcend the official discourse in order to reflect their own beliefs and influence policy options.

Third, drawing on various ideological sources and reform experience, Chinese reformers led by Deng have attempted to gradually transform the orthodox doctrine into a more elastic and pro-business ideology which, despite lack of an elaborate intellectual framework, still retains some essential socialist values and has tremendous implications on reform policies. Deng's 'socialism with Chinese characteristics' symbolizes such conscious efforts for doctrinal renovations through which initially partial, unsystematic ideas are gradually elaborated, modified and codified into a more formalized doctrine.

B The concept of ideology

It is hardly adequate to find a single and all-inclusive definition of ideology. One survey asserts that there are at least 27 elements in the concept of ideology.[3] Ideology has been defined as 'ideas which help to legitimate a dominant political power';[4] 'the link between theory and action';[5] and 'sets of ideas by which men posit, explain and justify ends and means of organized action.'[6] Schurmann, writing on China, defines ideology as 'a manner of thinking characteristic of an organization . . . a systematic set of ideas with action consequences serving the purpose of creating and using organization.'[7] All these interpretations are meaningful in their proper contexts, but any attempt to reduce

[3]Malcolm B. Hamilton, 'The Elements of the Concept of Ideology,' *Political Studies*, Volume 35, No. 1, March 1987, p. 18.
[4]Quoted in Terry Eagleton, *Ideology – an Introduction*, London, VERSO, 1991 p. 1.
[5]Zbigniev Brzezinski, *Ideology and Power in Soviet Politics*, Westport, Conn., Greenwood Press, 1976, p. 98.
[6]Martin Seliger, *Ideology and Politics*, New York, the Free Press, 1976, p. 14.
[7]Franz Schurmann, *Ideology and Organization in Communist China*, Berkeley, University of California Press, 1966, p. 18.

them into a single meaning perhaps risks undermining the rich discursive diversity and potency of the concept.

In this study the following is suggested as a working definition of ideology: It is essentially a set of ideas with a discursive framework which guides and/or justifies policies and actions, derived from certain values and doctrinal assumptions about the nature and dynamics of history. The study will focus on a wide range of doctrinal ideas employed by China's post-Mao political and intellectual elite[8] to guide or justify policy alternatives. In this context, ideology covers both relatively more cohesive values which have shaped the thinking of some of political elites and less coherent ideas which do not possess an elaborate intellectual structure but, nonetheless, represent value-oriented theoretical justifications.

Communist ideology is frequently classified by political scientists into two ideal types: Seliger's 'fundamental' and 'operative' ideology,[9] Moore's 'ideology of ends' and 'ideology of means'[10] and Schurmann's 'pure' and 'practical' ideology.[11] While at a fundamental level it refers to the body of theories considered as 'universal truth,' such as the end-goal of communism, class and class struggle, democratic centralism and the historical mission of the proletariat, at an operative level it designates sets of political ideas and values put forward by political elites to guide or justify their concrete policies and actions. It is not always easy, however, to draw a clear distinction between fundamental and operative ideology. There is frequently a degree of overlapping between the two; yet each is sufficiently distinguishable for analytic purpose and a separate treatment with focus on the latter, as intended for this book, is therefore feasible.

Theoretical distinction between the two levels or two dimensions of ideology is important when one attempts to understand how two communist leaders, who share common ideological allegiance, are often in conflict with each other. They are probably committed to the same pure principles, but they are different

[8]Political elite is defined as the top leaders of the Party and/or state. Intellectual elite refers to China's leading intellectuals whose theories and ideas have influenced the course of Chinese political and economic developments since 1978, most of whom are also members of the Party.
[9]Seliger, 1976, p. 109.
[10]Barrington Moore, *Soviet Politics – the Dilemma of Power, the Role of Ideas in Social Change*, Cambridge, Mass., Harvard University Press, 1950, pp. 402–403.
[11]Schurmann, 1968, pp. 21–45.

at the operative level of ideology which in turn could produce very different policies. In fact, most controversies among the communist elites tend to occur in the field of operative ideology regarding how to guide party policies, and relate more to the specific political and economic issues of a particular country.

C Methodology

There has long been disagreement among scholars of Chinese politics over the essence of China's political life, and perhaps variants of the power model have been used most extensively as an analytical approach to Chinese politics. This school emphasizes personalities and power as the primary basis for political factional activity. This approach is relevant in analyzing leadership politics, as the model assumes a conflict pattern of policy formulation and consensus building, reflecting the interests of competing groups. This model is often used in analyzing post-Mao Chinese politics characterized by the tension between the reformers, who are increasingly determined to promote a market-oriented economy and greater political tolerance, and the more conservative leaders whose political views are confined to balancing the economy and improving the Leninist political system.

While incorporating some features of the power model in this study, I also think the model is insufficient in explaining the complexity of Chinese politics. The model tends to neglect two important elements of Chinese politics, namely, the role of the intellectual and that of ideology. The level of interaction between the political and the intellectual elites has become increasingly significant and sophisticated in the post-Mao era. The old relationship between the state and the Chinese intellectuals was marked by the total subordination of the latter to the former, while the new relationship is the relative autonomy of the latter to the former. Konrad and Szelenyi have developed the concept of 'dual functions' of the intellectual for legitimatizing and transcending the existing social order.[12] They attempt both to legitimize and interpret the prevailing social order and to question and challenge it. This 'schizophrenia' frequently leads to tensions between themselves and the authorities. In this study, the

[12]Gyvrgy Konrad and Ivan Szelenyi, *The Intellectuals on the Road to Class Power*, Brighton, Harvester Press 1979, p. 22.

concept of 'dual functions' of the intellectual is employed to explain the underlying causes for many ideological controversies. This concept can also be extended to what is conventionally called the patron-client relationship among the Chinese political elites.

Ideology is another area which is downplayed in the power model. Ideology is only treated at face value on the assumption that at the heart of the issue is the fact that decision-makers do not believe in the ideology they advocate and they rely more on their experience and non-ideological resources for solutions to China's problems. But as explained at the beginning of this chapter, one major force that has shaped post-Mao Chinese political life is still the conflict between competing ideologies and between political actors holding divergent perspectives of the nature of economic and political reforms and of what constitutes genuine socialism.

While acknowledging that reforms involve political actors with different beliefs clashing with one another, one should bear in mind the difficulty involved in verifying the intensity of their beliefs. This is, however, not the major concern of this study. My focus is placed more on the functional role and political use of competing ideologies rather than on how strong a given leader is loyal to his professed ideology. In this context, an attempt has been made to focus on the actors' discursive framework. I draw useful elements from Quentin Skinner and Joseph Schull's interpretation of ideology as a form of discourse often used for establishing ideological conventions to affect actions.[13]

This approach holds that 'the power of ideology is based on respect, not faith' and 'one's actions will be shaped by an ideology in so far as one must conform to its conventions; one need not "believe" in the ideology but in order to be taken seriously as a participant in the relevant ideological discourse, one must be committed to it.'[14] The author of this study does not entirely share the argument against the power of faith, but accepts the emphasis placed on 'respect' and 'conventions.' This approach seems to explain more convincingly the process of ideological evolution, in which actors with diversified beliefs or different

[13]See Quentin Skinner, *The Foundation of Modern Political Thought*, Cambridge, U.K. Cambridge University Press, Vol. 1, pp. xii-xiii, and 'Conventions and the Understanding of Speech Acts,' *Philosophical Quarterly*, Vol. 20, No. 79, April 1970, pp. 118–38 and Joseph Schull, 'What is Ideology? Theoretical Problems and Lessons from Soviet-Type Societies,' *Political Studies*, (1992) XL., pp. 728–741.
[14]Joseph Schull, op. cit., p. 728.

degrees of ideological commitment within an ideological movement choose to embrace, develop or reject elements of a given ideology, compatible with the above-mentioned 'schizophrenia' phenomenon of interpretation and transcendence. This approach is also useful in explaining the importance of building discursive conventions in the ideological political system as they can often decisively influence policy formulation and execution once they are officially sanctioned.

In this context, Weber's concept of 'elective affinity' is also employed in analyzing the relationship between the doctrine and its followers. According to Weber, the followers of an ideology 'elect' those features of the ideology with which they have an affinity of interests because 'ideas, selected and reinterpreted from the original doctrine, do gain an affinity with the interests of certain members of special strata; if they do not gain such an affinity, they are abandoned.'[15] A number of other concepts in social sciences have been used where appropriate and their sources indicated, such as substantive or purposive goal and 'hard' or 'soft' state.

However, while employing these concepts for analytical purpose, this study consists primarily of empirical research based on an extensive survey of primary sources ranging from official documents, policy statements, memoirs, and newspaper articles to personal interviews. This combined approach of empirical and theoretical study, as the author believes, is an effective way to handle the complex interactions between diversified ideological trends and policy alternatives discussed in this book and to better explain and understand the complicated process of Chinese politics.

As for the structure of this study, the author attempts to combine historical and thematic approaches. From an historical perspective, the course of ideological and political change since the Third Plenum in 1978 is characterized by cycles with periods of advance and periods of retreat.[16] The whole period from 1978

[15]H. Gerth and C. Wright Mills, *From Max Weber: Essays in Sociology*, New York, Oxford University Press, 1946, p. 63.

[16]Most China experts from China and the West agree to the cyclical nature of Chinese politics. See, for instance, Ruan Ming, *Lishi zhuanzhedian shang de huyaobang*, (Hu Yaobang at the Turning-Point of History), Hong Kong, Global Publishing Co. Ins. 1991, H. Harding, *China's Second Revolution: Reform after Mao*, Washington, D.C., the Brookings Institute, 1987, and C. L. Hamrin, *China and the Challenge of the Future: Changing Political Pattern*, Boulder, Westview Press, 1990.

to 1992 can be usefully divided into four cycles, and each cycle begins with reformist values, initiatives, and experimental implementation to be followed by ideological criticism and readjustment. Subsequently, pressure is built for a new round of reform initiatives. However, each cycle by no means represents a mere circular movement, returning to where it starts; some new features of ideology and reform are added to each new phase.

This cyclical pattern has derived partially from the complex nature of China's economic reform programme which has, in its process of evolution, stimulated many political, economic and social problems. Decentralization and open-door policies have frequently led to budget deficits, inflation, an over-heated economy, corruption and political dissent, thus building up pressure for economic and political re-centralization. But market-oriented reforms and their supporters are also increasingly urged by their own interests for greater autonomy and decision-making power, which in turn demand greater reform and opening. The division between reformers and more conservative leaders on the nature, scope and speed of reform have contributed to this cyclical pattern. Emphasizing the cyclical pattern does not imply that Chinese politics is simple and fit for compartmentalization. On the contrary, it is too complicated to be neatly divided. This study only attempts to adopt this analytically distinguishable pattern of change as a useful time frame for the purpose of a more focussed analysis of ideological trends and economic reforms and to better trace and elaborate some repeated themes of ideological controversies.

Within this cyclical framework, I attempt to organize the substantive part of my study in a manner parallel to what I designate as the four cycles. In each chapter, I first outline the trajectory of ideological developments by examining the broad ideological trends with focus on their origins and themes, and where appropriate, their relationship with the general orientation of economic reform. On the basis of this vertical approach, I attempt to make a thematic or horizontal analysis of a few selected issues involving ideological influence on economic reform policies, the political use of ideology for authority-building, and the interaction between ideological values, policies and actions. This blended approach, I hope, can best capture and explore the evolving nature of the interactions between ideologies and reform policies and the process of doctrinal renovation.

The substantive part will be preceded by a chapter presenting a quick review of ideology and modernization in China (Chapter One) in order to give an overall picture of the subject in a broader historical context, since much of post-Mao development has close relevance to what happened in the Maoist era and before. The 14th CPC Congress held in 1992, which summarizes Deng's doctrine on 'socialism with Chinese characteristics,' is treated separately as a chapter because it marks the beginning of a new reform drive or perhaps another cycle. This treatment is further justified by the fact that the Congress gives an official version of Dengism which coincides with the authors' attempt to recapture the main components of Deng's doctrine.

Chapter One

IDEOLOGY AND CHINA'S MODERNIZATION IN HISTORICAL PERSPECTIVE

A Overview

Ever since the mid-19th century, generations of the Chinese have endeavoured to modernize the country under the guidance of different ideologies. In the aftermath of a series of humiliating defeats inflicted by the Western powers in the 19th century, Zeng Guofan, Zuo Zongtang and Li Hongzhang initiated China's first major attempt for 'self-strengthening' under the slogan of 'Chinese learning as the essence, Western learning for utility' (zhongxue weiti, xixue weiyong) from the 1860s to the 1880s. They recommended strong warships and guns, established language schools, arsenals and dockyards, and sent students to Europe and the United States. But the whole process ended up in failure largely due to the flawed strategy of transplanting advanced foreign techniques while maintaining the conservative official ideology and anachronistic institutions, both of which stifled new ideas, creativity and individual initiatives.

The second major attempt, led by Kang Youwei and Liang Qichao, stood for significant institutional reforms including the establishment of a constitutional monarchy, parliamentary system and industrialization. Their Hundred Day's Reform was aborted in 1898 in the face of the fierce ideological and political resistance from the conservative Manchu aristocracies. But the Qing Court was shaken and had to adopt certain reforms three years later which, unfortunately, led to a chaotic decentralization.

Dr. Sun Yat-sen symbolized the third major attempt for modernization with the idea of democracy and republicanism. But Sun's parliamentarianism was crippled by military interventions and corruption. The period from the collapse of the Qing in 1911 to the Guomindang's coming to power in 1927 was chaotic with warlord governments controlling different regions of China and no nation-wide modernization effort was possible. Amid general disillusion with democracy, Chiang Kai-shek came to power, representing the fourth attempt to establish a modern and unified China, guided by Confucian ideology and elements of fascism. But his rule was weakened internally by civil wars with the communists and challenged externally by Japan. Though tremendous efforts were made, Chiang was unable to promote a full-scale modernization of China. It is worth noting that there has been a clear utilitarian purpose for advocating democracy or dictatorship in Chinese modern history, and the advocates' point of departure is always whether a doctrine can first make China economically strong and militarily powerful rather than the fulfillment of individuals. This constitutes an important feature of Chinese political culture which remains true today.

The prolonged state of turmoil and war hindered economic development as well as effective state action to assist modernization. According to S. Swamy, China's overall economic growth was extremely slow with per capita GNP growing by just 3.3 per cent per decade from 1870 to 1952.[1] However, there was a visible growth of certain modern industrial sectors under indigenous Chinese ownership or foreign ownership, especially in Shanghai and surrounding areas, and in the treaty ports and Manchuria.

The establishment of the People's Republic of China in 1949 created the national unity and state power necessary for a comprehensive nation-wide modernization programme. In this context, Mao Zedong represented the fifth attempt for modernization. Under Mao's radical version of Marxism and Leninism his efforts produced mixed economic and political results and culminated in the disastrous Cultural Revolution. Since 1978, Deng Xiaoping initiated China's sixth attempt for bringing this huge country into the mainstream of modern life. The goal of his reform programme is to make China an efficient modern economy by the middle of the 21st century within the

[1]Subramanian Swamy, 'The Response to Economic Challenge: a Comparative Economic History of China and India, 1870–1952,' *Quarterly Journal of Economics*, February 1979, p. 31.

framework of 'socialism with Chinese characteristics.' Against this general historical background, let us look more closely into the ideology/policy relationship during the pre-Deng period from 1949 to 1978.

B The Soviet Model (1953–1957)

From 1949 to 1952, tremendous efforts were made to restore the war-destroyed economy. A relatively prudent ideological line was followed which stressed a gradual 'transition from the new democracy stage to socialism' rather than a rush to socialist industrialization. The government carried out a sweeping and fairly successful land reform which provided poor peasants with land and promoted the recovery of the rural economy. The Chinese leadership encouraged private entrepreneurs and used their managerial, commercial and technical expertise to effect economic recovery.

With this recovery completed and the Korean War ended, the Chinese leadership initiated the First Five-Year Plan (1953–1957), during which, China rapidly constructed an economy based on the Soviet model. A socialist economy required replacing the anarchy of the market with central planning. Hence, a highly centralized administrative system was established in which all key economic and social organizations were nationalized. The whole economy was run as a single party-state bureaucracy with political-economic-social functions. Pursuing a Stalinist modernization strategy with priority given to the rapid growth of heavy industry, central planners determined all significant resource allocation and production targets, including enterprise inputs and outputs and their prices.

China's adoption of the Soviet model was primarily due to the fact that China utterly lacked experience in large-scale industrial development. The Soviet experience was attractive to the Chinese communists in several ways: It was ideologically sound and compatible with the communist aspiration of the Chinese political elite; the Soviet Union achieved its industrialization on the basis of a large and relatively backward country; the Soviet Union was also isolated from outside assistance and threatened by external forces. The prospect of equally rapid industrialization strongly appealed to the Chinese leadership.

The First Five-Year Plan produced impressive results: industrial output value grew at an annual rate of 18 per cent, while agricultural output value rose by an annual average of 4.5 per cent.[2] Despite the initial economic achievements, the Stalinist mode of modernization soon revealed its problems: the replacement of market with central planning led to the absence of competition and the growth of excessive bureaucracy; and extraction of resources from agriculture for growth in heavy industry hindered rural development. The top-down system was marked by poor feedback, inefficiency and waste. All this made continued high growth very difficult. During this period, two competing revisions of the Soviet model gradually emerged, namely, the Maoist model and the moderate Leninist model.

C The Maoist model I: The Great Leap Forward (1957–1960)

Sharing much of the Stalinist view of rapid industrialization, Mao Zedong invented his version of a more radical approach to modernization. Influenced by his guerrilla and mass-line experience, Mao was not satisfied with the Stalinist excessively centralized bureaucratic control of the economy. Nor was Mao content with the political 'revisionism' in Eastern Europe and the USSR set loose by Khrushchev's denunciation of Stalin.

The two distinctive features of the Maoist approach were the role of ideology and the massive labour mobilization. Mao abandoned his original plan of a gradual transition to socialism. Instead, he completed the 'socialist transformation of agriculture, industry, commerce and handicrafts' by 1956. Mao reversed the Hundred Flowers movement of 1956 and initiated the Anti-Rightist campaign. He also abandoned the line of the 8th CPC Congress which had declared the end of large-scale class struggle in China. He then accelerated the pace of collectivizing the rural and urban economies. With the establishment of the commune in 1958, Mao shelved the more moderate Second Five-Year Plan (1958 -1962) and started to promote ideological uniformity and the Great Leap Forward. Mao's deviation from the Soviet model was aimed at reestablishing China as the centre of world socialist revolution and moving rapidly towards a prosperous communist society through an ideologically inspired transformation of 'production relations.' Mao encouraged the

[2]Ma Hong (ed.), *Modern China's Economy and Management*, Beijing, Foreign Languages Press, 1990, pp. 18–19.

political activists to amalgamate China's 700,000 collective farms into just 24,000 people's communes with centralized accounting and hierarchy to achieve the economy of scale and, by doing so, virtually eliminated the 'private plot' and income differences between villages within the commune.

During the Great Leap Forward, quality and variety were neglected for the sake of greater quantities. With planning in chaos and market forces suppressed, much output was of very low quality. The most serious losses were in agriculture, where the Leap led to 'an averaging annual fall of 9.7 per cent' in agricultural production[3] and a major famine that caused the death of about 15 million people. 'In terms of loss of life' the Leap 'may have been the worst on human record.'[4] Some scholars claimed that the Great Leap Forward cost China 'almost a decade' of economic growth.[5]

D The moderate Leninist model (1961–1965)

The failure of the Great Leap Forward led to a substantial retreat from the Maoist radical policies. A moderate Leninist model for modernization, identified with Liu Shaoqi, Zhou Enlai and Chen Yun, had been considered towards the end of the First Five-Year Plan and now was adopted. The Party decided on the policy of 'readjustment, consolidation, filling-up and raising standards' with regard to the national economy. This moderate approach was characterized by Chen Yun's idea of overall balance through improved central planning, ideological uniformity and the supplementary role of the market in order to achieve overall coordination and balance among economic sectors and geographical regions. Deviating from the Stalinist and Maoist models, this approach favoured agriculture and light industry and desired to improve living standards along with industrialization. This approach was also committed to a national economy based on regional specialization rather than on local self-reliance.

Under this new approach, systematic retrenchment took place on all fronts. More realistic growth rates were set. In urban

[3] *ibid.*, p. 21.
[4] Carl Riskin, *China's Political Economy – the Quest for Development since 1949*, New York, Oxford University Press, 1988, p. 136.
[5] See *ibid.*, p. 133.

areas, investment priority shifted from steel and machinery to the production of fertilizer; the experiments with people's communes were stopped and thousands of capital construction projects came to a halt. The output value of heavy industry in 1962 dropped by 58.8 per cent and its proportion in the total industrial output value reduced from 66.7 per cent to 53.5 per cent.[6] Workers' participation in management was replaced by greater authority for managers. Individual material incentives were used in enterprises. In rural areas, the communes were reduced in size, accompanied by a devolution of responsibility and authority from the communes and brigades to the teams. 'Private plots' and rural markets were restored, and strict limits were set on collective accumulation. The commune farming was replaced with output quotas assigned to families. As a result, economic recovery took place. Good harvests were achieved from 1962 onwards, and industrial growth was restored. By 1964, Premier Zhou Enlai announced that the recovery was complete and a Third Five-Year Plan was ready for implementation in 1966.

E The Maoist model II: The Cultural Revolution (1966–1976)

The retreat from the Great Leap Forward improved the Chinese economy, but in Mao's perception, his power was in decline; China was changing 'her colour'; the Communist Party had been led astray by revisionist and bureaucratic tendencies and China was further away from Mao's idealistic goal of communism. Mao attributed the failure of the Great Leap Forward to the slow pace in the ideological transformation of the society and the existence of non-socialist elements. Mao shifted his attention to the need to purge the superstructure which was undermining the economic base.

Mao further developed his view that the development of the forces of production should be subordinated to the development of the correct relations of production. Mao put forward the slogan of 'grasping revolution, promoting production' on the belief that a new type of relations of production free from revisionist or bourgeois tendencies could emancipate the new forces of production which would lead to a socialist modern China.

[6]Ma Hong, 1990, p. 22.

Consequently, the moderate Leninist approach gave way to the Maoist radical approach with even greater emphasis on ideological mobilization. At the height of the Cultural Revolution, economic growth stagnated or even declined and considerable fluctuations occurred in government policies towards free markets, private plots and enterprise management. Technological progress became stagnant. Self-reliance prevailed over international trade. Exports were not viewed as demand stimulus but rather as a means to earn the hard currency to fill the gaps in domestic supply.

At the Fourth National People's Congress held in 1975, Zhou Enlai attempted to reintroduce the moderate Leninist approach. He set forth the goal of the 'four modernizations of agriculture, industry, science and technology and national defence' and made it clear that to achieve the goal it was necessary to make changes in governmental policies. Zhou even invoked one of Mao's statements on the need for a technical revolution and for borrowing technical know-how from foreign countries.[7] But such views immediately encountered criticism from the radicals for reversing the gains of the Cultural Revolution. Such criticism began to focus on Deng Xiaoping, who had been designated by Zhou for implementing the economic modernization programme. Deng attempted to revive the moderate Leninist approach which had helped restore Chinese economy from the disastrous Great Leap Forward, but his initial successes were quickly overshadowed by a more fierce power struggle in the Party which led to his downfall and the rise of Mao-designated Hua Guofeng.

In summary, despite Maoist radicalism, China succeeded in laying a fairly extensive industrial basis for its economic development from 1949 to 1976. China's gross material product grew at an annual average rate of over 7 per cent from 1953 to 1978, and net material product at almost 6 per cent. In the same period, its economic structure 'shifted rapidly away from agriculture towards industry with agriculture's share of gross material product falling from 57 to 28 percent.'[8]

However, these achievements have to be viewed against a

[7]Chou Enlai, 'Report on the Work of the Government,' *Peking Review*, No. 4, 24 January 1975, p. 24.
[8]Peter Nolan and Dong Furen, *The Chinese Economy and Its Future*, Cambridge, U.K., Polity Press, 1990, p. 8.

number of serious problems: first, such rapid growth of output was achieved in a wasteful fashion, requiring an increasing amount of capital to produce a given unit of output. Second, the heavy industry bias only allowed consumption to grow very slowly. China's average annual growth rate of real consumption per person was 2.2 per cent from 1952 to 1976.[9] Third, the adoption of a misguided population policy led to an increase of population from 575 million in 1952 to 975 million in 1978, an average annual growth rate of 2 per cent, which traded off much of the gain in economic growth. Fourth, the long-term picture tends to conceal the imbalanced development and short-term fluctuations in China's economic performance. Some periods, notably between 1949 and 1957 and between 1961 and 1965, witnessed more progress thanks to more moderate economic policies, while the Great Leap Forward created the unprecedented famine and the Cultural Revolution seriously disrupted economic development. Fifth, Mao's policy of self-seclusion reduced China's share of world trade from around 1.4 per cent in the mid-1950s to just 0.4 per cent in the mid-1970s and hindered China's economic development and technological progress.[10] Last but not least, Maoist radical ideology on class struggle led to a demoralization of the work force whose desire for a better life was suppressed by Mao's doctrine for class struggle.

[9] *ibid.*, p. 9.
[10] *ibid.*, p. 8.

Chapter Two

THE FIRST CYCLE: FROM THE DEBATE ON THE CRITERION OF TRUTH TO SOCIALISM WITH CHINESE CHARACTERISTICS (1978–1982)

Ideological debates and their impact on economic reform policy seem to operate in cycles. The first cycle started with the 1978 ideological debate on the criterion of truth initiated by Chinese reformers, which marked the beginning of a profound deviation from Maoist radicalism to Deng's reformism. Different doctrines competed with each other for dominance in shaping China's future in this era of transition.

Two themes emerged during this period: first, this cycle marked the beginning of Deng's attempt to transform the ideological foundation of Chinese society and in this process, Deng presented most of his embryonic ideas which were later to be gradually formulated into a doctrine. Second, the beginning of the cycle was marked by controversy between the Cultural Revolution Left and the post-Mao reformers. However, as the reform went further, a split emerged in the reformers' camp and controversies between more radical and more conservative reformers (hereinafter referred to as reformers and conservatives respectively) over the pace, scope, content and nature of reform began to predominate Chinese politics and economic policies.

A Major ideological trends

1 The debate on the criterion of truth

Chinese leaders were faced with a crisis of political confidence in the aftermath of the Cultural Revolution: the official doctrine was discredited and the legitimacy of the Party and the government was weakened in the eyes of the people. But the crisis also presented opportunities for a change of direction. The Chinese leaders had little dispute over the existence of such a crisis but differed significantly with regard to how to revitalize their doctrine and save their declining authority.

The Cultural Revolution Left led by Mao's chosen successor Hua Guofeng was to revive the ideological and charismatic authority that had characterized the Maoist era. The view allegedly associated with Hua was that of 'upholding whatever policy decisions Chairman Mao made, steadfastly carrying out whatever Chairman Mao instructed' ('Two Whatevers'). But this stereotyped criticism of Hua should not prevent us from seeing Hua's modest attempt at shifting policy emphasis within a Maoist discursive framework. Hua chose to highlight those elements in Maoism which favoured economic development and contact with foreign countries. While still stressing class struggle as the key task and Mao's slogan 'grasp revolution and promote production,' Hua called for greater labour discipline and payment according to work. Yet Hua was handicapped by the fact that his legitimacy depended entirely on Mao's charisma, and he had to maintain the authority of Maoism. Furthermore, Hua did not show any original vision of China other than reemphasizing the Maoist models of development such as Dazhai and Daqing which stressed ideological education and hard work as the Chinese way of developing agriculture and industry. 'He had no ideas of his own but the "two whatevers",' Deng observed on Hua in 1989.[1] Hua's ambitious modernization programme, a revival of the revised 1975 plan, was initiated at the Fifth National People's Congress in March 1978 but without intention to change the existing political and economic structure.

[1]Deng Xiaoping, 'We Must Form a Promising Collective Leadership that Will Carry out Reform,' (May 31, 1989), *Selected Works of Deng Xiaoping*, Vol. 3 (1982–1992), Beijing, Foreign Languages Press, 1993, (Hereinafter referred to as Deng Xiaoping, Vol. 3), p. 290.

Consequently, the question involved was whether there should be an imperative for ideological change. At a time of deep political crisis when public outcry for change was high, Hua committed a political mistake by stressing 'continuity' with the past rather than 'change' and failed to present new and inspiring ideas with a directing power. In contrast, having experienced the Cultural Revolution and economic deterioration, Deng understood that the prevailing crisis provided a major catalyst for change and he seized the opportunity as he had done in 1975. Reformers led by Deng perceived a crisis-induced ideological change as inevitable if the Party was to regain the trust of the people which had existed in the early years of the People's Republic.

It is useful to draw on an analogy made by G. Galeotti and A. Breton between popular trust and capital investment. The concept concludes that communist governments do not keep on investing in popular trust and their capital of trust is thus constantly depreciated, which breeds prevailing distrust. At a certain point, people are no longer willing to cooperate with the party because the two sides (people vs. the party) are not engaged in fair and equal exchanges with one side being sincere and the other side cheating. Furthermore, ideological indoctrination is perceived by people as a major mode of cheating.[2] In Chinese politics, Hua still believed that the mainstream of Maoism could secure the trust of the people, while Deng Xiaoping realized that the Party should lose no time in reinvesting in people's trust by changing the whole ideological basis of political authority from the Maoist excessive emphasis on politics and revolutions to economics and modernization. To reinvest in the trust of the people and appreciate the capital of trust, reformers sought to reassess Mao, rehabilitate the persecuted, abandon radical ideology and policies and usher in a workable modernization programme so as to bring tangible benefits for the people. All this entailed a fundamental ideological transformation and a profound reform of China's existing economic and political structure.

Reformers demonstrated a degree of prudence in ideological innovations. Without deviating too much from the prevailing ideological convention about the greatness of Mao Zedong

[2]G. Galeotti and A. Breton, 'An Economic Theory of Political Parties,' *Kyklos*, Vol. 39, 1986, pp. 47–65.

Thought, Deng spoke of both the high relevance of Mao Zedong Thought and the need for a return to the fundamentals of Mao Zedong Thought. Implicitly rejecting Hua's 'two whatevers,' Deng said that it was necessary to 'use genuine Mao Zedong Thought taken as an integral whole in guiding our Party, our army and our people.'[3] According to Deng, the point of departure of Mao Zedong Thought was not the theory of class struggle but 'seeking truth from facts,' an idea Mao had developed during the war years.[4] Deng proclaimed this notion to be the very foundation of Mao's thought on the understanding that primacy of practice as the basis of the 'integral whole' of Mao Zedong Thought could be used to endorse acts in discord with Mao's specific words.

This relative prudence was conditioned by both political and ideological imperatives. Politically, Deng was acutely aware of the need for greater support from the Party rank and file, many of whom still believed in Mao, and he had to win the leadership struggle against Hua and get his reform programme off the ground in a less confrontational environment. In terms of power balance, pro-reform forces were still not strong enough to stage an open challenge to Hua. Moreover, his failings notwithstanding, Mao was the undisputable leader of the Chinese Revolution to which Deng had devoted much of his life. In this sense, political attitude towards Mao was a matter of the Party's identity and legitimacy. Deng hence endeavored to maintain a degree of continuity with the past while calling for certain important changes.

Ideologically, Deng shared some of Mao's values and basics of Marxism. In certain ways, Deng was returning to a more classical version of Marxism which emphasizes the economy as the basis and the theory of 'existence determines consciousness' and to its basic methodology rather than its utopian themes. This return to basics itself was a kind of liberalization for the

[3]Deng Xiaoping clearly rejected the 'two whatevers' in his private talks with some leaders of the Party in May 1977, claiming that 'if this principle (two whatevers) were correct, there could be no justification for my rehabilitation, nor could there be any for the statement that the activities of the masses at Tiananmen Square in 1976 were reasonable.' But in his letter to the CPC Central Committee, Deng confined himself to discussing the 'integral whole' of Mao Zedong Thought. See Deng Xiaoping, 'The 'Two Whatevers' do not Accord with Marxism' in *Selected Works of Deng Xiaoping* (1975–1982), pp. 51–52.
[4]*ibid.*, pp. 128–132.

people who were no longer expected to strive for the humanly impossible, and now there were relatively objective criterion for good performance and behaviour.

But this prudent attitude gave way to a more direct challenge to Hua's 'two whatevers' when Deng's constituency grew with more veteran cadres being rehabilitated. The debate on the criterion of truth initiated by Hu Yaobang, then vice president of the Central Party School, was a turning-point from political prudence to a more aggressive confrontation with reform opponents. The debate started with the publication of a controversial article entitled 'Practice is the Sole Criterion of Truth,' originally prepared by a scholar from Nanjing University, in *Lilun Dongtai* (Theoretical Trends), an internal journal of the Party School, whose readership included all the Party's top leaders, then in *Guangming Ribao* on 10 May and *Renmin Ribao* on 12 May 1978.

Any theories, including Mao's, according to this article, must be tested to see if it is truth. The discourse immediately angered the Cultural Revolution Left. Wang Dongxing condemned the article as 'targeting at Chairman (Mao)'s thought.' Ideologues argued that Marxism and Mao's theory were already proved as 'universal truth' and any demand for further testing was tantamount to 'spreading doubts' and negating their validity. Hua Guofeng urged the CPC propaganda departments 'don't get involved' and 'don't make comment.'[5] Even Hu Qiaomu, then a supporter of Deng's reform, urged Hu Yaobang to put an end to the debate for fear of top-level political wrangling. Hu Yaobang almost agreed to tone it down[6] when Deng Xiaoping expressed his support in a speech at the conference on political work of the army by calling for 'seeking truth from facts.' General Luo Ruiqing, then Secretary-General of the CPC Military Commission, came out to back Hu Yaobang by carrying an article in support of the debate in *Jiefangjun Bao* (Liberation Army Daily) on 24 June 1978, a clear sign of military backing for reform and change. Such support from Deng and the military indicated a decisive shift of the power balance in favour of a new ideological convention.

[5]Hu Shen (ed.), *Zhongguo gongchandang de qishinian* (the Seventy Years of the Chinese Communist Party), Beijing, CPC Party History Press, 1991, p. 487.

[6]Ruan Ming, *Lishi zhuanzhe dian shang de Hu Yaobang* (Hu Yaobang at the Turning-Point of History), Hong Kong, Global Publishing Co. Inc., 1991, p. 14.

Although many local leaders still respected Maoist conventions, this power tilt in favour of change precluded any genuine debate on this issue. The ideological discourse now became a rallying point in the leadership struggle on which all politicians must 'biaotai' (take a stand openly), a political tactic developed in the Chinese communist movement by which a discursive framework was created to compel all cadres in the Party hierarchy to express openly their support for the Party's prevailing convention whether they actually agree or not. Such normative consensus tended to dramatically raise the political cost of any overt resistance to the convention. Buttressed with their growing strength, reformers quickly enforced a normative convention among leaders across the country on the need for ideological change and policy adjustment, as shown in the fact that provincial leaders took turns to express their support for the new ideological discourse, although their commitment might vary from simple lip service to a complete embrace. Respect from the Party cadres for the new official convention enabled the reformers to define their policy agenda for economic and political changes.

To reformers, there were three principal reasons for their affinity with the new doctrine. First, they understood that Mao's ideological legacy had lost much credibility with the population mainly due to the Cultural Revolution, but it still prevented a leadership consensus from emerging on much desired changes, as Mao's statements were still held sacred by many Party cadres. Under the circumstances, the objective of the reformers had to be a reassessment of the prevailing ideological framework. It is therefore not surprising that the major deviation from Maoist economic and political policies started with a debate on epistemology which challenged the philosophical basis of Maoist convention.

Second, the theme of 'practice is the only criterion of truth' was important for economic reforms because the criterion of practice was essentially defined by reformers as economic performance. The Cultural Revolution Left had argued that a practice which created a higher standard of living at the expense of the communist collective ideals would be considered as a failure. This view was refuted by the reformers as 'extreme leftism' which negated the basic Marxist principle that socialism should be able to create much higher productivity and hence higher living standards than capitalism. This performance-oriented approach, controversial as it was, was well received by the population in general, who was more attracted by businesslike, practical and tangible performance rather than the empty slogans characteristic of Mao's utopianism.

Third, this ideological debate provided an effective instrument for reformers to build up their authority in the leadership struggle. At the preparatory conference for the Third Plenum held from 10 November to 15 December 1978, the much publicized discourse already enabled Hu Yaobang to be strong enough to manipulate the agenda of the meeting to such a degree that Hu was able to invite more reform-minded people to the conference and introduce the debate directly to the conference when the struggle with Hua Guofeng made it necessary.[7] Hua's followers resorted to the old ideological resources and refused to accept the new discursive framework on which the convention had already taken shape. This causal power of ideology had rendered the Cultural Revolution Left in a 'no win' situation at the conference. As a result they also failed in setting the policy agenda. Deng Xiaoping seized the opportunity to declare that the debate was 'very good and necessary,' and 'the more I think about it, the more it is a political issue involving the fate of the Party and the country.'[8]

The Third Plenum established a reform-oriented policy agenda and signaled a watershed between Maoist past and Deng's era of reform. The decision adopted at the Plenum stressed the need for a dramatic reform of economic management that

> carrying out the Four Modernizations requires great growth in the productive forces, which in turn requires diverse changes in those aspects of the relations of production and the superstructure not in harmony with the growth of the productive forces, and requires changes in all methods of

[7] *ibid.*, p. 28.
[8] This comment is contained in Ruan Ming's personal notes of Deng's talks prior to the Third Plenum. See Ruan Ming, op. cit. p. 95. A revised version appeared in Research Department, CPC Secretariat, *Jianchi gaige kaifang gaohuo* (Adhere to Reform, Opening and Invigorating the Economy – a Collection of Important Documents since the Third Plenum of the 11th CPC Central Committee), Beijing, People's Press, 1987 (Hereinafter referred to as 'JGKG'), p. 7.

management and actions and thinking which stand in the way of such growth.[9]

The significance of the ideological victory on the part of reformers was also manifested in many unfolding events. For instance, in the following year, the Fourth Plenum, 'proceeding from the thesis of practice being the criterion of truth,' declared the Cultural Revolution as a 'great calamity for the Chinese people' and rejected Hua Guofeng's position about the nature of the Gang of Four being ultra-right. On the contrary, it was defined as ultra-left, thus further changing the course of China from ideological radicalism to Deng's developmentalism.

Building on the favourable momentum generated by the debate, Deng made one of the most important political statements in his political career on 13 December 1978, in which he reconfirmed the significance of the truth debate in emancipating the mind and outlined his basic perceptions of economic reforms.[10] This statement indicated Deng's intention to create a new unifying theory based on generally accepted 'truth criterion' and to reject radical Maoism and induce new policies. But unlike Mao, whose ideology was in Mannheim's term 'total ideology,' Deng's ambition was more parochial and instrumental and the immediate impulsion of Deng's theoretical attempt was confined to the leadership struggle and China's modernization. The following ideas, though enunciated first in embryonic form, introduced into Chinese politics a new discursive framework which proved significant in the formulation of Deng's developmental theme of 'socialism with Chinese characteristics.' These idaas did not possess a sophisticated intellectual structure but produced strong impact on China's economic reform.

First, Deng gave top priority to the goal of modernization as the most important task of the Party. He compared realization of the four modernizations to 'a profound revolution' which should be led by an 'emancipation of minds,' claiming that

[9]Research Department, CPC Secretariat, *Jianchi sixiang jiben yuanze fandui zichan jieji ziyouhua* (Adhere to the Four Cardinal Principles and Oppose Bourgeois Liberalization – a Collection of Important Documents since the Third Plenum of the 11th CPC Central Committee), Beijing, People's Press, 1987 (Hereinafter referred to as 'JSFZ'), pp. 1–2.

[10]Deng Xiaoping, 'Emancipate the Mind, Seek Truth from Facts and Unite as One in Looking to the Future,' (December 13, 1978), *Selected Works of Deng Xiaoping* (1975–1982), Beijing, Foreign Languages Press, 1984 (Hereinafter referred to as Deng Xiaoping (1984)), pp. 151–165.

without an immediate significant economic and political reform and emancipation of minds, China's 'modernization programme and socialist cause will be doomed.'[11] The immediate conclusion Deng reached at the end of the Cultural Revolution was that the new basis for Chinese socialism could only be modernization, which, both as a goal and a process, constituted the only theme which could unite the people and rebuild the Party's authority. Deng attributed the prevailing popular discontent and poor economic performance to the 'ossified thinking' and rigid central command, highlighted the urgency for reform and modernization and argued for 'taking initiatives' and 'thinking boldly' in the process of modernization.

Second, Deng introduced the concept of 'economic democracy' and discussed it at two levels: (1) There should be a decentralization to give full play to the initiative of every region, every factory and every production team. Deng noted that if a production team has decision-making power over its economic activities, peasants

> will lie awake at night so long as a single piece of land is left unplanted or a single pond unused for aquatic production, and they will find ways to remedy the situation. Just imagine the additional wealth that could be created if all the people in China's hundreds of thousands of enterprises and millions of production teams put their minds to work.[12]

The idea of 'decentralization' is a hallmark of Deng's developmentalism. (2) It was essential to safeguard the 'democratic rights' of workers and peasants, including 'the rights of democratic election, management, and supervision' so that every worker and peasant would have the incentive to work for China's modernization.[13] Deng even advocated direct participation by the masses in managing enterprises. But similar to pursuits of the previous generations of modernizers, Deng's point of departure in advocating 'democracy' was utilitarian: to modernize the country. Stressing the participatory value was perhaps partly due to Deng's pressing need for popular support in the power struggle with Hua and partly due to the repressive

[11]*ibid.*, p. 161.
[12]*ibid.*, p. 157.
[13]*ibid.*, p. 157.

experience of the Cultural Revolution which had created a disenchanted population. But Deng later became more suspicious about the possible political consequences and the economic efficacy of such participation.

Third, Deng deviated from the convention about socialism being a progressive reduction in socio-economic inequalities, as Deng drew lessons from Mao's excessive egalitarianism which had reduced the people to the level of common poverty. Deng claimed that some people and some regions should be encouraged to get rich first as models for others to emulate. Deng justified this inequality as temporary phenomena with an ultimate aim of 'helping the people of all our nationalities to become prosperous in a comparatively short period.'[14] This idea, which was presented in a very straightforward discursive framework, proved extremely significant in inducing changes, promoting market-oriented economic reforms and establishing economic zones in China's coastal areas.

2 The four cardinal principles

With the gradual political relaxation of post-Mao China, there emerged vociferous political demands as shown in the Democracy Wall Movement. Numerous wall posters appeared in Beijing with two main themes: condemning political persecutions that had happened during the Maoist era and advocating democracy, justice and human rights. As analyzing this movement does not fall into the scope of this study, it suffices to point out a relevant fact: this movement was at least implicitly supported by the reformers at its initial stage, as illustrated by the fact that many arguments in the wall posters were in fact responding to the then leadership struggle between the reformers and the Left, and many ideas revealed in the wall posters were used by the reformers to challenge the Left during the Third Plenum's preparatory conference.[15] Consequently, it revealed that the reformers could possibly cooperate with democracy activists in resisting conservative offensives, but, buttressed with state power, they could also manipulate the pace, scope and degree of such cooperation.

In March 1979 Deng decided to set a limit on political liberal-

[14] *ibid.*, pp. 163–164.
[15] Ruan Ming, 1991, p. 29.

ization by advancing the 'four cardinal principles' – a commitment to Marxism-Leninism-Mao Zedong Thought, Party leadership, socialism and the proletarian dictatorship.[16] This constituted a major authoritarian component of Deng's formative doctrine. Some radical reformers called them 'four sticks' for punishing liberals.[17] Politically, Deng condemned the Democracy Wall Movement which had become more radical by demanding for a comprehensive liberalization of the Chinese political system. Wei Jingsheng, a movement activist, singled out Deng Xiaoping for criticism of a dictatorial-style leadership, and there emerged a rising demand for freedom of speech and other human rights. This shift from advocating democracy to stressing authority and discipline was triggered by Deng's fear of any possible spread of unorthodox ideas which could engender grievances and hostilities towards the Party in the aftermath of the Cultural Revolution and undermine the foundation of communist rule, which Deng believed was indispensable for holding China together and China's modernization.

The revival of a more authoritarian attitude and conservative discourse had an immediate political imperative. Deng seemed determined to take a middle course between those who considered the line of the Third Plenum as a betrayal of socialism and communism and an excessive step towards the Right and those having disaffection with the Party and the socialist system as clearly expressed in the Democratic Wall Movement. When the demands of the Movement began to challenge the fundamentals of the Party, Deng made it clear that no criticism of the Party should go beyond a certain limit. To demonstrate this point, orders were given for the arrest of Wei Jingsheng and other political activists in Beijing, Shanghai and Guangzhou between late March and early April, 1979. To maintain a broad support for economic reform, Deng now assured more cautious reformers and ideological conservatives that he would not tolerate political dissent to go beyond control. Deng's personal experience of decades of wars and political chaos persuaded him to regard pro-democracy movements as a step towards

[16]Deng raised these four principles in a speech at a work conference on theoretical work on 30 March 1979. See JSFZ, pp. 9–23, and the English translation of the speech is 'Uphold the Four Cardinal Principles,' (March 30, 1979) in Deng Xiaoping (1984), pp. 166–191.

[17]For instance, Liu Binyan made a number of such statements in his speeches and lectures in the mid-1980s.

anarchism as prevailed in the Cultural Revolution, which, in Deng's view, could push China into endless wrangling and even civil war. Deng's decision to suppress the Democracy Wall Movement did not seem to produce too great a political repercussion in China, as Deng's popularity was still high and the memory of the chaos of the Cultural Revolution remained fresh.

In his statement in March 1979, Deng argued passionately for the four cardinal principles and introduced a more conservative discursive framework for ideological discussion. On Marxism-Leninism-Mao Zedong Thought, Deng held that China, with her size and population, needed a unifying ideology to get people united and make the country strong. Aware that the old orthodox doctrine was losing its appeal, Deng hoped to revive what he believed was useful from Marxism, or what he called the fundamental principles and methods of analysis in Marx and Mao. Deng stressed that one should adhere to their methodology rather than their specific claims.

Deng's defence of Marx and Mao should not be simply regarded as a tactic for placating the conservatives in the Party. Deng indeed saw himself as a defender of Mao's philosophical framework. Deng's own experience as an army commander and strategist during the war years led him to share many of Mao's assumptions, such as analysis of principal contradictions, a conscious emphasis on fundamentals and long-term perspectives and constantly relating tactics to strategies, politics to economics, policies to goals and the present to the future. This approach enabled Deng to demonstrate a remarkable consistency, and occasionally a vision, but also frequently caused ideological confusion in the process of reforms.

As for the leading role of the Party, Deng endorsed Leninist elitist discourse. Recalling lessons from contemporary Chinese history when Chinese republicanism had degenerated into rule by warlords, Deng rejected liberal discourse about a multi-party system. Deng shared with many Chinese the deep-rooted concerns of stability of China with over 1 billion people and a prolonged history of war and unrest. As a believer in Lenin's theory of the party and the Chinese traditional rule of the elite, Deng held that since the Party had acquired the power at great human cost, it should defend its power and promote a top-down and controlled process of modernization and social change. This meant that the Party would encourage a considerable economic liberalization yet permit no significant challenge to its rule. For Deng, abandoning Party leadership would be tantamount to anarchism. Deng asked rhetorically, without the Party,

> Who would organize the socialist economy, politics, military affairs and culture of China, and who would organize the four modernizations?[18]

However, Deng's authoritarianism also implied the need to explore a more effective leadership and an improved style of Party's work.

Deng asserted that socialism had narrowed the gap between China and the developed countries in the past three decades, despite the 'mistakes' committed by the Party, and that socialism should make use of 'useful elements of capitalist countries,' but not their political system; a reminder of 'Chinese learning as the essence, Western learning for utility.' Without clearly defining socialism, Deng, however, indicated his initial idea on Chinese-style socialism. Drawing inspiration from Mao, Deng claimed that just as Mao initiated the path of the rural area encircling the cities in the Chinese revolution, 'we must likewise act in accordance with our own situation and find a Chinese path to modernization.'[19]

Deng considered the dictatorship of the proletariat as indispensable to defend socialism at home and safeguard China's sovereignty against 'imperialism and hegemonism.' In line with Leninist discourse, Deng described the dictatorship of the proletariat as state machinery including army, police, court and prison which served to protect 'people's democracy.' Deng condemned the practice of the state machinery during the Cultural Revolution as fascist but concluded that the present conditions in China still required state machinery. Deng's attitude never wavered on this issue. As a seasoned politician and soldier, Deng's affinity with the 'dictatorship of the proletariat' was not only aimed at suppressing criminal activities but also pro-Western political dissidents. The discourse on the withering away of the state, a classical Marxist concept, served to illustrate Deng's position. In the late 1970s, Deng Xiaoping held fairly regular

[18]Deng Xiaoping (1984), p. 178.
[19]*ibid.*, p. 171.

consultations with some intellectuals to solicit their opinions about state affairs. Hu Qiaomu, Deng Liqun and Yu Guangyuan, three prominent Party theoreticians, were often invited by Deng to such discussion sessions. On one occasion Deng was briefed about Yu Guangyuan's allegedly espoused view that the state 'entered a moribund stage as soon as the proletariat seized political power.' Deng was disturbed by this, for he held that the withering away of the state was to be a protracted process of unknown length and that the prevailing task was to strengthen the state to ensure order and stability. According to Su Shaozhi, 'As a result, he (Deng) temporarily excluded Yu from further consultation sessions.'[20]

The fact that the four cardinal principles were not clearly defined, however, caused much confusion. For instance, is the earlier Marx part of Marxism? What is socialism? How does one practise the leadership of the Party in the process of economic liberalization? Like his early ideas on 'economic democracy,' these ideas only represented Deng's initial attempt to build a doctrine. He was in the process of seeking to define and specify a more coherent ideological framework for his modernization programme, as shown later when Deng tried to elaborate these principles.

But Deng's immediate concern was the socio-political function of his ideas, just as Barrington Moore asserted, 'the power of ideas does not depend upon their logical coherence alone, but also upon the social functions that they perform.'[21] Deng deemed it an urgent political priority to stop immediately any open challenge to the Party. Hence, his four principles were advanced to impose a discursive convention on the people to fulfil the socio-political function of an official ideology.

The four principles have caused much ideological and political confusion in the course of reform as shown in various ideological drives, partly because Deng resorted to an unpopular Maoist discursive framework, which was perceived as a revival of Maoist leftism, although Deng had to a certain extent deviated from Mao. This framework made it easy for Deng to win the support of conservatives for the reform and ensured a gradual departure from the orthodox so as to reduce ideological

[20]Su Shaozhi, 'A Decade of Crises at the Institute of Marxism-Leninism-Mao Zedong Thought,' *The China Quarterly*, No. 134, June 1993, p. 335.
[21]Barrington Moore, 1950, p. 224.

and political risks. But it gave opportunities to conservatives and even the Cultural Revolution Left to launch various attempts to set the reforms back in the name of defending the four principles. All ideological campaigns were launched under the four principles, thus alienating intellectuals and other reform supporters away from the economic reforms that Deng desired.

The ambiguity of the new discourse, as expected, aroused controversy but also provided opportunities for interpretation and transcendence. On 3 May 1979, Zhou Yang, Vice President of the Chinese Academy of Social Sciences, addressed a symposium marking the 60th anniversary of the May 4 Movement and called for further emancipation of the mind. According to Zhou, the youth movement in 1919, the Yanan rectification campaign in 1942 and political awakening since the Tiananmen Incident in 1976 represented 'three great campaigns of emancipating the mind,' and in commenting on one of the four principles, Zhou asserted that Chinese socialism was still fluid and evolving, and its ultimate form was still to take shape through more practice and experiment.[22]

In contrast to this effort at transcending the official discourse, in his speech to mark the same occasion, Hua Guofeng did not make any comment on the truth criterion debate or the 1976 Tiananmen Incident. Rather, he gave a narrow interpretation of the four principles, calling for the need to hold high the banner of Marxism-Leninism-Mao Zedong Thought in China's modernization endeavour. Hua declared that without the correct ideological guidance, the youth movement could get nowhere and Chinese socialism would fail.[23]

There was a propaganda campaign to publicize the four principles. Most articles strictly interpreted the official discourse. For instance, one article in defence of China's record of socialist economy carried in *Beijing Ribao* (Beijing Daily) claimed, without indicating the source of the data:

> From 1949 to 1977, China's gross industrial output increased 28 times. . . . Within 28 years, China has achieved what many capitalist countries did over several centuries. This is

[22]*Renmin Ribao*, 7 May 1979.
[23]*Renmin Ribao*, 25 April 1979

> a clear demonstration of the superiority of the socialist system.[24]

Another article in *Hong Qi* (Red Flag) claimed that 'those who advocate inferiority of socialism to capitalism are either doing so out of ignorance or out of ulterior motives' and that socialism was a society free from exploitation, thus a sharp contrast to 'exploitation, plunder, serious crime and decadence' of capitalist society.[25]

This classical and narrow interpretation of the new discourse still carried the tone of the Cultural Revolution, indicating that the Cultural Revolution Left found in these principles a useful weapon against the current trend of liberalization so as to protect their vested interests derived from the Cultural Revolution establishment. But the conservative discourse apparently did not win support from Deng, who advocated a more centrist approach to the four principles as shown in an article in *Renmin Ribao*, which distinguished two types of socialism: 'scientific socialism' and 'false socialism' and asserted the need to 'adhere to' and 'develop' Marxism and expressed a position which was later attributed to Deng that the only criterion for judging socialism is whether it can promote the rapid development of productive forces. The article attacked the leftists as the real enemies of the four principles because they only paid lip service to the principles while carrying out 'false socialism' which caused the Party to lose credibility.[26] Zhao Ziyang, then the Party secretary of Sichuan Province, criticized the ultra-leftist approach to the principles which only 'brings the four cardinal principles back to the distorted fallacy . . . of Lin Biao and the "Gang of Four",' but Zhao also criticized the ultra-rightism which 'doubts and opposes the four cardinal principles.'[27]

Reformers, afraid of being constrained by the narrow interpretation in promoting their own priorities, elected a broader and more flexible interpretation of the principles by stressing the need to both 'adhere to' and 'develop' them so as to facilitate economic and political reforms. Unlike Maoism, the embryonic and general nature of Deng's ideas also provided greater room for a process of creative interpretation and 'elective affinity'

[24]*Beijing Ribao*, 25 April 1979.
[25]*Hong Qi*, No. 5, 1979, p. 12.
[26]*Remin Ribao*, 11 May 1979.
[27]*Renmin Ribao*, 23 May 1979.

while Deng largely retained the power of arbitration and, generally speaking, a more reform-oriented centrist position.

3 The first campaign against bourgeois liberalization

Following the 1978 Third Plenum, China entered a period of rapid change. In rural areas the household responsibility system began to be implemented in many places, and in urban areas, Zhao Ziyang's Sichuan experience in decentralization was tried as an experiment. The first relatively free direct election of deputies to the county-level people's congresses was held in the autumn of 1980. Deng made his most authoritative speech on political reform on 18 August 1980 (not published in China until July 1983) in which Deng criticized over-centralization and bureaucratization. The Third Session of the Fifth People's Congress replaced Hua Guofeng with reformer Zhao Ziyang as premier of the State Council and deputies were allowed to question various cabinet ministers. In November 1980 the trial of the Gang of Four was staged.

However, the economic dislocations due to Hua's ambitious modernization programme and the new experiments in decentralization caused rising inflation and budget deficit, and limited political liberalization aroused suspicions on the part of many veteran Party leaders. Disagreement between advocates of reform and stabilization emerged with a strong ideological tone. A clear trend towards ideological conservatism was emerging since late 1980. This also indicated a shift of ideological tensions away from those between the reformers and the Cultural Revolution Left to those within the reformer's camp between reformers who wanted to further reform experiments and opening to the outside world and conservatives who urged for improved central command and tighter ideological control.

In addition to the above mentioned political and economic causes, the new conservative ideological trend was in part a reaction to an external factor: the 1980 Polish crisis and its possible impact on China where economic reform and political relaxation were creating a centrifugal force. The linkage between domestic and external events sometimes becomes crucial in changing China's domestic political orientations. For instance, the 1956 Hungarian Uprising was one major reason for Mao's reemphasis on the class struggle. On 24 September 1980, Hu

Qiaomu wrote a letter to Hu Yaobang warning of the possible impact of the Polish crisis on China in general and Chinese workers in particular. Hu Qiaomu wrote: 'The ideological, economic, political and cultural influence from outside China is a big problem for us.' He cautioned that China's reform could also lead to a situation similar to that in Poland where 'there were official trade unions and independent trade unions.'[28] Chen Yun stated that China must pay attention to the 'issue of propaganda' and the 'issue of economics.' Otherwise, Chen warned, 'the incident in Poland could also occur in China.'[29]

In contrast, reformers led by Hu Yaobang seemed determined to push through economic and political reforms. Liao Gailong, a senior researcher at the Policy Research Office of the CPC Central Committee, produced a revised report on political reform in early October, in which he outlined some unprecedentedly bold reform proposals ranging from establishing two chambers similar to the US Congress under the People's Congress to democratization of the Party, the government and enterprises. His thinking seemed to represent a group of 'Marxist democrats' in the Party. He traced China's systemic problems to Stalin and even Lenin. According to Liao,

> after the Russian Communist Party had become the ruling party, Lenin did not place the Party organization on a democratic basis,... Lenin's political theories emphasized the aspect of violent suppression of the dictatorship of the proletariat, and neglected its democratic aspect.[30]

Liao referred to Mao's statement of July 1957:

> We must bring about a political climate which has both centralism and democracy, discipline and freedom, unity of purpose and ease of mind for the individual, and which is lively and vigorous.[31]

On 15 October, Hu Yaobang also reaffirmed Mao's formulation and observed that Mao 'was unable to realize it' in his lifetime. Hu stressed that this task 'has now fallen upon us.' Hu was

[28]Ruan Ming, 1991, p. 50.
[29]*Ibid.*, p. 51.
[30]Liao Gailong, 'Zhonggong genshen gaige fangan' (CPC Reform Proposals in 1980), *The Seventies*, March 1981, pp. 38–48.
[31]*ibid.*

one of the first Chinese leaders who claimed that democracy 'is not only a means, but also an end.'[32]

Liao and Hu attempted to use this new discourse for shaping up new conventions. For instance, they interpreted the Polish crisis in terms of democracy and people's trust to reflect their own beliefs and aspirations. According to Hu Yaobang, the Polish Communist Party 'turned its back on the people and thus it lost the trust and sympathy of the people despite its past heroic struggle for them.' Such trust and sympathy 'went to the Catholic Church, because it is patriotic, while the Party is not.'[33] Therefore both Hu and Liao stressed the need to improve the relations between the Party and workers through democratization. And Liao went further to suggest that trade unions should undergo 'thorough reform' and become the 'loyal spokesmen' for the interests of workers while the Party exerted its influence only through its members working in the trade unions.[34]

But this more liberal discourse did not prevail when concern was growing at the top leadership about economic dislocations and possible political unrest. This ideological drift was further complicated by a top-level leadership struggle for establishing individual leaders' authority on reforms. Parallel with ideological alarm to the Polish crisis and the more orthodox discourse, was an attempt on the part of the more conservative reformers to project Chen Yun as another paramount leader on a par with Deng Xiaoping. In November 1980, Deng Liqun made four speeches at the Central Party School on the subject of 'Learning from Comrade Chen Yun on Economic Work.'[35] He claimed:

> The first man who has mastered the objective law of China's democratic revolution is Comrade Mao Zedong; while the first man who has mastered the objective law of China's socialist revolution and construction is Comrade Chen Yun.

He criticized many senior leaders like Lu Dingyi and Fang Yi

[32]Hu Yaobang, 'Guanyu sixiang zhengzhi gongzuo de ruogan wenti' (On Some Problems of Ideological and Political Work), 15 October 1980, *Dangfeng Wenti*, p. 88.
[33]*ibid.*, pp. 96–98.
[34]Liao Gailong, op. cit., p. 43.
[35]Deng Liqun, *Xiang chenyun tongzhi xuexi zuo jingji gongzuo* (Learning from Comrade Chen Yun in Doing Economic Work), Beijing, CPC Party School Press, 1981, (Internal Publication).

for their liberal statements made during internal discussions concerning the Party's draft resolution on Mao to be adopted the next year. Moreover, Deng Liqun organized the publication of Chen Yun's selected works to be 'studied earnestly by the whole Party.'[36] This attempt to back Chen Yun was a further indication that a rift was emerging in the reformers' camp as to who should have the ultimate authority on at least economic matters at a time when the Cultural Revolution Left's camp was shrinking.

In a work conference held in Beijing in December 1980, Chen Yun was confident enough to call for 'fundamentally readjusting the Party's guideline in economic work.' At the same time, he was the first to use the concept of 'bourgeois liberalization' to describe the ideological relaxation and he called for a struggle against such a trend. Unlike Schram's assertion that Liao Gailong's report on drastic political reform represented Deng's ideas,[37] Deng had in fact retreated in March 1979 from his 1978 position on democracy and participatory values. In the more conservative ideological atmosphere, Deng, who was still to consolidate his political authority, showed a far more cautious attitude towards political reform. Moreover, believing in the absolute need for stability, Deng was deeply concerned with the possible impact of the Polish crisis on China and feared a fast political reform and liberal discourse could lead to an ungovernable situation. His fear was revealed in his statement against the unorthodox ideologies. Deng himself shelved his proposal for political reform and began to focus on tighter political control. This time, he stated:

> We should criticize and oppose the tendency to worship capitalism and to advocate bourgeois liberalization. We should criticize and oppose the decadent bourgeois ideas of doing everything solely for profit, seeking advantage at the expense of others and always putting money first. We should criticize and oppose anarchism and ultra-individualism. We shall continue to promote exchanges with friendly Western countries and to learn whatever is useful to us

[36]Ruan Ming, 1991, p. 52.
[37]Stuart Schram, 1984, p. 20.

from capitalist countries. But we must carry this struggle in the ideological and political spheres through to the end.[38]

Deng's authoritarian tone, however, did not imply a change of his stand on decentralization. Deng still cautioned against the Party's excessive intervention in the functions of the government and enterprises. He specifically mentioned that the Party should divorce itself from much of the day-to-day 'running' of government and enterprises. The Party should instead strengthen the ideological education of its members and educate the masses about the need for unity and stability in a style similar to the traditional elitist way of communication and governance in Chinese history. In this context, Deng criticized the Party's ideological workers for their failure to 'propagate the four cardinal principles actively, confidently and with good results,' but he also cautioned them against any 'crude way' in handling ideological issues.[39]

The trend against ideological liberalism reached a new high in 1981. By adopting the same political tactics that Mao had used, such as choice of literary targets and the use of radical slogans, the conservatives singled out a literary work and its author as representative of 'bourgeois liberalization' for criticism in the media in April 1981. Their immediate purpose was to repress the liberal trend, which still maintained its vigour in the intellectual circles despite the conservative discourse since the 1980 work conference. The conservative-controlled army newspaper launched a criticism of the screenplay entitled *Unrequited Love* written by Bai Hua, a veteran army writer. The screenplay described a painter returning from abroad to serve his country, who ended up dead due to political persecution. Thus, Bai Hua raised the question, 'You love your motherland, but does your motherland love you?' The film, based on the screenplay, was condemned for casting a poor image of the Party and Mao and profaning the sacred, patriotic sentiments of the people for their motherland.[40]

But the resemblance between this critical discourse and that of Mao's immediately caused popular resentment, especially among Chinese intellectuals and some top leaders. Their experi-

[38]Deng Xiaoping (1984), 'Implement the Policy of Readjustment, Ensure Stability and Unity,' (December 25, 1980), p. 350.
[39]*ibid.*, pp. 344–355.
[40]*Jiefangjun Bao*, 21 April 1981.

ence of the Cultural Revolution was still fresh and their collective memory of the political persecution made them immediately identify the literary criticism as a sign of another political persecution campaign, which would produce much wider implications, and they resisted it spontaneously. *Renmin Ribao* and most of the provincial papers refused to continue the criticism, a sign of top-level ideological differences. At Beijing and Fudan Universities, wall posters condemned the leftist criticism of the liberal writer.[41] The Chinese intellectuals resisted the criticism of liberal thinking, and one of Bai Hua's poems was even honoured with a national prize, apparently with the approval of certain top leaders. All this suggested not only a rift within the top leadership on ideological issues but also a decisive change of popular attitude from the old era of 'complete subordination to the authority' to a new era in which intellectuals had greater freedom to choose whether to embrace the official line. Naturally, the top-level differences on the issue reduced the political cost of the intellectuals' non-cooperation.

In reaction to this, Deng seemed to have sensed two extreme trends: an increasingly hostile sentiment towards the Party, on the one hand, and an attempt to return to the Maoist days of ideological persecution, on the other. By his balancing act, Deng hoped to tackle both issues. He looked beyond the screenplay to the whole issue of society challenging the Party leadership. In reference to some liberal views, Deng claimed on 17 July 1981, they 'went far beyond certain wrong, anti-socialist statements criticized during the anti-Rightist struggle of 1957.' Deng described these anti-socialist elements as 'having a murderous look on their face' (shaqi tengteng), a very strong phrase in Chinese indicating that these people were now ready to fight a life-or-death struggle. Deng stressed the need to criticize Bai Hua's work for its 'erroneous tendency' of 'bourgeois liberalization.'[42]

Deng further defined the discursive terms of his four principles by claiming that 'the keystone of bourgeois liberalization

[41]Qi Xin, Zaipi baihua he ziyouhua qingxiang (Another Round of Criticism of Bai Hua and Liberal Trend), *The Seventies*, October 1981, p. 90.
[42]Deng Xiaoping, 'Dangqian sixiang zhanxian de ruoganwenti' (Concerning Problems on the Ideological Front), in JSFZ, pp. 153–157 and its English translation is contained in Deng Xiaoping (1984), pp. 367–371. (The official translation of 'shaqi tengteng' is simply 'how aggressive . . .' See p. 368).

is opposition to Party leadership.'[43] Therefore, Deng held that Party leadership should be the core of the four principles. In 1979, Deng gave equal importance to the four principles. In 1980, he gave more importance to socialism.[44] Now he gave priority to Party leadership. This could be considered as Deng's reaction to the social trends which had evolved from a general suspicion of socialism to directly questioning the authority of the Party. Deng argued that Bai Hua's work only created one impression on its reader:

> The Communist Party and the socialist system are bad. It vilifies the latter to such an extent that one wonders what has happened to the author's Party spirit. Some say the movie achieves a fairly high artistic standard, but that only makes it all the more harmful. In fact, a work of this sort has the same effect as the views of the so-called democrats.[45]

Deng further claimed that for a country of China's size, 'without Party leadership there definitely will be nationwide disorder and China would fall apart.'[46]

Another explanation of this discursive shift was that with the evolution of economic reforms Deng himself came to realize that the present concept of socialism was confusing and should be redefined. For instance, was the market-oriented reform a deviation from socialism? To what degree, should socialism allow non-public ownership? How did one justify the many apparently capitalist methods in the development of Chinese economy? On all this, Deng's ideas were still vague. But regarding Party's leadership, Deng had developed a clearer concept, which referred mainly to an enhanced organizational and ideological leadership and to a separation of the Party from the day-to-day 'running' of economic activities.

Deng's emphasis on the role of the Party also reflected the ideological resources he mainly relied upon: the Leninist tradition of Party elitism; the Chinese tradition of elitism; his per-

[43]Deng Xiaoping (1984), p. 369.
[44]Deng Xiaoping, Muqian de xingshi he renwu (The Present Situation and Tasks), (16 January 1980) in JSFZ, pp. 49 and its English translation is contained in Deng Xiaoping (1984), pp. 224–258. Deng claimed then that 'the four cardinal principles require us first and foremost to uphold socialiism.' p. 241)
[45]*ibid.*, p. 369.
[46]*ibid.*, p. 369.

sonal experience of the Chinese Revolution and the unifying role of the Party. He consistently held that only the Party was able to unify a country which had been called 'a sheet of loose sands.'

Another important development in the ideological tensions of this period was the reformers' deliberate efforts to transform the Maoist approach to an ideological struggle. Radical reformers like Hu Yaobang certainly did not like the campaign against bourgeois liberalization. But once launched by the conservatives, reformers, including Deng, endeavoured to confine such campaigns. They also attempted to transform, in the language of game theory, the past zero-sum game which involved a head-to-head conflict and an all-or-nothing situation, into a positive non-zero-sum game in which both players (the campaigners and their targets) could gain something.[47] Their approach was to prevent the campaigners from playing rough while offering the target rewards for a reasonable amount of cooperation. Deng, for instance, challenged the rude manner in which the army newspaper handled Bai Hua's work and cautioned the newspaper against repeating the mistakes of harsh treatment of intellectuals practiced in the Cultural Revolution. He claimed that some arguments and tactics used in the newspaper 'were not carefully thought out' and one must learn from past lessons. 'We must not,' Deng asserted, 'take the old path and resort to political movements.'[48]

Deng urged for more reasoning and persuaded the army newspaper not to publish anything more on the subject.[49] Deng also made deliberate efforts to confine this kind of criticism to the intelligentsia and did not allow it to expand into economic reforms or other areas. As a result, Hu Yaobang persuaded Bai Hua to criticize himself and confess his 'ideological errors.' Hu then quickly declared that Bai Hua

> has recognized his mistakes through (outside) criticism and made self-criticism. This is very good. By doing this, the issue of *Unrequited Love* came to a satisfactory end . . . Com-

[47]For a discussion on various games, see Martin Shubik, *Game Theory in the Social Sciences: Concepts and Solutions*, Cambridge, Mass., The MIT Press, 1984.
[48]in JSFZ, p. 90 and Deng Xiaoping (1984), p. 369.
[49]*ibid.*

> rade Bai Hua is still a Party member and a writer, and he will continue writing.

Hu clearly wanted to drive the point home that the present approach to intellectuals was different from the past. Hu commented:

> People now can see that the guideline and approach adopted by the Party's Central Committee are very different from those in certain periods in the past. Such a difference has shown that our Party has indeed drawn useful lessons from the past mistakes and setbacks.[50]

This short revival of the conservative ideological campaign was significant in several aspects: First, it was an indication of the strength of the conservative forces inside the Party and the military, who were deeply disturbed by the on-going economic and political liberalization. Second, Deng was determined to keep the leading role of the Party, and he was ready to criticize any ideological tendencies which challenged the Party. But Deng and Hu intended to adopt, in contrast to the heavy-handed methods of the Cultural Revolution, a relatively mild approach (so-called 'criticism and self-criticism'), in an attempt to check any deviations from the Party's line without alienating the intellectuals from the Party. Third, despite Deng's intention to keep the middle course, the campaign increased the political cost of reform by reinforcing the collective memory of past ideological movements, which did not favour the bold thinking and creativity that reformers desired in the reform process. This first major campaign also created a precedent in post-Mao era for ideological campaigns which always gather the support of ideologues and anti-reformers. Reoccurring several times since 1978, such ideological campaigns had an unfavourable impact on China's economic reform.

4 The 12th CPC Congress and socialism with Chinese characteristics

The preparation for the Party Congress, as usual, was marked by competing ideologies trying to influence the setting of policy

[50] Wenxue yishu he jingshen wenming (Literature, Arts and Spiritual Civilization), *Liaowang*, No. 2, 1982, p. 4.

agenda and personnel reshuffling. Since early 1981, Hu Yaobang was preparing a new ideological platform for the 12th CPC Congress. Two issues were controversial: First, what should constitute the core of 'socialist spiritual civilization,' a concept put forward by some Party veterans to parallel China's modernization programme ('socialist material civilization')? For the masses, Hu Yaobang stressed that the emphasis should be placed on raising the general level of education and science rather than communist ideology, which was the 'belief' system of the Party members. But conservative ideologues argued that the latter should be the priority.

This was illustrated by an article in *Jiefangjun Bao* written by Zhao Yayi, a veteran army propaganda chief, entitled 'Communist Ideology is the Core of Socialist Spiritual Civilization' in August 1982,[51] just prior to the convening of the 12th CPC Congress. The publication expressed the conservatives' efforts to reassert their influence before the Congress. The author of this article argued that there should be a class-based position in analyzing the previous civilizations. According to the author, capitalist civilization had caused 'countless grave disasters' to humanity in general and the working class in particular such that it should not be incorporated into the Party's programme to be adopted at the Congress. The author was apparently not in favour of Deng Xiaoping's open-door policy, which encouraged the inflow of Western management and technology.

Furthermore, the article challenged Hu Yaobang and Deng Xiaoping's view on the importance of culture and education so as to produce qualified and competent people for China's modernization. The author argued that one's education should not be a condition for his political consciousness and that well-educated intellectuals should learn from many poorly-educated people if the latter had more lofty ideals. Disturbed by this apparently 'leftist discourse,' Hu Yaobang immediately ordered a stop to further publishing this article, and the army newspaper had to release a self-criticism on the article a month later.

The second issue was that of a developmental model for China. In 1977–1978 the Yugoslavian and Romanian models

[51] *Jiefangjun Bao*, 28 August 1982.

were highly valued on both ideological and economic grounds. Since then reformers and their newly-established think tanks conducted substantial research on different models of development. For instance, the Institute of Marxism-Leninism-Mao Zedong Thought sent groups to study the experience of Hungary, Italy, France, the Netherlands and Switzerland and attended such forums as 'Socialism in the World' held in Yugoslavia. Officials and economists were sent to some 'Little Dragons' and many other countries to study developmental experience ranging from processing zones to export-oriented strategies. Inside China, Hu Yaobang ordered specialists to conduct research on what China would be like in the year 2000, which gave an impetus to searching for new ideas. Such studies all suggested that China should not copy any foreign experience, not even that of socialist countries. Given China's bitter experience with the Soviet model, the existing problems with the East European models and China's political culture in favour of Chinese uniqueness, it was fairly easy to reach a quick consensus that there was no fixed model for China's development and that China should explore its own approach to modernization. Hu openly stated this idea prior to the 12th Congress and Deng developed this into a new discourse of what he called 'building socialism with Chinese characteristics,' which later became the synonym of Deng Xiaoping's doctrine.

The 12th CPC Congress was held in September 1982 amid high expectation of economic reforms. Deng attributed to it an historical watershed comparable to the 7th CPC Congress in 1945, which established a relative ideological uniformity in the Party and laid a political basis for Mao's eventual victory in 1949. In terms of ideology and its discursive framework, the 12th Congress was noted for three themes: First, emphasis on 'socialist spiritual civilization' and intra-Party democracy. Second, the decision on Party rectification; and third, Deng's concept of 'socialism with Chinese characteristics.'

On the issue of 'socialist spiritual civilization,' Hu Yaobang claimed:

> In the process of transforming the objective world, people also transform their subjective world, and the production of spiritual values and the spiritual life of society also

develop . . . Material civilization provides an indispensable foundation for socialist spiritual civilization which, in its turn, gives a tremendous impetus to the former and ensures its correct orientation. Each is the condition and the objective of the other.[52]

In analyzing the 12th CPC Congress, Lowell Dittmer regarded Hu's statement as 'making culture/ideology a function of economics,' but Hu's last remark revealed a lapse 'from transitivity to reciprocal causation.'[53] On the whole, Hu presented a balanced discursive framework that combined culture and education with communist belief, but Hu's emphasis was placed on education, culture and science, work ethics and moral integrity.

Pragmatism was also shown in linking the new discourse with improving the functional efficiency of the Party. In his political report to the Congress, Hu interpreted 'socialist spiritual civilization' as an impetus to promote the intra-Party democracy and improve the conduct of the Party. Describing the intra-Party democracy as the best guarantee of 'socialist spiritual civilization,' Hu attempted to tackle the tough issue of Party reorganization and rectification, claiming that only by solving these issues could 'spiritual civilization' be achieved. The linkage of the new ideological discourse with proposals for functional rationality provided added authority to reformers' restructuring programme.

Hu's political report built up a new discursive framework for the Party's restructuring. He severely criticized such problems as 'over-concentration of power, proliferation of concurrent and deputy posts, organizational overlapping, lack of clear-cut job responsibility, over-staffing and failure to separate Party work from government work,' which were blamed as incompatible with 'socialist spiritual civilization.'[54] The Congress decided to abolish the chairman system, to establish the Secretariat and to turn the Central Committee into three concurrent organs – the central committee, the commission for the inspection of

[52]Hu Yaobang, Quanmian kaichuang shehuizhuyi xiandaihua jianshe de xinjumian (Open up a New Situation in Socialist Modernization – Report to the 12th CPC Congress), in JGKG, pp. 205–226 and *Renmin Ribao*, 8 September 1982.
[53]Lowell Dittmer, 'The 12th Congress of the Communist Party of China,' *China Quarterly*, No. 89, March 1983, p. 119.
[54]*Renmin Ribao*, 8 September 1982.

discipline and the central advisory committee. Though a significantly weakened reform plan compared with that of 1980, the attempted functional separation of powers within the Party was a step towards more intra-Party democracy. As proved in later years, these institutions did to a limited extent check and balance each other.

The new power structure was generally more in favour of the reformers. As Hu Yaobang became the head of the Secretariat and Zhao Ziyang Premier, both would work at the 'front line.' The Politburo became the second line and was to play the role as a 'board of directors.'[55] This restructuring granted much enhanced power to Hu and Zhao in the daily management of the Party affairs and economic reforms.

In line with Deng's call for improving the efficiency of the Party, Hu also stressed the need to separate the function of the Party from that of the government. Hu claimed:

> Party leadership is mainly political and ideological in matters of principles and policy and in the selection, allocation, assessment and supervision of cadres. It should not be equated with administrative work and the direction of production by government organs and enterprises.

This formulation could be considered another step towards a clearer elaboration of Deng's discourse on Party leadership. Although the attempted new convention facilitated Party restructuring at the central committee level, it proved difficult to implement across the country mainly because of local cadres' opposition due to their vested interests. This is the main reason why reformers also decided to launch a Party rectification campaign throughout the country.

The campaign was aimed at improving the Party's organizational purity and checking the 'unhealthy tendencies' (corruption, economic crimes, etc.), which were allegedly caused by the 'vicious influence' of the Cultural Revolution and the 'corrosive effect of bourgeois ideology under the new situation.' Bruce Dickson noted that one major difference between the present rectification and those in the Maoist period was that 'it is less concerned with the Maoist belief in the ability of the

[55]Zen Jianwei, Xinlao jiaoti jiwang kailai (The New Replacing the Old and Carrying forward the Cause), *Liaowang*, No. 10, 1982, p. 2.

party to change people's thinking than it is in the desire to simply control their behaviour.'[56]

Keeping with the Leninist tradition of party-building, Chinese communists tended to associate the strength of the Party with ideological unity and organizational purity. Ideological unity was more based on Hu's interpretation of 'socialist spiritual civilization' so as to ensure broad respect for the reformers' policies such as promoting intellectuals and professionals to responsible positions. To achieve an enhanced functional efficiency of the Party, both reformers and conservatives agreed on the pressing need to completely remove the Cultural Revolution Left from different localities and grass-roots units and replace them with pro-reform candidates. Deng singled out three types of people for removal: those who rose to prominence during the Cultural Revolution by following Lin Biao and the Gang of Four; those who were seriously factionalist in their ideas; and those who indulged in beating, smashing and looting. Chen Yun claimed that those 'who have already been promoted must be resolutely removed from the leading bodies.'[57] It was also planned that at the final stage of the rectification campaign, there would be an institutional arrangement for a re-registration of all Party members to as to enhance the Party's organizational purity.

To achieve this purpose, reformers carefully planned a process of theoretical study to establish a new ideological convention within the Party rank and file. The Party members were required to study a set of written texts and Party documents, including the new Party constitution, in order to establish the code for the criterion of the Party members' proper behaviour before any administrative actions were taken. At the Second Session of the 12th CPC Central Committee held in October 1983, the 'Decision on Party Rectification' was officially adopted. It explicitly stressed the importance of ideological conformity through the study of a new set of texts, which included the recently published selected works of Deng Xiaoping and several speeches by Chen Yun. Obviously, the rectification campaign was used to reinforce the ideological authority of Deng Xiaoping and

[56]Bruce Dickson, 'Conflict and Non-Compliance in Chinese Politics: Party Rectification, 1983–87,' *Pacific Affairs*, Vol. 63, No. 2, Summer 1990, p. 181.
[57]JSFZ, p. 48.

Chen Yun in the course of reform, although more emphasis seemed to be placed on Deng's works, which had been claimed as an 'enrichment to Mao Zedong Thought.' Both Deng and Chen understood the importance of enhanced ideological authority which can be easily translated into political authority.

At the Congress, Deng Xiaoping advanced perhaps the most important ideological concept in his political career: 'building socialism with Chinese characteristics.' Deng stated,

> In carrying out our modernization programme we must proceed from Chinese realities. . . . We must integrate the universal truth of Marxism with the concrete realities of China, blaze a path of our own and build a socialism with Chinese characteristics.[58]

Deng's new discourse was significant in several ways. First, it showed Deng's determination to explore a unique path of reform and modernization. To this end, Deng needed a broadly interpreted socialism and a more permissive discursive framework to initiate and justify experiments. Second, Deng began to deviate from the moderate Leninist approach, which was still the prevailing convention, although Deng was not yet in a position to seriously challenge this convention. Deng did not have Mao's absolute authority, especially in the economic field. Such an authority had to be earned. The new discourse could be regarded as an important step taken by Deng to build up his authority.

The third point was often neglected by Deng watchers: this new formula also reflected Deng's strong sense of nationalism. It was put forward at a time of rising Chinese nationalism partly triggered by the Reagan administration's heavy-handed ideological approach to China and Taiwan. This seemed to convince Deng to abandon his earlier hope for significant closer ties with the United States. Deng decided in 1982 to distance China from the United States by pursuing an 'independent foreign policy.' In his same speech to the Party Congress, Deng stated bluntly that 'no foreign country should expect China to become

[58]Deng Xiaoping, 'Opening Speech at the Twelfth National Congress of the Communist Party of China,' (September 1, 1982), Vol. 3, p. 14.

its vassal (fuyong) or swallow the bitter fruit by undermining China's own interests.'[59]

One constant source of Deng's ideological values was China's modern humiliating experience with the Western powers; this experience had nurtured Deng's nationalist inclination. He viewed the existing world markets as favouring more developed countries, and he saw power relations as unfavourable to economically backward countries like China. This frame of mind was a decisive determinant of Deng's belief in realpolitik, in the strengthening of China's national power and in retaining Chinese identity. At Deng's initiative, the Party Congress put forward the goal of quadrupling China's industrial and agricultural output by the year 2000. Deng repeatedly stressed that this target only meant moderately decent living standards for the Chinese (per capita income around $800–1,000), but in terms of 'overall national strength,' Deng claimed that China would be much stronger. Deng hoped to attract Western capital and technology, but he had a fairly critical assessment of what he perceived as reality. He remarked four months before the Party Congress:

> It isn't easy to get funds and advanced technology from the developed countries. There are still some people around who are wedded to the ideas of the old-line colonialists; they are reluctant to see the poor countries develop, and attempt to throttle them. Therefore, while pursuing the policy of opening to the outside world, we must stick to the principle of relying mainly on our own efforts, . . . [60]

In another statement made in 1979, he grouped China's friends into two types: those who supported China's stability and 'wish to see China strong' and those who 'merely wish to expand trade with China.'[61] As a nationalist, Deng was deter-

[59]This is a literal translation of Deng's remark. The official translation is: 'No foreign country should expect China to be its vassal or to accept anything that is damaging to China's own interests.' See Deng Xiaoping, 'Opening Speech at the Twelfth National Congress of the Communist Party of China,' (September 1, 1982), Vol. 3, pp. 14–15.

[60]Deng Xiaoping (1984), 'China's Historical Experience of Economic Construction,' (May 6, 1982), pp. 383–384.

[61]Deng Xiaoping (1984), 'Uphold the Four Cardinal Principles,' (May 30, 1979), p. 184.

mined to make the country strong by attracting foreign capital, technology and management techniques, but Deng refrained from a complete embrace of the West, fearing the loss of China's identity as a major power. Deng called for guarding against the corrosive influence of 'external decadent ideologies.' It was reasonable to conclude that one purpose of Deng's discourse on 'socialism with Chinese characteristics' was to highlight the Chinese national and ideological identity and independence from both the Soviet communist model and the Western capitalist model.

Deng did not further elaborate his concept of socialism with Chinese characteristics, nor did Hu Yaobang in his report to the Congress. This vagueness suggested that Deng was apparently still to explore a more coherent ideology for his reform programme. By keeping the concept general, normative and flexible, Deng was able to ensure a wide discursive acceptance of the new formula. This was already significant for reforms and reformers. On the one hand, the concept retained the ideological consistency by stressing 'socialism' which was essential for leadership consensus. On the other hand, it allowed for more theoretical innovations and flexible policies under 'Chinese characteristics.' One reformist economist commented that 'the concept is so ideologically flexible that we have enough room to manoeuver within it.'[62] Methodologically, this discourse showed Deng's philosophical root in Mao's 'unity of opposites,' namely, a unity of the general (socialism) and the specific (Chinese characteristics). This concept, apparently acceptable to all, paved the way for an agreement on the general orientation of economic reform. The 12th CPC Congress adopted a compromise convention: the primary role of planning was affirmed while the supplementary role of the market was also noted. Greater openness to the outside world was balanced by the renewed call for resisting Western ideological influence.

Soon after the Congress, Deng discussed the issue of socialism with the visiting North Korean President Kim Il Sung. Deng once again stressed development as the primary goal of socialism. In a sharp contrast to Mao's 'politics in command,' Deng told Kim:

[62]Wang Xiaoqiang's conversation with the author on 27 November 1991 in Cambridge, U.K. Wang was ex-Deputy Director of the Institute for Research on the Restructuring of the Economic System.

> We must concentrate on economic development. In a country as big and as poor as ours, if we don't try to increase production, how can we survive? How is socialism superior, when our people have so many difficulties in their lives?[63]

Deng described the alleged Gang of Four's concept of 'poor socialism' and 'poor communism' as 'sheer nonsense.' Deng claimed:

> at the first stage of communism, . . . we must do all we can to develop the productive forces and gradually eliminate poverty, constantly raising the people's living standards. Otherwise, how will socialism be able to triumph over capitalism? . . . When economy is highly developed and there is overwhelming material abundance, we shall be able to apply the principle of from each according to his ability, to each according to his needs.[64]

Although Deng related the present economic development to the future of communism, Deng's primary concern was China's immediate task of removing poverty, and his whole formative doctrine of Chinese-style socialism was built around this theme.

B Ideology and reform policies

1 Challenging Hua's economic policies

One major objective of reformers in establishing a discursive framework on the criterion of truth was to challenge the prevailing Maoist economic conventions, which Hua Guofeng still attempted to defend, and to provide a new ideological foundation for reformist policy alternatives.

It is a common practice in an ideological political system that the ruling party makes a general assessment of doctrinal relevance of the prevailing situation at every critical turning-point of history. When Hua Guofeng restarted the four modernizations programme, his assessment of the prevailing situation

[63]Deng Xiaoping, 'We shall Concentrate on Economic Development,' (September 18, 1982), Vol. 3, p. 21.
[64]*ibid.*

was that the main obstacle to rapid economic growth was largely, if not entirely, the result of the 'sabotage of Lin Biao and the Gang of Four.' Hua claimed that the gradual elimination of this political obstacle could lead to a process of rapid economic development. The causal impact of Maoist economic convention was not an issue, and the radical Maoist models such as Daqing and Dazhai were still praised, while the Gang of Four was labelled as the 'fake left, real right'.

While certain extreme economic policies of the Cultural Revolution were abandoned and the notion of enterprise profitability and the principle of 'distribution according to one's work' rehabilitated, many of the Cultural Revolution's economic conventions and institutions remained intact, such as self-sufficiency and revolutionary committees. Political 'stability and unity' were considered the purpose of economic development. The absence of a fundamental departure from the Maoist convention was reflected in many articles. In 'Great Guiding Principles for Socialist Construction' written by the State Planning Commission and published in *Renmin Ribao*,[65] the main emphasis in promoting the economy was still placed on class contradictions and class struggles with 'grasping revolution and promoting production' as the key in solving all problems. According to Yu Qiuli, Minister in charge of the State Planning Commission, the struggle against the Gang of Four would be the powerful impetus to economic growth and the roots of China's economic problems did not lie in the central planning system itself but rather in the 'failure to correctly implement central planning and its requirements.'[66] The media still criticized Liu Shaoqi's economic policies. It was in this ideological context that Hua set out his ambitious modernization programme.

Hua's ambitious modernization plan was actually a revival of Deng's 1975 plan, a ten-year period for the first stage which called for 400 million metric tons of grain, a 60 million ton capacity for steel production, and an overall 10 per cent annual increase in industrial production by 1985. This plan was to be followed by several five-year plans to move China 'into the front

[65]*Renmin Ribao*, 12 September 1977.
[66]*Remin Ribao*, 25 October 1977.

ranks of the world economy.'[67] The unrealistic modernization programme produced policies in favour of heavy industry, a high accumulation rate, a high growth rate, a rapid rural mechanization and a substantial increase in imports. Hua was still both conditioned by the Stalinist doctrine of economic development and the Maoist 'leap forward' which seemed to have neglected to a considerable extent China's actual conditions and 'absorptive capacity.'

From early 1978 onwards, however, some rehabilitated economists and Party officials began to privately question the validity of Hua's approach. Questions such as the 'law of value' and 'economic methods' were raised and discussed in certain closed meetings due to the ideological and political sensitivity of the subjects.

The debate on the criterion of truth in May 1978, however, decisively changed the situation in the sense that it provided a new and more permissive climate for rethinking many of Hua's policies and offered a new discursive framework for discussing formerly sensitive issues. Since the new discourse had even challenged the validity of Mao's instructions, everything else could be subject to reexamination. As a result, there emerged an explosion of discussions on many formerly taboo subjects in the Chinese media.

The first major policy statement critical of Hua's programme was made by Hu Qiaomu, the president of the newly established Chinese Academy of Social Sciences. At the State Council, Hu delivered a speech on 'observing objective economic laws and speeding up the four modernizations,' in which he discussed some basic principles which would entail a moderate economic reform. Hu reassessed Stalin's theory on the incompatibility between the 'law of value' and the 'law of planned and proportionate development.' He introduced the concept of underdeveloped productive forces to stress the need for a significant deviation from Stalin's theory, and he observed that the two laws could be made mutually interdependent under socialist conditions characterized by underdeveloped productive forces. In other words, a socialist country should respect the 'law of value' in its planned economy and China should readjust certain prices so as to reflect the balance between supply and demand

[67]Hua Guofeng, 'Report on the Work of the Government,' *Peking Review*, No. 10, March 1978, p. 19.

and grant greater autonomy to enterprises under central planning. These remarks raised an ideologically sensitive issue of whether socialist central planning should allow a market role in the form of price mechanism. The fact that Hu's speech was not published until 6 October 1978, almost five months later, indicated a serious controversy about the speech among the top leaders.[68]

Since then, many theoretical discussions touching upon almost every aspect of Hua's economic approach were reported in the Chinese media. Among the issues discussed openly from 1978 to 1980 were: 'What should be the major contradiction in the new era (class struggle or economic development)?'; 'Why has there been a consistent pattern of imbalance in favour of heavy industry at the expense of agriculture and light industry?'; 'What is the purpose of economic development?' and 'What should be China's development model?' A clearly pro-reform discursive framework was emerging from these discussions.

One way to build such a reformist framework was still the traditional method of indoctrination. The institutionalized Party cells at the grass-roots level organized political sessions to study official articles and the Party's designated documents. For instance, study sessions on the criterion of truth were held in almost all enterprises and government institutions in late 1978, and the same was true of the discussion on the purpose of socialist production in late 1979. This kind of institutionalized indoctrination was employed to facilitate the creation of pro-reform conventions so as to influence the Party rank and file and ordinary workers with pro-reform values. In such study sessions, people were informed about the new policies and discussed their relevance to localized reality.

While it was a 'participation without influence' as described by Andrew Nathan,[69] such practice, in comparison with that in the Cultural Revolution, was reduced in frequency and intensity, and participants were far more open and frank in presenting their views. The ideological materials were also more relevant to the political and economic reality of the country. For instance,

[68]Hu Qiaomu, 'Observe Economic Laws, Speed up the Four Modernizations,' *Renmin Ribao*, 6 October 1978.

[69]Andrew Nathan, *Chinese Democracy*, London, I. B. Tauris & Co. Ltd, 1986, p. 227.

a key-note article used in such studies was 'Why Is It Necessary to Discuss the Purpose of Socialist Production?'[70] which claimed that according to Marxism the purpose of production was to 'meet the increasing material needs of the people;' therefore it was necessary to redress the imbalance between light industry, agriculture and heavy industry. Opponents to the new policy simply ignored the fact that the Chinese 'workers, peasants and intellectuals still live a hard life.' Moral judgment notwithstanding, reformers still widely used ideological indoctrination in late 1970s and later to undermine the ideological basis of undesirable economic policies and to prepare new conventions for Deng's economic reforms.

The new ideological convention based on seeking truth from facts justified a deviation from many prevailing policies and the adoption of more realistic ones. For instance, the Third Plenum itself initiated a number of new policies in deviation from Hua's modernization programme such as vigorously developing light industry and greater decision making power for rural communes and brigades. But the Cultural Revolution Left still possessed power and influence at the top-level of leadership where the commitment to the new convention was not yet fully established.

Consequently, reformers had to introduce new policy alternatives with tremendous ideological precaution. Many interpretations of Maoist ideological values and policies were slightly altered with a shift of emphasis rather than categorically rejected. For instance, while the Decision at the Third Plenum reaffirmed Mao's 'taking grain as the key link and ensuring an all-round development,' reformers now placed more emphasis than before on 'all-round development.' Therefore, farmers' 'side-occupations' or individuals' initiatives in growing fruit, vegetables and livestock that had long been considered as 'capitalist tails' were encouraged to 'develop simultaneously' and 'should not be interfered with.' The Decision also set out some general principles such as 'giving priority to mobilizing the initiative of hundreds of millions of Chinese peasants' and encouraging measures which 'develop rural economy' rather than gave all the details of policies.[71]

This approach adopted by reformers was aimed at, on the

[70] *Renmin Ribao*, 24 November 1979.
[71] JGKG, p. 3.

one hand, reducing political resistance and controversy to the minimum and ensuring a top-level political consensus so as to get reforms off the ground speedily, and on the other hand it also encouraged grass-roots experimentation to produce results which could in turn induce further doctrinal changes. Given the top-level political constraints, reformers seemed to often rely more on the causal impact of practice on doctrinal innovations as shown in China's rural reform: grass-roots economic reforms produced tangible results, which then influenced top-level politics and consequently induced greater doctrinal renovation.

With the growing strength of reformers and the spread of grass-roots reform experiments, a more direct confrontation in the field of economic policies between reformers and the Cultural Revolution Left became inevitable. In the process of such conflicts, reformers frequently raised policy issues to the level of ideology and discussed them in the new pro-reform discursive framework so as to accuse reform opponents and their policies for violating the Party's prevailing conventions. The rehabilitated economic planner Chen Yun led this challenge. In sharp contrast to Hua's economic policies which gave weight to heavy industry and accumulation, Chen Yun had been an advocate of an economic ideology that retained Stalin's concept of central planning and proportional development but stressed balance over speed, consumption over accumulation, and light industry over heavy industry.

Chen Yun was critical of Hua's ambitious modernization programme, including his plan for the massive importation of advanced foreign technology and capital equipment from the West and Japan. Chen used the new ideological formula of 'seeking truth from facts' to its full extent by literally challenging Hua Guofeng: 'if we say seeking truth from facts, then what facts is China faced with?' According to Chen, the basic facts were: first, China had a population of 1 billion, of which 800 million were peasants; this justified his claim of priority in agriculture. Second, modernization in a country of China's size could only be achieved on the basis of its existing industry. Hua's large-scale import plan was therefore criticized as an attempt to have an imported modernization, which ignored China's foreign currency status and 'absorptive capacity.' Chen also cautioned against using foreign loans in financing these projects. Chen cited ideological differences between socialism and capitalism as one reason to warn against any unrealistic dream about Western assistance when he stated that 'we must see clearly that foreign capitalists are also capitalists.' Chen, in fact, maintained his position on the issue when the reformers later planned large-scale borrowing.[72] At the conference on economic work held in April 1979, Chen Yun once again raised the issue of economic readjustment to the ideological level by arguing that 'at present the biggest problem is not economic readjustment but ideology.' According to Chen, the old Stalinist economic thinking which stressed heavy industry at the expense of agriculture had created a national economy of 'high speed, high accumulation, poor results, and low consumption.'[73]

A leadership consensus on two issues was reached at this conference: first, Chen Yun's call for a three-year period of 'readjusting, restructuring, consolidating, and improving the national economy' was officially approved. The readjustment policy included a strategy for the vigorous development of agriculture, light industry and international trade and second, Zhao Ziyang's Sichuan experience in urban reform was approved. Its main feature was to delegate greater decision-making powers to local authorities and enterprises over the use of investment funds and economic activities. If the truth debate signaled a decisive victory for reformers in the ideological field and the Third Plenum a decisive victory of the reformers over the Cultural Revolution Left in the political field, then this conference marked a decisive victory for the reformers in economic policy. The truth debate could be regarded as the major catalyst for this chain of changes which placed China on a new path of development because the debate provided an entirely new convention credible enough to challenge the old conventions and offered a new discursive framework innovative enough to induce and legitimize meaningful policy debate and deviations.

[72]Chen Yun, Jianchi anbili yuanze tiaozheng guomin jingji (Adhere to the proportionate principle in readjusting the national economy), 21 March 1979, JGKG, pp. 21–25.
[73]*ibid.*, p. 27.

2 The reassessment of the role of the market

One immediate impact of the new convention on economic reform was manifest in theoretical debates. Thanks to the truth debate, economics was finally considered as a science with its autonomy free from ideological interference. However, Chinese economic discourse and policy debate were still influenced and constrained by the old ideological conventions from the very beginning of reform. The main controversy occurred around the market issue, which had long been regarded in classic Marxism as the antithesis of socialism; therefore, the market-oriented reforms in a socialist context were bound to arouse controversy. The constant ideological campaigns had further complicated the market issue.

The new doctrine, however, permitted many economists and economic officials to question the fundamental causes of China's economic problems and the market's role in economic reforms. To outsiders, such controversies may seem metaphysical and meaningless, but to Chinese reformers and conservatives alike, they carry extremely significant political and policy implications.

Since, the truth debate started, many economists began to reassess the market's role in the Chinese economy. At a symposium held in Wuxi of Jiangsu Province in April 1979, over 300 scholars gathered to discuss the issue of market economy. Three views emerged: the first one held that planned economy and market economy should integrate with each other. The second school held that 'socialist market economy constitutes a new form of market economy based on public ownership of the means of production.' But the predominant view assumed that socialist economy should be planned economy, and the concept of combining market economy with planned economy was 'ambiguous' and as 'illogical' as 'mixing the whole with the part.'[74]

At a meeting held from July to September 1979 on accelerating the four modernizations initiated by the State Council, more progress towards acceptance of market mechanisms was made. The concept of 'combining planned economy and market economy' was formally raised in discussion. But the term 'market

[74]Wu Jinglian, *Jihua jingji haishi shichang jingji* (Planned economy or market economy), Beijing, Chinese Economics Press, 1993, pp. 134–135.

economy' still proved too ideologically sensitive. In the end, top-echelon economic officials and most economists reached a consensus on the definition of the present stage of Chinese economy as 'the commodity economy combining planning regulation with market regulation.' In September 1980, this concept was officially incorporated into the report, prepared by the Office of Economic Reform under the State Council, entitled 'Initial Proposals on Economic Structural Reform.' The report stated that the 'orientation' of China's economic reform should be market oriented: while adhering to the predominant public ownership, China should make use of economic laws 'in light of the demand of commodity economy and economy of scale' and 'transform the present single mode of planning regulation into the mode of market regulation under the guidance of planning.'[75]

Deng's view on market economy was, however, more positive. In November 1979, Deng told a delegation from Encyclopedia Britannica, Inc. when being questioned about whether socialism can adopt market economy:

> It is surely not correct to say that market economy is only confined to capitalist society. Why cannot socialism engage in (gao) market economy? . . . A market economy existed already in the feudal society. Socialism may also engage in market economy.[76]

But Deng's idea, bold as it was, did not possess any operational power, because Deng did not explain in late 1979, when private ownership and private economy were still not permitted under Chinese law, how a market economy could operate. But Deng's idea was provocative. Addressing the market economy mainly from a political and ideological perspective, Deng seemed to suggest: (1) a market economy should be ideologically acceptable in socialist China; (2) socialist public ownership should not necessarily conflict with the market; and (3) experiments in applying a market economy in China should be tolerated. Straying too far from the prevailing convention, Deng's remarks were only known to a small circle of leaders and intellectuals and were not made public until the early 1990s,

[75]*ibid.*, pp. 135.

[76]Gao Lu, 'Shehuizhuyi shichang jingji tifa chutai shimo' (the Origin of the Wording 'Socialist Market Economy'), *Jingji Ribao*, 14 November 1992.

although Deng made some less straightforward remarks to a similar effect in early 1980s. This fact itself showed the prudence with which Deng treated ideologically sensitive issues and the limited authority Deng had on economic matters. It perhaps also suggested that Deng himself was not yet confident enough about the market's role.

The ideological sensitivity and insecurity about the market were also illustrated by the fact that Deng dealt with the problem by alternately emphasizing and then de-emphasizing the market's role in the late 1970s and early 1980s. But what distinguished Deng from many other leaders was that Deng always allowed market-oriented experiments to continue and constantly justified these practices as socialist. Deng had made a consistent effort to gradually develop his pro-market doctrine.

Ideological controversy over the market's role was particularly sharp in the 1980/1981 drive against bourgeois liberalization and around the 12th CPC Congress. Such debates were not simply academic. They had profound policy implications. For instance, what kind of economic polices should China adopt to redress her persistent pattern of economic imbalance? Should priority be given to the policy of readjustment or to that of reform? Chen Yun held that a readjustment mainly through administrative means could improve central planning and thus reduce the sectoral imbalance. Meanwhile, more radical reformers believed that a centrally planned economy was the root cause of such imbalance and that market mechanisms such as prices, loans, and interests should be employed to restructure the Chinese economy and restore sectoral imbalance. Therefore they held that China's economic reform should be clearly market-oriented. But Chen Yun's view on economic readjustment gained predominance thanks in part to the first drive against bourgeois liberalization in the mid-1980, which virtually silenced any call for the market-orientation of China's economic reform.

Renmin Ribao's editorial 'Firmly Grasp Readjustment as a Crucial Factor'[77] highlighted Chen Yun's opinion. It claimed that 'there is at present the view that the root cause of our economy's imbalance has been the present system of economic management. Unless the system undergoes thorough reforms, China's

[77]*Renmin Ribao*, 27 May 1980.

readjustment will get nowhere. In our opinion, such a view is lop-sided.' In June and July, the same paper published a series of editorials calling for economic readjustment and greater prudence and caution in economic reform.

At the work conference of December 1980, Chen Yun and Li Xiannian argued for 're-centralizing' the economy and called for a clear commitment to putting 'readjustment' before 'reform.' Chen stressed the need for reimposing ideological and social controls while ensuring careful planning and tighter control over imports and prices. Chen and Li also urged a comprehensive review of reforms, including those in the SEZs. The post-Great Leap readjustment in the early 1960s was hailed as a model of readjustment and cautious reforms. Deng Xiaoping seemed to have to acquiesce to Chen Yun's authority in the economic field, where Deng's authority was still weak, although Deng was gradually building his own authority through rural reform and the SEZs. He expressed support for Chen Yun's arguments for re-centralization. Deng said that during the forthcoming period, 'the focus should be placed on readjustment. Reform should serve readjustment, . . . reform should be conducive to readjustment rather than hinder it.' But Deng also tried to differentiate the present readjustment from the old one of the early 1960s, claiming that the present policy was more limited and taken by the Chinese leaders of their own accord. Ideologically, Deng was now on the defensive and stressed that his effort for emancipating the mind was within the four cardinal principles and therefore compatible with upholding Marxist orthodoxy.[78]

As the drive against bourgeois liberalism was mounting since the early 1980s, the conservatives even started a kind of witch hunt. In January 1981, the Research Office of the State Council, headed by Deng Liqun, claimed that they were ready to 'launch a decisive battle against bourgeois liberalization by writing on 200 questions relating to theory, culture, education, science, and the press.'[79]

In April 1981, when the first campaign against 'bourgeois liberalization' was at its peak, the Research Office prepared a report which grouped Chinese economists into four categories according to their ideological commitment to planning and the market. Pro-market economists like Xue Muqiao and Lin Zili

[78] JGKG, pp. 100–110.
[79] Ruan Ming, 1991, p. 55.

were classified as the fourth category subject to criticism. A number of articles were published to criticize the opinion that 'the socialist economy is a commodity economy' on the grounds that socialism can only adopt central planning, the characteristic of which was mandatory planning. These articles also rejected the concept of a socialist planned commodity economy because it 'finally reduces socialist economy to commodity economy and abandons planned economy.' Pro-market economists were criticized as attempting to reform China's economic management according to the 'principle of capitalist market economy.' Even moderate ideas like 'planning at macro-level and market regulating at micro-level' were criticized, as they would 'weaken socialist planned economy' and 'make 'macro-planning' meaningless like a figurehead' or a detested 'burglar' (liangshang junzi).[80]

At the grass-roots level, people were confused with policy changes and some people commented, 'it is not easy to invigorate the economy; but it takes only three days to stifle it.' Some people even 'turn pale at the mere mention of "bao" (contract responsibility system).' Many local cadres began to turn away from reform experiments and returned to the 'beaten track.'[81]

Chen Yun's authority was further enhanced when he put forward his economic ideology of the 'bird-cage theory,' which compared central planning with a bird-cage and the economy with a bird. The readjustment or reform only expands the inner-space of the bird-cage just large enough for the bird to fly comfortably but without escaping from the cage. This is a far cry from the reformist market-oriented reform aimed at breaking the cage or creating a new cage responsive to market signals. But Chen's theory was generally accepted at the top-level of leadership and constituted the major discursive framework for more conservative reformers in the whole process of reform. Chen Yun's reinforced personal authority was rivaling that of Deng, and Chen was definitely more authoritative than Deng on economic matters.

There were several reasons behind the general acceptance of Chen's theory and policy options. First, the economic situation was grim. Trial experiments in enterprise autonomy had pro-

[80]Wu Jinglian, op. cit., p. 136.
[81]*Liaowang*, No. 7, 1981, p. 16.

gressed much too fast, despite Zhao Ziyang's caution in March 1980. By April 1980, 16 per cent of enterprises had been participating in the 'self-management' experiments, accounting for 60 percent of total industrial output value (state sector). Sectoral imbalances and disproportions were much more serious than had been originally expected. Under the circumstances, Chen's 'bird-cage theory' seemed more intellectually coherent and operationally predictable than any other reformist theory. The fact that it had been tested during the post-Great Leap economic recovery gave it added authority. In contrast, the reformers were unable to offer any credible policy alternatives that could immediately stop the seemingly 'run-away' economy, especially in industry and commerce, despite their clear preference for more market-oriented reforms, and second, ideologically, Deng shared Chen's concern on possible unrest as a result of internal decentralization and the external influence, exemplified by the Polish crisis. The 1980–1981 drive against bourgeois liberalization was undoubtedly a major stimulus to more conservative ideological and political thinking as it drastically increased the political cost of resisting Chen's more orthodox theoretical formulations.

But in politics there are trade-offs between interest groups. More radical reformers were able to accept this retreat in urban reform only when they had ensured that rural reform would be allowed to continue and no ideological or policy retreat in rural reform would be permitted. Deng Xiaoping specifically claimed that there should be no dispute about the rural responsibility system. Those against the new practice could wait and see while those for the practice should be allowed to continue their experiment.[82] As China's reform process suggests, the reformers' favorable strategy is incrementalism. By gradually reducing the apparent marginal benefit to reform opponents and sceptics, and by initiating pro-business ideological and discursive revisions to create new conventions favourable to market-oriented reforms, incrementalism increases the political cost of overt resistance to reform policies. Therefore, reformers are frequently content with reforms confined to certain areas until proven successful and they then justify these reforms ideologically and extend them to other areas.

[82]Deng Xiaoping, 'Excerpts from Talks Given in Wuchang, Shenzhen, Zhuhai and Shanghai,' (January 18–February 21, 1992), Vol. 3, p. 362.

Incrementalism is also manifest in the reformers' cautious deviation from the more conservative ideological convention. For instance, Zhao Ziyang managed to stress reforms within the more conservative ideological context. Based on the proposals presented by newly established think tanks, Premier Zhao Ziyang put forward ten-guiding principles to the National People's Congress in December 1981. While largely in conformity with Chen Yun's economic thinking, these principles contained elements slightly different from Chen's. Zhao showed sufficient respect for Chen Yun's central planning ideology by stressing the importance of balance and public ownership. Zhao also placed emphasis on the long-term stability of the rural responsibility system and on opening China to the outside.

The fact that no reference was made to the Daqing experience in Zhao's ten principles might have caused anxiety among the Cultural Revolution Left, whose influence was dwindling but not yet exhausted. A few days after Zhao's report, *Renmin Ribao* published a circular which, though incorporating more pragmatic ideas, called for continued efforts to learn from Daqing in industry. But neither Zhao's report nor the revival of the Daqing experience changed the overall convention based on Chen Yun's 'bird-cage theory,' although reformers clearly preferred a market-oriented approach. On some informal occasions, however, Zhao deviated more readily from Chen Yun's doctrine. For instance, in an inspection tour in 1981, Zhao stressed his preference for a greater market role:

> Coupons are issued whenever there is a shortage as if they could solve all the problems. In fact, the problems are not solved. On the contrary, the reactive role of the market is thus suppressed.[83]

With decentralization and top-level leadership divisions on reform orientation, China entered a stage of greater political diversity and local initiatives. Many provincial leaders were bolder than ever before to take their own initiatives in creatively interpreting the imposed top-level conventions. For instance,

[83]Jia Wenyin and Niu Zhenwu, Tiaozheng de zhuyao mubiao shi jingji jiegou helihua (The Main Objective of Readjustment is to Rationalize Economic Structure), *Liaowang*, No. 1, 1981, p. 12.

when re-centralization was introduced in late 1980, Guangdong province, probably with Zhao's support, adopted effective measures to address the fear of a policy shift during the drive against bourgeois liberalization by putting forward some ingenious ideas in the tradition of dialectics like 'three combinations': to combine readjustment with flexible measures, to combine re-centralization with invigoration (of the economy); and to combine retreat with advance. By October 1981, 94 percent of enterprises in Guangdong adopted a responsibility system.[84] This difference between the supposed top-level ideological convention and local creative interpretation illustrates an emerging phenomenon in post-Mao era that decentralization had contributed to greater local ideological flexibility, especially when more conservative trends came to predominate at the top leadership. As a result, reforms could still continue in some provinces and in certain fields despite a generally unfavourable ideological climate.

Furthermore, these local initiatives in turn influenced the top-level politics and ideological conventions. If good economic performance can be registered, then local ideological innovations may be incorporated into the new official doctrine to justify existing reforms and induce further reforms.

The second major controversy over the market's role occurred around the 12th CPC Congress. At the crucial time of preparing for the Congress in 1982, reformers began to increase their efforts to shape up pro-reform conventions and influence the agenda-setting prior to the Congress. While Hu Yaobang was concentrating on the new ideological platform for the Congress, as discussed in the first part of this chapter, Premier Zhao was trying to revive the momentum for economic reform. In the spring of 1982, Zhao expressed the view that the readjustment had been successfully completed and it was time for new reform initiatives. This judgment led to a more reform-oriented final draft version of the 6th Five-Year Plan. The plan now explicitly set forth the goal for diversified economic ownership and encouraged the vigorous development of external economic relations and trade. Compared with the ten principles in December 1981, the plan was more market-oriented. It altered two important elements: the call for prudence in economic

[84]Qi Xiu, Zhengce dailai le sudu (Policy Brings about Speed), *Liaowang*, No. 7, 1981, p. 17.

reform was replaced by the demand for courageous economic reform; the call for a balance between self-reliance and open-door policy was substituted with the demand for a greater opening to the international market.

But conservatives were also preparing to influence the agenda of the Congress. For instance, Chen Yun gave a widely publicized talk on planned economy in the spring of 1982, in which he stated:

> Ours is a socialist planned economy. A planned economy should be primary in industry, and there should be no exception in agriculture. The primacy of the planned economy supplemented by market regulation must continue even with the adoption of the (rural) responsibility system. . . . Agriculture, in conformity with planned economy, is in the long-term interests of peasants.[85]

Chen cited such examples as a fixed quota for raising and purchasing pigs and no decrease of arable land for growing grain.[86]

In August 1982 when the political report to the 12th CPC Congress was being drafted, Hu Qiaomu distributed a letter written by five economic officials in an attempt to prevent the Congress from adopting a radical pro-market economic agenda. This letter raised the most sensitive and persistent ideological question in China's fifteen years of economic reform: Is the reform policy socialist or capitalist? The letter claimed that if enterprises became 'independent economic entities' and if all operations of enterprises were to be regulated by market forces, then 'it will weaken planned economy and socialist public ownership.' The authors of the letter further stated that 'although we still have commodity production and exchange of commodities, we must not describe our economy simply as a commodity economy.' Such a concept will 'blur the distinction between a socialist planned economy and a capitalist anarchic economy.' Some conservatives even claimed that 'natural economy,' 'capitalist commodity economy' and 'socialist planned economy' respectively marked three stages of social development. If the

[85]Zhu Minzhi and Zhou Aiguo, Chuyi zai zhongnanhai. . . . (The New Year, at Zhonghanhai . . .), *Liaowang*, No. 2, 1982, pp. 2–3.
[86]*ibid*.

socialist planned economy was 'downgraded' to commodity economy, then it would no longer be socialism. Therefore the purpose of reform was said to expand and improve mandatory planning.[87] The conservative discourse compromised the content of the political report adopted at the 12th CPC Congress, which declared that 'China practices a planned economy on the basis of public ownership' and a certain portion of products were to be subject to market regulation, but this portion was 'supplementary to,' 'subordinated to,' and 'secondary to' state planning.[88] Following this, almost no concepts other than this official version were permitted in the Chinese press until late 1984, when the Party adopted the decision on urban reform.

The concept of 'socialism with Chinese characteristics' that Deng had advanced at the Congress seemed to be still a vague concept, though it ultimately induced and justified many pro-reform discourses and practices. But drawing on studies by pro-reform economists, Hu Yaobang continued the reformers' strategy of incrementalism and introduced a specific reformist concept of 'guidance planning' which was apparently acceptable to all parties. Distinguished from the Stalinist 'mandatory planning,' the concept, as Robert Hsu claims, was similar to Western 'indicative planning' in its suggestive nature and its reliance on indirect economic incentives for implementation.[89] This new discourse was the reformers' theoretical innovation within the generally agreed discursive framework. As with many sensitive ideological issues, it was designed to address the defects of mandatory planning without undermining the planning nature of the socialist economy or its discursive convention. The Congress endorsed Chen Yun's view that central planing was primary and the market was secondary. As Hu's idea constituted an incremental deviation from the prevailing convention seemingly acceptable to all, the Congress also incorporated Hu's idea into the Party's political report. The new concept proved effective in shaping up pro-reform conventions and sanctioning reformist policies.

[87] *Jingjixue Wenzhai,* (Economics Abstracts), No. 1, 1985, pp. 5–6.
[88] JGKG, p. 158.
[89] For more detailed account of this idea and its origin, see Robert Hsu, *Economic Theories in China 1979–1988*, Cambridge, U.K., Cambridge University Press, 1991, pp. 35–6 and 46–7.

3 The beginning of rural reform

During most of the 1970s, much of the Cultural Revolution Left's opposition to private economy originated from its radical ideological conventions that private economy would lead to the return of capitalism. Household sidelines and family-based farming were the 'tails of capitalism,' which were assumed to hinder the transition from socialism to communism as they tended to reinforce the peasants' 'petty bourgeois mentality' and to provide a breeding ground for a new class of rural exploiters.

The truth debate certainly introduced a more relaxed and permissive atmosphere that encouraged reform experiments. But contrary to the conventional belief that the Party reformers initiated the rural reform at the Third Plenum, this reform, which decisively changed the fate of China's 800 million peasants, was initiated in Anhui Province by some peasants, who were simply too poor to continue the same way in the commune system. There was no convincing evidence that the relaxed political atmosphere had encouraged them. On the contrary, like in the difficult times of the past, they ran high personal risks to start their own experiment. The twelve households, who pioneered what was later called 'the household responsibility system,' in fact signed a secret deal on 21 December 1978, coinciding with the Third Plenum's convening date, in which they vowed that if their bold attempt went wrong, they were 'prepared to be imprisoned and executed.'[90] It was clear that strong political pressure and an hostile environment did not encourage their practice and that these peasants had not perceived the dawn of a more relaxed atmosphere.

Furthermore, while the Third Plenum was claimed to be the beginning of the new era, the decision on rural work adopted at the Plenum explicitly banned leasing land for household farming (fentian dangan) and fixing quotas on a household basis (baochan daohu). But the practice was tolerated and even spread rapidly to many other provinces. How can one explain this apparent paradox? In fact, this was just one of many political paradoxes that occurred during post-Mao economic transition. An ideological explanation is suggested as follows: It reflects a tension between two competing ideological conventions;

[90]Documentary film: Shinianchao (Ten-Year Tide), Personal notes.

namely, the emerging overarching convention encouraging pragmatism and reform experiment, as embodied in the new doctrine of 'seeking truth from facts,' versus various localized conventions specifically banning certain practices associated with capitalism in agriculture and other areas.[91] It is in this context that one should look at the competing ideologies and officialdom's 'elective affinity' for them. Deng Xiaoping advocated the new overarching ideology so as to induce and justify policies which could be considered unacceptable in localized conventions. Reformers in different localities found the overarching ideology in line with their desires and interests and cast suspicion about localized conventions. Furthermore, the overarching convention had effectively reduced the cost of non-compliance with localized conventions. If the political cost of resisting the localized conventions was lowered further (for instance, when reformers had strong backing at the top leadership or the reform experiments in question produced favourable results), reformers would tend to resist the localized conventions by playing up the overarching convention.

The beginning of the rural responsibility system was a good example. A number of provinces tolerated and even encouraged the new practice under the overarching convention. Zhao Ziyang was perhaps right when he remarked to a visiting American journalist:

> The contract responsibility system was not our brainchild. It was invented by Chinese peasants. We simply followed the new idea of 'seeking truth from facts' and tolerated its experimentation. The experience of Chinese peasants convinced us of its efficiency and we legalized and extended it across the country.[92]

Governor Wan Li of Anhui Province did not stop such practices that most cadres knew, from their experience of the early 1960s, could yield better economic results. It was reported that some rural cadres came to Wan Li after reading a reader's letter in *Renmin Ribao* criticizing the leasing of land for household farming as practising capitalism. Wan was bold enough to retort,

[91] I draw inspiration from Joseph Schull's brief comment on the two concepts in his study. See Joseph Schull, op. cit., p. 735.

[92] Zhao's conversation with Harrison Salisbury on 5 November 1987. Personal notes.

'the newspaper does not till the land. Nor does it grow crops. Just ignore it. We do what we should do.'[93]

The pro-reform overarching convention played an effective role in facilitating the adoption of those policies which, according to the localized conventions, were still associated with capitalism and reduced the political cost of policy execution by softening or even neutralizing the edge of conservative critiques. The new overarching ideology, combined with other factors, had a clear bearing on 'localized conventions' and frequently generated a kind of political tolerance unprecedented in China's post-1949 history. This was shown in a slogan by the Party Secretary of Guangdong Province Ren Zhongyi, 'to the outside, more open; to the inside, looser; to those below, more power' (duiwai, gengjia kaifang; duinei, gengjia fangkuan; duixia, gengjia fangquan).[94] In the early 1980s, over 140,000 peasants from Wenzhou of Zhejiang Province travelled elsewhere to market their products. They were labelled as 'embracing capitalism' and as 'a contingent of bribery.' Local officials were not sure whether the peasants' spontaneous activity would be officially sanctioned, but they knew it was conducive to the local economy and were 'not in a hurry to ban the new practice,' which was in line with the new overarching ideology of 'seeking truth from facts.' Later they even used a Taoist expression of 'letting things take their own course' (wuwei erzhi) to describe their style of political tolerance in the early 1980s.[95]

Deng partly designed greater tolerance for market-oriented activities, as sanctioned by the overarching ideology, to achieve the credibility of reform policies, because his ideas encouraged less administrative intervention and facilitated a greater consistency of pro-business experiments and spontaneity. Deng himself set an example in handling the case of 'Fool's Sunflower Seeds' (a peasant made a fortune out of selling dried salted sunflower seeds) in the early 1980's. As Deng recalled in 1992:

> In the initial stage of the rural reform, there emerged in Anhui Province the issue of the 'Fool's Sunflower Seeds'.

[93]Documentary film, op. cit.

[94]E. F. Vogel's translation of the last part of this slogan ('to those below, more leeway') is elegant but inaccurate. See E. F. Vogel, *One Step Ahead in China – Guangdong under Reform*, Cambridge, Mass., Harvard University Press, 1989, p. 88.

[95]*Jingji Cankao Bao* (Economic Reference News), 20 November 1993.

> Many people felt uncomfortable with this man who had made a profit of 1 million yuan. they called for action to be taken against him. I said that no action should be taken, because that would make people think we had changed our policies, and the loss would outweigh the gain. There are many problems like this one, and if we don't handle them properly, our policies could easily be undermined and overall reform affected.[96]

But all leaders are not reform-minded. Many are more concerned with ideological righteousness, on which they perceive their career depends. Due to the bitter experience of the Maoist class struggle and merciless political persecutions, the Chinese political culture had shaped a kind of passive mentality in the officialdom towards reform and change and a primary concern for ideological righteousness and political safety rather than innovations and creativity. Rural reform is again a useful illustration. It started with an uphill battle. Some cadres were perhaps indeed motivated by ideological predilection, fearing a capitalist restoration and increased 'class polarization' in the rural areas, while others reacted to the reforms from their own vested interests. Mao Zhiyong, then the first Party secretary of Hunan Province, admitted later that 'after the Third Plenum in 1978, some people wanted to practise the responsibility system. We did not agree (to their request). In certain areas (we) even banned it.'[97] In his authoritative book on Chinese socialist economics published in 1981, Xue Muqiao, a top-ranking pro-reform economist, still held that the ownership system should be collective in the form of communes, brigades and teams. For Xue, the team (not household yet) should still be the basic level of ownership and the base accounting level.[98]

At the conference of the provincial Party secretaries convened in September 1980, a heated debate occurred about the political nature of the household responsibility system. For instance, Gansu Province had widely adopted the system while Jilin Province and the suburbs of Shanghai had not. Some believed the contract responsibility system, on the basis of production teams,

[96]Deng Xiaoping, Vol. 3, p. 359.
[97]*Zhonggong Yanjiu* (Research on Communist China), November 1985, p. 14.
[98]Xue Muqiao, *Zhongguo shehuizhuyi jingji wenti yanjiu* (A Study on China's Socialist Economy), Beijing, People's Press, 1979, p. 59.

was still socialist, but on the basis of individuals or individual households, it became capitalistic. In the end, the reformers succeeded in reaching a consensus that judgment on rural experimentation would be withheld to allow for further experiments. The final document of the conference only confirmed that the 'household responsibility system does not deviate from the socialist track,' but the reform was not imposed across the country.[99]

Deng recalled later that at first only one third of Chinese provinces vigorously promoted the responsibility system. The rest took a 'wait and see' attitude or tried to resist the new practice. Deng described his incremental approach as 'having more time for actions' by avoiding prolonged ideological disputes, and he suggested his preference for a deferral of value judgment on controversial issues until the experience of the new practice yielded results.[100] It was not until the Sixth Plenum in June 1981 that the old convention was abandoned and the household responsibility system was officially asserted.

The campaign against bourgeois liberalization created a certain degree of confusion in rural areas, despite the reformers' efforts to confine it to the non-economic activities, as it was widely perceived as an attempt to change the overarching ideology. In an ideological political system, a perceived revision of the overarching ideology always generates an impact across the entire range of policies. When the campaign started, some local cadres began to claim that economic prosperity would lead to 'revisionism,' 'polarization,' and 'capitalism.'[101] In some areas, work teams were sent to redress the 'excess' of the household responsibility system and it was also reported that there were people who wanted to reverse the reform policy despite its spectacular achievements.[102]

But on the whole, the reform in rural areas was not seriously affected by the short-lived campaign, because of an emerging consensus among top-level reformers. Deng indicated his clear preference for the responsibility system, while Chen Yun

[99]Zen Jianwei, Shike xiangzhe bayi nongmin (Always Taking Account of 800 Million Peasants), *Liaowang*, No. 2, 1981, pp. 2–4.
[100]Deng Xiaoping, Vol. 3, p. 362.
[101]Niu Zhenwu, Qingchu zuo de yingxiang zhuyao kao xuexi (Removing Leftist Influence Mainly Relies on Study), *Liaowang*, No. 5, August 1981, pp. 28–29.
[102]*Liaowang*, No. 2, 1981, p. 18, and No. 9, 1981, p. 7.

regarded it as a necessary ideological concession to capitalism. Chen observed that one could

> permit more factors of capitalism to exist under the premise of making no changes in the fundamental system of socialism itself. The value of the existence (of such factors) is to be affirmed and their right to existence is to be protected. This sort of transformation calls for determination, courage, discretion, and the need to keep cool heads on the part of all communist Party members. If we fail, then China will revert from a socialist society to a capitalist society. The price of such a concession is indeed high. But we have no choice.[103]

Moreover, resistance to the Left not only came from top-level reformers, but also from ordinary peasants, who had benefitted from the new policies. For instance, work teams sent to stop the reforms were coldly received by peasants and could hardly find an audience in those areas. The new practice was officially confirmed once again in the Party Central Committee's No.1 document in 1982, which concluded that the contract responsibility system, whether based on households or production teams, was socialist.[104]

However, with regard to the official dismantling of the commune system, which had been so closely identified with Mao for over two decades, reformers adopted an incremental approach. Wan Li observed in 1982:

> Prudence is necessary when approaching the reform of the commune institutions. We should not require each level to reform from top to bottom by prescribing a time limit for fulfillment. Until suitable new organizational forms can replace production brigades and teams, we should not recklessly change existing forms and bring about a disorderly situation.[105]

The reformers followed a pragmatic approach by transforming the substance of the commune system while retaining the nomi-

[103]Chen Yun's Utterances at a Politburo Meeting, *Issues and Studies*, No. 7, July 1980, pp. 94–95.
[104]Gao Shangquan, *Zhongguo de jingji tizhi gaige* (China's Economic System Reform), Beijing, People's Press, 1991, p. 330.
[105]*Renmin Ribao*, 23 December 1982.

nal existence of the institutions. In one way this reduced the ideological resistance to rural reforms and tapped what can be called transitional values of the previous system, such as a differentiated phasing-out of the work-point system, which ensured a relatively smooth transition from the old system to the new.

This approach was time-consuming but resulted in a firmer and more reliable constituency in support of reform. Rather than antagonizing many of those with vested interests, like rural cadres, by immediately abolishing the old system, Chinese reformers, sometimes unintentionally, managed to make use of the transitional values of the old system. At the same time, reformers took steps to gradually involve these people in the reform process and let them have a stake in the reform's success. This incremental approach to reforming the old system, which recognized its transitional value, marked a sharp difference between Chinese reformers and 'shock therapy' believers. When the new convention and the efficacy of the new practice were solidly established not only in terms of tangible results, but also in public perception and political culture, the commune system was halted and replaced in 1983 by the pre-1949 county and township system. This return to the household economy as the basic unit of production was described in Marxist discourse by Du Runshen, a leading agricultural economist, as an effort for 'exploring the path of socialist agriculture with Chinese characteristics.'[106]

4 The establishment of the Special Economic Zones

The establishment of the Special Economic Zones (SEZs) was incompatible with the orthodox ideological conventions. After the downfall of the Gang of Four, Hua Guofeng initiated a large-scale import programme for Western technology and equipment. This already marked a deviation from the Maoist convention of complete self-reliance. Hua's primary ideological support for this approach was Mao's 1956 speech 'On the Ten Great Relationships' which had not been published until December

[106]*Renmin Ribao*, 7 March 1983.

1976. In the speech, Mao stated that China should 'learn all that is genuinely good' from foreign countries.[107]

Hua attacked the Gang of Four's closed-door policy, which had called for almost complete autarky. However, Hua's open-door policy, constrained by the Maoist ideological framework, was confined to foreign trade. For instance, it was declared in 1977 that China would not accept any international loans, foreign 'assistance' or direct investment. Chinese officials still regarded export promotion zones in many developing countries as a manifestation of contemporary imperialism and new colonialism. By extension, China should not copy them.

Economic realism associated with the truth debate finally enabled some Chinese decision-makers to see the advantages of such zones to economic development, and the idea of some sort of economic zones was brought to the work conference held in March 1979. Deng supported the idea by drawing inspiration from his early revolutionary experience and claimed that 'during the war, wasn't Yanan a special zone?' Deng derived his belief in the zone idea from the two views he had expounded in 1978: first, that some people and some regions should be encouraged to get rich to set examples for others to emulate; and second, that China must open itself to the outside world to 'absorb advanced foreign technology, managerial experience and capital.' But perhaps equally important was the fact that Deng needed a pilot zone to experiment market-oriented economic reforms and to accumulate experience and build up his own authority on economic matters.

Since the new idea strayed significantly from the accepted conventions, there emerged much scepticism about whether the idea was 'ideologically sound' or 'politically correct.' The reformers again adopted an incremental approach and were cautious in every step they took towards establishing the special economic zones and were ready to make compromises if needed.

After all, China was the first socialist country to adopt a zone policy, while all other export promotion zones in developing countries only promoted the growth of capitalism. Even the use of the name of 'export promotion zone' like other developing countries could be ideologically controversial in China. Most

[107]*Peking Review*, 1 January 1977, pp. 10–25.

reformers understood from their experience in Chinese politics that the Chinese zones had to be described as something unique and compatible to China's socialism.

In September 1979, Vice Premier Gu Mu, an ardent supporter of the experiment, talked about the opening of 'special districts' in Shenzhen and Zhuhai. But this name could imply that central government was ready to tolerate a greater freedom, which could even be stretched to mean 'politically special.' In the end, Deng took the decision to use 'special economic zones.' By this, Deng ruled out any possibility of any special political policies, as he observed, 'It will not be good to call them special political zones.'[108] Suggesting Deng's concern about the sensitive linkage between economics and politics, the name of the Special Economic Zones (SEZs) demonstrated a useful compromise acceptable to all parties. The reformers were happy with special pilot areas for experimenting with economic reforms, which were bound to have political implications, while the conservatives were content that the SEZs were confined only to economics.

Which areas should be chosen as the SEZs was another thorny issue. The first four zones were Shenzhen, Zhuhai, Shantou and Xiamen located respectively in Guangdong Province and Fujian Province. Their geographic proximity to Hong Kong, Macau and Taiwan was a strong advantage in terms of attracting overseas Chinese investment. However, all of them were economically poor and weak in human resources and infrastructures. The fact that they all were set up in areas far away from the political and economic centres of China suggested a fear in the minds of the top-level decision makers about any possible unfavourable political and economic consequences from these bold experiments.

Shanghai, China's largest industrial city with a well-trained work force and a large pool of scientists and technicians and extensive overseas connections, could have been favourably considered for such an experiment if there had been a more liberal and market-oriented ideological convention. It was possible that due to the central planners' opposition or fear of their opposition, or the influence of Chen Yun, a native of Shanghai, who had tremendous influence over Shanghai's planned economy,

[108]Deng Xiaoping yu shenzhen tequ (Deng Xiaoping and Shenzhen SEZ), *Liaowang*, overseas edition, No. 39, 28 September 1992, pp. 3–7.

that Deng did not insist on Shanghai being made into a special zone. In 1992 Deng candidly expressed his regret:

> In retrospect, one of my biggest mistakes was leaving out Shanghai when we launched the four special economic zones. If Shanghai had been included, the situation with regard to reform and opening in the Yangtze Delta, the entire Yangtze River valley and, indeed, the whole country would be quite different.[109]

Paying attention to ideological sensitivity in every step of the reform process was one characteristic of the Chinese reformers in their efforts to avoid ideological or political confrontation with the conservatives and speedily get the reform project off the ground. But the principal drawback of this incremental approach was many missed opportunities, as illustrated by the experience of Shanghai.

The reformers also attended to other concerns of the SEZ sceptics which, if not handled properly, could also be elevated to the level of ideology. For instance, one of Chen Yun's major concerns was financial, given China's budget deficit. He made it clear that trade, not investment, should be the focus of China's international economic policy, as he believed that trade could be more readily controlled and balanced, whereas foreign investment might make China more vulnerable to outside political and economic influence. To ally Chen's worry, the reformers made efforts to convince sceptics like Chen that the zones would help China earn hard currency and thus relieve domestic budget deficits with the inflow of foreign investment.[110]

Despite all this, suspicion about the SEZs did not fade easily. The 1980/1981 alarm about 'bourgeois liberalization' revived criticism of the SEZs. They were compared to the foreign concessions of the nineteenth and early twentieth centuries in China. This apparent analogy was established to criticize such special privileges as tax breaks and internal borders. The rights of foreign enterprises to freely recruit Chinese employees and repatriate profits and establish wholly foreign-owned enterprises were regarded by conservative ideologues as betraying China's

[109]Deng Xiaoping, Vol. 3, p. 363–364.

[110]George Crane, *The Political Economy of China's Special Economic Zones*, London, M. E. Sharpe, 1990, p. 32.

economic and political sovereignty or as so-called 'Hong Kong-ization.' Such open-door policies were tantamount to 'selling out the country.' They asked that if wholly foreign-owned subsidiaries were allowed to repatriate profits earned in China, 'are we not regressing to capitalist exploitation?'[111]

The work conference of December 1980 sent another chill to the zone idea, as the conference decided to give priority to readjustment and slow down the pace of the SEZs. When the campaign against the bourgeois liberalization came to its peak in 1981, Hu Qiaomu and Deng Liqun attacked the notion of state capitalism in the SEZs. They argued, 'after three decades of socialism, (the notion) could cause ideological confusion (sixiang hunluan) if one talks glibly about state capitalism and in particular state capitalism involving foreign capital and the special and flexible policies' for the SEZs. This indicated their strong displeasure for the socialist 'concession' to state capitalism.[112]

The reformers argued in defence of the zones. They held that the SEZs were not concessions because they were not subjected to the extraterritorial rights enjoyed by foreign nationals in pre-1949 days. Foreign businessmen must operate under Chinese law. Preferential treatment extended to foreign investors was mutually beneficial, and therefore the SEZs would not be transformed into 'colonies.' Lenin's New Economic Policy was the standard discursive framework in support of the zone idea, as the reformers claimed that Lenin endorsed the idea of socialist countries making use of state capitalism and foreign capital for promoting their economic development without abandoning their sovereignty and ideology. The reformers admitted that some exploitation did exist in the zones. However, this was a kind of 'buying out policy' similar to the method used against the national bourgeoisie in the early fifties and justified by Lenin's New Economic Policy.

Moreover, such a policy was indispensable if China was to acquire the much needed capital and technology necessary for China's modernization. They argued that the SEZs would go a long way in helping to achieve the reunification of Hong Kong, Macau and Taiwan, as the success of the SEZs would build China's credibility among compatriots and narrow the economic

[111] *ibid.*, p. 36.
[112] Ruan Ming, 1991, pp. 58–61.

gaps between China and those areas. The 'special' nature of the SEZs also allowed the reformers to perceive their efforts as pioneering economic reforms for the whole country.[113]

Controversies over the theoretical justification of the zones still continued in 1982. One issue under debate concerned still the political nature of the SEZs. But the discussion began to be more policy-oriented. In other words, the development strategies of the SEZs were discussed in relation to an ideological judgment over their political nature. If the SEZs were politically sound, they could be further expanded and if not, they should be limited or even reduced. Most SEZ advocates still used Lenin's New Economic Policy to justify the SEZs. According to Lenin, state capitalism involved cooperation between socialist state power on the one hand and large-scale national and multinational capitalist enterprises on the other. The state would exercise control over the activities of the capitalist enterprises but also allow them some room for making profits. This school argued that the SEZs possessed a 'dual nature,' involving both socialist (Chinese) and capitalist (foreign) elements. Exploitation of Chinese labour was described as a 'cost' or a tuition that must be paid to achieve the goal of socialist modernization. From this perspective, the zones should be properly expanded as the zones complemented rather than threatened Chinese socialism. But the more conservative school held that in the zones, two antagonistic modes coexisted and competed with each other. Therefore the zones must be carefully controlled and monitored. The more liberal school, on the contrary, contended that the zones were socialist because capitalist forces were allowed to enter the zones to develop China's socialist economy; hence, the SEZs were serving socialism and should be vigorously promoted. Such debate continued off and on during the whole process of China's economic reform.[114]

[113]Based on my conversation with Xu Jingan, Chairman of the Shenzhen Commission for Restructuring the Economic System in March 1993 in Shenzhen. Some comments are also contained in Xu Jingan, *Shenzhen tequ de jueqi yu zhongguo xiandaihua* (The Rise of Shenzhen SEZ and China's Modernization), Nanjing, Nanjing University Press, 1992.
[114]George Crane, op. cit., pp. 40–9.

Chapter Three

THE SECOND CYCLE: FROM NEW VERSIONS OF MARXISM TO THE NEW TECHNOLOGICAL REVOLUTION (1983–1984)

The year from January 1983 to early 1984 witnessed another noticeable cycle in ideology and policy which once again highlighted the ideological sensitivity of China's reform efforts. The year 1983 started with the reformers' attempts to accelerate the pace of reform and inject vigour to the Chinese social sciences. The resulting new interpretations of Marxism immediately encountered a conservative ideological offensive under the banner of anti-spiritual pollution, which quickly spread from theoretical circles to other fields. To save reforms from the ideological frenzy, reformers seized the opportunity to launch a counter campaign on the overriding importance of a new technological revolution, thus significantly diluting the conservative campaign.

Compared with the first cycle, this cycle was relatively short, but it also provided useful insights into the tensions between competing ideologies and their impact on reform policies. Two themes are particularly important in this chapter: First, the non-dogmatic approach to reforms has provided Chinese intellectuals with an opportunity to transcend the official discourse so as to demand a more fundamental change of China's political and economic system. Such attempts, however, tend to produce mixed results as shown in the surge of a new reform drive and the ensuing conservative counter-offensive. Second, a technological revolution has a tremendous appeal to Chinese reformers, who see in it an opportunity to resist the conservative ideological drive, an inspiration for new ideas and a chance for

China's modernization, as shown in Deng's sharper deviation from the convention based on the 'bird-cage theory.'

A Major ideological trends

1 New versions of Marxism

The reformers meant that the year 1983 should be a year of reform. Hu Yaobang advocated 'comprehensive and systemwide reform' and claimed that 'reform is the task for all fronts, all areas, all departments and all units.' In order to establish a new ideological convention to promote reforms, Hu Yaobang called for a non-dogmatic approach to Marxism and an exploration of new ideas and brave policies to facilitate the new drive for economic reforms.[1] By adapting Marxism to the new reality, reformers hoped that many pro-reform policies could be better implemented.

Against this background was a revival of new thinking on Marxism. A group of influential Party intellectuals attempted to both interpret and transcend the official discourse by developing new interpretations of Marxism flexible enough to suit their own goals. For example, Su Shaozhi, Director of the Institute of Marxism-Leninism-Mao Zedong Thought, published an article entitled 'Developing Marxism in the Reform and Building Socialism with Chinese Characteristics.'[2] Su made a distinction between the Marxist conclusions of universal application and those of non-universal application, calling for a new version of Marxism that could explain and guide China's unique reform and rejecting the 'old antiques' (chennian gudong), a suggestive reference to some classical Marxist concepts. He warned that sticking to dogmatism would provide 'refuge and a hotbed for leftism' and 'ideological pretexts for the critics of the reform.'

The most influential, however, was the intellectual attempt to transcend the Marxist discourse on humanism and alienation. Speaking at a symposium on Marxism, Zhou Yang placed humanism at the centre of Marxism, calling for a reevaluation of 'bourgeois humanism' and once again raising the concept of 'alienation' contained in Marx's early writings.[3] The concept of 'alienation' originated from classical German philosophy. Both

[1]*Renmin Ribao*, 14 March 1983.
[2]*Renmin Ribao*, 11 March 1983.
[3]Zhou Yang, Guanyu Makesizhuyi de jige lilun wenti de tantao (Discourse on Several Theoretical Issues in Marxism), *Renmin Ribao*, 16 March 1983.

Hegel and Feuerbach discussed 'alienation' in their writings. It meant that in the process of development, a subject produces through its own activities an antagonistic object which, as an external and alien force, stands opposed to the subject itself. Marx used this concept to criticize the alienation of labour in a bourgeois society and the alienation of human nature caused by alienated labour. According to Marx, wealth was created by the workers, but in turn capitalists used the wealth to exploit the workers.[4] The same logic applied to money. Man created money, but money in turn controlled man. He also declared communism as the only solution to the problem of alienation, because it eliminated private ownership and exploitation. Zhou Yang, however, argued that alienation occurred not only in capitalist countries but also in China and in China's ideological and political domains as well as economic and other fields.

In contrast, the orthodox school emphasized that alienation was only an historical phenomenon which emerged in capitalist society and would never happen in socialist society, although some theorists in the Soviet Union and Eastern Europe admitted long ago that alienation did happen in socialist society. In China this subject had been raised in June 1980 by Wang Ruoshui, who openly asserted that there was serious alienation in China. Wang described the personality cult and 'modern superstition' as ideological alienation. He said: 'a leader arose from among the people. But as a result of propaganda or the personality cult, he became divorced from the people and the people in turn had to obey his order unconditionally,' alluding to Mao's personality cult during the Cultural Revolution. Wang observed the existence of political alienation: a public servant of the people, as a communist cadre was supposed to be, became the master over the people.[5] In 1983, Zhou Yang further developed Wang's discourse on alienation. Zhou Yang made an analysis of humanism and alienation, arguing that alienation was against humanism and that the aim of communism was to realize the full development of man and overcome various forms of alienation. Zhou also raised the issue of economic alienation: 'in economic construction,' due to lack of experience and knowl-

[4]Marx's idea of alienation is expounded in his *Economic and Philosophical Manuscripts of 1844*, in particular pp. 120–27, New York, International Publishers, 1964.
[5]Quoted in Jin Zhong, *From Mao to Deng*, Hong Kong, Celeluck Co., Ltd. 1990, p. 197.

edge of building socialism, 'we did many foolish things and in the end we reap what we have sown.'[6]

The resurrection of the Marxist discourse on alienation had three main causes. First, it was a serious attempt by reform-minded intellectuals to acknowledge the alienation of people from their government and from their economic system in the hope that facing this issue squarely could usher in 'a profound revolution' to reform China's political and economic system. Second, the intellectuals' efforts coincided with those by the top-echelon reformers, who were busy planning more complex urban reforms. This would require a more flexible interpretation of Marxism as the new ideological basis for urban reforms. Although the elements of their ideological convergence may not be necessarily identical, exploring a new and pro-reform discursive framework was part of their shared goal. Third, the reformers wanted to attract more people, especially intellectuals and the youth, who were increasingly cynical about Chinese politics and the official discourse, to work for the reform programme. The Party, if able to provide a more humanistic ideology and a more inspiring discourse, could be more attractive to intellectuals and the youth.

But in contrast to intellectual interest in different theoretical interpretations of Marxism, Deng still focused his attention on the more pragmatic dimension of his Chinese-style socialism. At the end of a tour of Jiangsu province, he seemed to be inspired by the 'socialist' experience of the city of Suzhou, a rising economic power house of that province where the total per capita agricultural and industrial output had approached $800, fairly close to Deng's 'year 2000' goal for the whole country. Deng's personal interest in the Suzhou experience was reflected in the discussion he had with the local leaders. Deng asked 'what society was like with that level of output?' According to Deng, the reply was:

1. People had adequate food, clothing and other consumer goods, so that they no longer had to worry about their basic needs;
2. There had enough housing, with 20 square metres per person, . . .
3. There was basically full employment in cities and towns;

[6]Zhou Yang, op. cit.

4. Rural people were no longer pouring into big cities;
5. Primary and secondary education had become universal, and funds available for education, culture, sports, public welfare and other undertakings; and
6. People's ethical standards had risen, and the crime rate had decreased.[7]

This picture serves to reveal Deng's concept of Chinese-style socialism or Deng's picture of China by the end of the 20th century. Unlike Barry Naughton's assertion that Deng 'had never even hinted at his ideas about what kind of society ought to emerge' as a result of economic development,[8] Deng's keen interest in the Suzhou model suggested that Deng's 'economics in command' was associated with some traditional socialist values and programmes.

2 The campaign against spiritual pollution

The intellectual transcendence of Marxism aroused discontent among many Party veterans and ideologues. As early as January 1983 when Hu Yaobang was talking about the emancipation of the mind and bolder reforms, Deng Liqun spoke on the same occasion about 'firmly opposing and overcoming the bourgeois ideology of commercializing everything.' On 24 and 25 September 1983 respectively, Deng Liqun gave speeches to a committee under the State Council and to postgraduates in Beijing, stressing the need for upholding the four principles, building socialist civilization and eliminating spiritual pollution.[9]

One reason for the emerging ideological differences could be that both sides intended to influence the planned Party rectification campaign. Arguments about Marxist humanism or alienation may not have shaped policy agenda, as the discussion was still confined to the intellectual elite, but these ideas had influenced the overarching ideology and its discursive framework (more flexible or rigid? more innovative or dogmatic?), which in turn could change the political cost of compliance or non-compliance with a given policy.

[7]Deng Xiaoping, 'Remarks after an Inspection Tour of Jiangsu Province and Other Places,' (March 2, 1983), Vol. 3, pp. 34–35.
[8]Barry Naughton, 'Deng Xiaoping: the Economist,' *The China Quarterly*, September 1993, No. 135, p. 502.
[9]*Renmin Ribao*, 25 and 26 September 1983.

The conservative forces were actively preparing a nationwide education campaign in communist ideology. They succeeded in producing a study outline in the hope to make it the major document for the Party's rectification campaign, and they even distributed it for discussion across the nation. The document contained much implicit criticism of reform policies, ranging from money worship to polarization, from mishandling of bonuses to betraying Chinese sovereignty. The outline insisted on the incorporation of communist ideology into all reforms and stressed that patriotism meant belief in the socialist system and communism.[10]

For Deng Xiaoping, the rectification campaign was part of his overall strategy to rebuild the Party by improving its efficacy. Hence, he constantly urged the replacement of uneducated cadres with better educated ones and respect for knowledge and expertise. But he never agreed that modernization meant Westernization. This idea was embodied in his concept of 'socialism with Chinese characteristics.' He stood for modernization without Westernization, an idea derived in part from his experience, as a Chinese nationalist, with the West and in part from his belief in many socialist critiques of Western values. Consequently, Deng was in constant conflict with the inflow of Western values.

The official effort to 'eliminate spiritual pollution' was incorporated into the 'Decision of the CPC Central Committee on Party Rectification.' The Decision called on Party members to

> enhance their understanding of the theories of Marxism-Leninism and Mao Zedong Thought and the policies based on them . . . ; dare to combat all hostile forces disrupting socialism; fight against decadent bourgeois ideology, against acts of creating spiritual pollution and against the abuse of power and position for personal gains so that they will set a good example for the broad masses of Party members; and guide the masses to make efforts to become people with high ideals and morality, cultural knowledge and a sense of discipline.[11]

[10]Gongchanzhuyi de shijian yu gongchanzhuyi de sixiang jiaoyu (The Practice of Communism and Education in Communist Ideology – Study Outline), *Hunan Ribao* (Hunan Daily), 25 October 1983.
[11]See *Beijing Review,* No. 41, 17 October 1983, pp. I-XII.

In a speech delivered on 22 October Deng elaborated his criticism of 'spiritual pollution.' He defined 'spiritual pollution' as

> the spread of the corrupt and decadent ideas of the bourgeoisie and other exploiting classes and the spread of distrust of socialism and communism and leadership by the Communist Party.[12]

Deng also singled out the intellectual discourse on alienation and humanism as examples of 'spiritual pollution' because these concepts encouraged the distrust of socialism and of the Party. Deng argued in Leninist discursive terms against discussing humanism 'in abstract terms' and called for a distinction between socialist humanism and capitalist humanism. He did not regard freedom of expression as an intrinsic value of human beings and opposed any spread of 'counter-revolutionary views.' Proceeding from his belief in developmentalism, Deng claimed:

> The standards of living and the level of education of our people are not high, and discussion of the value of the human being or of humanism isn't going to raise them. Only active efforts to achieve material and ethical progress can do that.[13]

Many articles were published to criticize the discourse of alienation. A notable one was a speech by Hu Qiaomu in January 1984,[14] who argued that economic alienation could not exist in socialist society as there was no exploitation under socialism. Bureaucratism should not be linked with alienation, because to do so would blur the difference between socialism and capitalism. *Renmin Ribao* published a commentary entitled 'Further Achieving Ideological and Political Unity in the Whole Party,' in which the problem of alienation was counterargued. The author stated:

> in fact, this viewpoint (Zhou Yang's) propagates that in the process of development, socialism will continuously produce alien forces and can never get rid of them. If this

[12]Deng Xiaoping, 'Party's Urgent Tasks on the Organizational and Ideological Fronts,' (12 October 1983), Vol. 3, p. 51. It is useful to note that 'jingshen wuran' is translated into 'mental pollution' rather than 'spiritual pollution' in Vol. 3.
[13]*ibid.*, p. 52.
[14]*Renmin Ribao*, 27 January 1984.

> is true, our socialist system will inevitably plunge into a desperate situation and will find no way out. Then what's the use of our emphasis on supporting and improving Party leadership?[15]

The strongest condemnation of the unorthodox discourse came from Wang Zhen, Vice President of China, in October 1983 at a conference of the newly established Chinese Society for the Study of Scientific Socialism. Wang claimed:

> There are people who say that our country is not yet socialist, or that ours is agrarian socialism. There are also those who are constantly propagating so-called 'socialist alienation,' saying something to the effect that socialism suffers not only from ideological alienation, but from political alienation and economic alienation. They even go as far as to say that 'the roots of alienation are to be found in the socialist system itself.' These views are entirely opposed to the Marxist scientific system.[16]

Both Deng and Wang sternly condemned Western ideological influence on China and Chinese intellectuals. Such influence was alleged to have reached an alarming proportion, and the allegedly corrosive Western ideas included a multi-party system, individualism, freedom of expression discussed in the abstract, money-worship, pornography and other 'decadent ideologies.'

Deng stood for purification, and regarded it as an important precondition for the efficacy of the Party as the leading force in China. Deng never believed in the functional necessity of a multi-party democracy based on adversaries for a market-oriented economy. To Deng, an enlightened and disciplined elite with shared beliefs could better ensure order and guide reforms. His writing and speeches revealed clearly his hope for a revival of the revolutionary moral force and a sense of discipline and sacrifice as a unifying force of the political elite for China's modernization. As observed by Thomas B. Gold in his article on 'spiritual pollution,' Deng

> wants economic development and a loyal technocracy to spur it, while not shrinking from sacrificing intellectual and artistic liberalization in the process. He advocated eliminat-

[15]*Renmin Ribao*, 20 December 1983.
[16]*Renmin Ribao*, 25 October 1983.

ing spiritual pollution not just for balancing competing factions and bolstering support for rectification; he really wanted a purification.[17]

Wang Zhen put forward three normative requirements for ending ideological confusion. First, the Chinese theoreticians and Party members should stand at the forefront of the struggle against the spiritual pollution by working, in Stalinist terminology, like the engineers of the human soul; second, it was necessary to establish a large Marxist theoretical contingent, which should exclude those who oppose Marxism under the disguise of 'theoretical research'; and third, it was essential to further propagate the 'theories of scientific socialism' to the masses.[18]

As a result, some liberal intellectuals like Wang Ruoshui and Hu Jiwei were removed from office, and Zhou Yang was compelled to make a self-criticism. Criticism was soon extended to many aspects of ordinary life, from fashion clothes to pop music.[19] The conservatives again adopted the strategy of controlling the media to spread the campaign and then compelling a 'biaotai' (take a stand openly) from cadres, intellectuals and professional institutions to create a conservative discursive convention, which would in turn influence decision-making and policy alternatives. Those who did not openly take a stand would risk being regarded as flagrantly disagreeing with the Party's political decision.

Deng Xiaoping supported some shift in the ideological line for both ideological and political reasons, as he insisted on Chinese-style socialism, and he would not be 'too soft on the Right.' But he did not want, as some hardliners tried, to make this drive another political purge or extend it to other fields, especially the ongoing economic reforms. For Deng, the paramount task for the Party was economic development. Even ideological struggle should be judged by its relevance to development. For Deng, the greatest danger of ideological heresy was its possible causal impact on the credibility of his reform programme. Both Hu Yaobang and Zhao Ziyang were also

[17]Thomas B. Gold, 'Just in Time – China Battles Spiritual Pollution on the eve of 1984,' *Asian Survey*, No. 9, 1984, p. 123.
[18]*Renmin Ribao*, 25 October 1983.
[19]*Liaowang*, No. 3, 1983, p. 45.

against the expansion of the scope of the campaign and its ultra-leftist discourse.

The reformers resisted such ideological excesses by three tactics. First, they downplayed the campaign. Hu Yaobang described the campaign as part of the Party's regular efforts for education of its members. An editorial in *Renmin Ribao* stated:

> At present, some foreign press agencies present our fight against spiritual pollution as a 'movement.' It is not a movement, but none other than an ordinary item of work in building socialist civilization. We are sure that in the future, the development of the situation will contribute to the dissipation of these misunderstandings.[20]

Second, they redefined the discourse of the campaign in order to redirect the campaign in favour of reform. Hu specifically stressed that the campaign 'must be conducted to promote economic development' rather than another political purge. An indication of this was Hu's attempt to associate 'spiritual pollution' with economic crimes, such as the embezzlement of public funds and corruption.[21] Third, they tried to confine the campaign to a limited area and decouple politics from economics. On 8 December, a Party directive placed the rural areas off campaign limits. On 18 December, the State Council issued a directive which specifically listed six areas of activities for scientific and technical personnel free from the campaign.[22]

As in the first campaign against bourgeois liberalization, most Chinese intellectuals refused to go along with ritual ideological struggle. For instance, reform-minded theorists working under the Secretariat's research group displayed their displeasure with their head, Deng Liqun, by requesting that their group move to the State Council headed by Zhao Ziyang,[23] and many theoreticians simply refused to obey the orders to write on things that toed the official line. The campaign died out towards the end of the year when *Renmin Ribao*'s New Year editorial barely mentioned spiritual pollution and once again stressed that work in all spheres must be subordinate to economic development.

[20] *Renmin Ribao*, 16 November 1983.
[21] *The Nineties*, No. 2, 1984, p. 6.
[22] *Renmin Ribao*, 18 December 1983.
[23] Wang Xiaoqiang's conversation with the author in Cambridge, U.K., on 27 November 1991.

By April 1984, the trend had changed from anti-rightism to anti-leftism. The press was once again filled with articles extolling pro-reform conventions such as virtues of entrepreneurship and new reform initiatives. The editorial of *Renmin Ribao* in April, which was based on a talk by Hu Yaobang, claimed:

> In our country, 'leftist' influences have penetrated very deeply, and it is not easy to eliminate the residual 'leftist' influence. Wang Ming's line was implemented for only four years, but it took us ten years to eliminate the influence of his line. After the founding of the People's Republic of China, 'leftist' errors continued, off and on, for twenty years, culminating in the extremes of the Cultural Revolution, and we will have to work with a great deal of energy before we can eliminate its influence. We must not neglect this point to the slightest degree in the course of Party rectification.[24]

In fact, the editorial constituted an explicit repudiation of the conservative discourse in September and October of 1983, which had stressed the rightist trend as the major danger to the country.

3 The new technological revolution

In the reform's high tide in early 1983, while engaged in intellectual transcendence, Chinese intellectuals also introduced into China the futurist writings from the West, which immediately aroused strong interest in the Party's top-level leadership. The technological revolution discussed in futurist writings broadened the vision of Chinese reformers and provided a new discursive framework for thinking and policy options. Alvin Toffler visited China in January 1983. Both Zhao Ziyang and Hu Yaobang met with him and had cordial conversations. The works of Western futurologists, such as Daniel Bell's *Coming of Post-Industrial Society*, John Naisbitt's *Megatrends* and Alvin Toffler's *Third Wave*, were translated and widely circulated in China. According to Toffler, the first wave was agrarian revolution, the second industrial revolution and the third information revolution. Naisbitt suggested that the knowledge theory of value should replace

[24]*Renmin Ribao*, 1 April 1984.

the Marxist labour theory of value.[25] Many Chinese researchers endorsed these basic arguments about the third wave and called for reform to meet the challenge of the new technological revolution.

But more conservative leaders were opposed to futurism, which called into question most Marxist themes on class, capitalism, imperialism, socialism and communism. For instance, Hu Qiaomu himself attempted to limit the audience to Toffler's lectures in China and in September 1983 when the anti-'spiritual pollution' campaign began, the Chinese translations of some futurist books, including Toffler's *Third Wave*, were taken off the shelves of bookstores. Some considered the new technological revolution as 'heretical opinions' and bourgeois 'sugarcoated bullet.'[26] Some scholars argued for caution about these new theories, especially, the possibility that China could skip certain stages of development; according to Toffler, the late-comers could avoid the worst of industrial revolution and go directly into information society. This theme reminded many of the old utopia of a short-cut to catch up with the West. However, other researchers cited examples such as Japan's catching up with Europe, and Singapore's emergence as a dynamic economy by using modern technology to skip some stages of development.[27]

Reformers' think tanks briefed Zhao Ziyang and Hu Yaobang on these developments. While conservative ideologues were busy preparing for a drive against spiritual pollution, Zhao Ziyang decided to give the futurist theory a push. On 9 October 1983, Zhao chaired a meeting on the subject and instructed a group of specialists to do a study on the new technological revolution and its possible impact on China.

Zhao's handling of this ideologically sensitive issue was typical of Chinese reformers' pragmatism. Zhao made a distinction between the unacceptable ideological facade and the acceptable substance. He stated that many scholars

> in capitalist countries advocated these views with their political purposes, because capitalism is in deep crisis . . .

[25]See John Naisbitt, *Megatrends – Ten New Directions Transforming Our lives*, New York, Warner Books., Inc., 1982 and Huang Shunji and Li Qinzhen, *Daganggan – zhenhan shijie de xinjishu geming* (Big Lever – The New Technological Revolution that is Shaking the World), Jinan, Shandong University Press, 1986.
[26]*Liaowang*, 2 January 1984, p. 27.
[27]Huang Shunji and Li Qinzhen, 1986, pp. 455–482.

> therefore, they are looking for a panacea to inspire people and overcome the predicament and attempt to find a 'splendid new times.' Fundamentally speaking, their views are contrary to the basic tenets of Marxism.[28]

However, Zhao redefined the thrust of futurism as value-neutral and it could be used for China's benefit, as he claimed:

> No matter whether they are correct, and whatever purposes they serve . . . we can acquire a piece of information that at the turn of the century . . . The present and immediately possible technological breakthroughs will be applied to production and society and bring about new changes in social life. This trend merits our attention, . . . we should study it conscientiously and, in light of our actual conditions, define the proper economic strategies and technological policies to be adopted for long-term plans, covering ten or twenty years, especially science and technology plans . . . The new world industrial revolution is an opportunity as well as a challenge.[29]

Zhao stressed that China should keep abreast of the new trends and find ways to narrow the economic and technological gap between China and the developed countries. Zhao also claimed that there were two possibilities: one was that China may narrow its 'economic and technological gaps' with the developed countries if China made good use of this opportunity by 'focusing on the utilization of new scientific and technological results and developing China's economy' or China may widen her gaps with the developed countries if she failed to 'handle this situation properly or ignore it.'[30]

The new discourse was also aimed at softening the edge of the on-going campaign against spiritual pollution and diverting people's attention from the campaign to economic reform and opening up. Zhao's statement was made public in October 1983 at the height of anti-spiritual pollution in Shanghai's *World Economic Herald*. In early November Hu Yaobang wrote a letter in support of Zhao's October comment. Hu criticized those who 'pay no attention to the new developments in the world.' Challenging the leftists and their ideological campaign, Hu claimed:

[28]*World Economic Herald*, 31 October 1984.
[29]*ibid.*
[30]*ibid.*

> some even regard the new achievements made by mankind in our time as heresy and capitalist sugar-coated bullets. In educating cadres in the economic field, whether the main task is to struggle against ignorance or so-called liberalization is a question that merits serious consideration.[31]

Reformer-controlled media immediately gave wide publicity to the new technological revolution and diluted the campaign against spiritual pollution. Checking the unpopular ideological campaign with a relatively popular ideological drive proved effective.

But as shown in Zhao's approach to sensitive ideological issues, Chinese reformers used Marxist discursive framework in discussing the Third Wave either out of their belief or out of their ideological precautions. Some scholars argued that the Third Wave could help eliminate what Mao called the three great differences between worker and peasant, between town and country, and between mental and manual labour. In other words, the new theory served to justify the Marxist analysis of the determining role of the productive forces,[32] which brought the world closer to the highest point of capitalism, a significant step towards the ultimate goal of communism. Ma Hong noted that although the new theory served the ideological function of legitimating the continued survival of capitalism, China should not overlook the possible benefit to arise from such a revolution. Su Shaozhi and Ding Xueliang claimed that Marx had predicted the information revolution and the post-industrial society discussed in the works by Bell.[33]

In February 1984, Deng Xiaoping supported the discourse on the new technological revolution by visiting a Shanghai exhibit on microelectronic technology. Deng spoke out on China's need for advanced technology. The Chinese propaganda apparatus now began a full-swing media campaign to promote awareness of the technological revolution that finally drowned out the hardliners' ideological fever against 'spiritual pollution.' From March 1984 onwards, the Chinese press dropped its criticism of spiritual pollution and began a publicity campaign to spread information on the technological revolution. Party and govern-

[31]Xinhua, 24 June 1984, quoted in Carol Lee Hamrin, *China and the Challenge of the Future*, Boulder, Westview Press, 1990, p. 77.
[32]*Guangming Ribao*, 4 and 9 January 1984.
[33]*Guangming Ribao*, 14 December 1983.

ment officials, including members of the Politburo and the Secretariat, were reported to have attended lectures on the new technological revolution. The discussion also influenced China's developmental planning. Substantive amendments were made to incorporate the strategy for developing new technologies into China's planning. Zhang Jinfu, a state councillor and minister of the economic commission, stated that Zhao's instruction had led to some changes in the Sixth Five-Year Plan.[34]

The new technological revolution also seemed to be one of the main sources of inspiration for Deng and his followers. As a discourse, the new technological revolution does not interpret the world as a bipolar ideological confrontation between capitalism and communism but rather as a set of challenges and opportunities. It was perhaps not a coincidence that in 1984 Deng made a number of apparently more inspiring and unconventional talks. In February 1984 Deng talked about 'finding new solutions for the many problems that cannot be solved by old ones.'[35] He began to raise a number of big issues on the relationship between socialism and capitalism and on the modernization of China.

In 1984, Deng presented more clearly his concept of 'one county, two systems' for solving issues like Hong Kong, Macau and Taiwan. He endorsed the expansion of the Xiamen SEZ and the idea of turning Xiamen into a 'free port.'[36] He even asserted that capitalism could contribute to socialism by claiming that 'the existence of capitalism in limited areas will actually be conducive to the development of socialism.'[37] Deviating from the Leninist convention on sharp confrontational relationship between the capitalist countries and the developing countries, Deng's prognosis was that there could be cooperation between them and that the developing countries should absorb Western capital, technology and managerial skills and Western countries

[34]*Guoji Maoyi* (International Trade), 12 (27 December 1983), pp. 3–4, Quoted in Carol Lee Hamrin, 1990, p. 78.
[35]Deng Xiaoping, 'A New Approach to Stabilizing the World Situation,' (February 22, 1984), Vol. 3, p. 59.
[36]Liu Jintian, Deng Xiaoping de licheng (Deng Xiaoping's Journey), Beijing, PLA Cultural Press, 1994, Vol. 2, p. 365–366 and p. 288.
[37]Deng Xiaoping, 'China will Always Keep its Promises,' (December 19, 1984), Vol. 3, p. 109.

would serve their own economic interests if they could help the developing countries, as it would contribute to market creation.[38]

Deng once again emphasized his developmentalism that the merit of an ideology and policy should be judged only by one criterion; namely, whether it could promote economic development. Countering arguments against the SEZs as 'Hong Kongization,' Deng called for building several 'Hong Kongs' in China. Deng also introduced a two-stage development goal: following a quadrupling of GNP by the year 2000, China would devote the first thirty to fifty years of the 21st century to economic development in order to approach the level of the developed countries. To match this long-term goal, Deng promised Hong Kong at least fifty years of a capitalist system beyond 1997 and suggested that there would be a gradual peaceful integration, which would be increasingly facilitated by China's modernization process. It seemed that the discussion of the new technological revolution served as an inspiration for Deng's more pragmatic thinking on the issues of socialism, capitalism and modernization, for his efforts for doctrinal renovation and authority building, and for his clearer deviation from the conventions based on Chen Yun's 'bird-cage theory.'

In the context of the ideological struggle, the discussion on the new technological revolution seemed to suggest that, compared with the concept of democracy and humanism, it was relatively easy to challenge the orthodox views in a discursive framework of science and technology in Deng's China. There were several reasons for this. First, Deng's commitment to science and technology could be exploited to resist conservative ideological offensives. Reformers had chosen a subject to which Deng was personally committed, thus winning Deng's crucial support in the struggle between reformers and ideologues; second, by stressing the increasingly greater gap between China and the West in science and technology, reformers were appealing to Chinese nationalism and the urgent need to restore China's past glory. The orthodox views thus caught more resentment, as the leftists were blamed implicitly for intentionally leaving China further behind other countries. It was interesting to note that nationalist sentiment was frequently exploited by both reformers and conservatives to revive the Chinese collec-

[38]Deng Xiaoping, 'We Must Safeguard World Peace and Ensure Domestic Development,' (May 29, 1984), Vol. 3, p. 66.

tive memory of their past glory and humiliation endured in modern history, and to portray explicitly or implicitly the other side as insensitive to this or as a betrayal of the national interests of China. Third, by placing the new technological revolution in a Marxist discursive framework, they reduced the political cost of adhering to the new doctrine. By declaring the thrust of futurism value-free, they attempted to decouple the ideological dimension from the substantive content of the subject. Consequently, they drew useful inspirations from it and managed to change the course of the on-going conservative ideological drive.

B Ideology and reform policies

1 Policy towards intellectuals[39]

One major obstacle to China's economic reform was the Maoist anti-intellectualism and the low level of education of Chinese cadres. In the 1950s, Maoist discourse maintained that the major contradiction in society was the struggle between the proletariat and the bourgeoisie. At that time, intellectuals were classified among the bourgeoisie and were branded 'bourgeois intellectuals.' Since intellectuals did not control any means of production except knowledge, they were labelled as 'intellectual aristocracy,' which in Mao's supposedly egalitarian society was a curse. As a result, the intellectuals suffered badly in the successive ideological campaigns launched by Mao after 1949.

Since Deng's return to power, reformers adopted a policy of encouraging intellectuals to play a greater role in the modernization process. In early 1982, the CPC Central Committee issued Document No.10 entitled 'Circular on Seriously Checking the Work Concerning Intellectuals.' This document required cadres at all levels to give equal treatment to intellectuals politically; to give them greater freedom in their work; and to show concern for their living conditions and help them solve their problems. But this drive met strong resistance, as the Maoist anti-intellectualism and deep-rooted leftist prejudice against intellectuals still had a grip on many cadres, who criticized intellectuals for their alleged 'arrogance,' 'inexperience' and 'political naivete.'

To attract intellectuals to the Party's reform programme, the

[39]In the Chinese context, 'intellectuals' refers to a broad category covering most specialists and professionals.

reformers renewed their efforts to establish a new convention in favour of intellectuals and knowledge. The method adopted by Hu Yaobang in 1983 to refute leftist contempt for intellectuals was to reinterpret their idol – Karl Marx. With the new interpretations of Marxism in early 1983, Hu Yaobang attempted to describe Marx as a genuine, non-dogmatic and courageous intellectual. Choosing the occasion of Marx's centenary anniversary in 1983 Hu Yaobang talked at length about Marx as the most accomplished intellectual and scientist committed to seeking a genuine understanding of complex and changing reality. By praising Marx in such a way, Hu made the word 'intellectuals' a good word and criticized the 'red' cadres for their anti-intellectualism. Hu further stated:

> It was necessary to oppose the erroneous tendency of separating intellectuals from the working class, counterpoising them to the workers and regarding them as an alien force, and to confirm the correct concept of intellectuals as a part of the working class, and to strengthen a hundredfold the unity between workers and peasants on the one hand and the intellectuals on the other.[40]

The reformers had a practical imperative for establishing a pro-intellectual convention, as they were making efforts to promote people with good education to leading posts in the Party on the belief that the Party must be composed of competent and professional people committed to reform. The 1983 statistics showed that the educational level of cadres (those on the government's payroll) was low: only 61 per cent had a high school education, and only one fifth had a college or university education.[41] Hu Yaobang stated that if China wanted to absorb all the achievements of modern science and technology and develop a modern economy, Chinese cadres must be better educated and understand the world trends. Hu argued:

> Knowledge and intellectuals are necessary for overthrowing the old world, and they are even more necessary for building the new world. . . . But it is precisely about this key question that our understanding has been inadequate for so long and it is why we have been obsessed for years by

[40] *Renmin Ribao*, 14 March 1983.
[41] *Liaowang*, No. 1, 1983, p. 25.

> erroneous ideas that depart from Marxism. Today, the correct attitude towards knowledge and intellectuals has therefore become a vital and urgent question.[42]

The reformers did not simply stop at the ideological justification for the intellectuals' greater role. Another method they employed was to combine the ideological drive with widely-publicized revelations in the media about the recent injustice and inhuman treatment that the intellectuals had suffered. Furthermore, the on-going discussion of 'socialist humanism' and a humanistic touch in these revelations gave added weight to the plight of intellectuals and made it more sensational to the general public.

The media reported several shocking cases. For example, Mrs. Zhu Yuefeng, an engineer, was reported to have committed suicide as a result of leftist persecution. Zhu was promoted to the post of deputy director of the Beijing No.7 Chemical Plant in late 1978. But her devotion to work and her expertise only aroused jealousy and hatred from certain Party officials including the director of the enterprise, who, a layman, framed many charges against her and refused to admit her to the Party.[43] Another widely reported case was that of Mrs. Jiang Xiongxu, a chemist, who lost her left eye in a chemical experiment and won three awards from the Hengyang municipal government for her contribution to chemical research. But some officials in her plant spread rumours about her and in the end banned her from entering her laboratory.[44] Describing such stories from a humanistic perspective, these reports instilled a strong sense of moral obligation and urgency in redressing the injustice. Commenting on the case of Jiang, *Renmin Ribao* stated in its editorial note that this case

> reminds us that if we fail to implement resolutely the Party's policy towards intellectuals, and if we fail to value the important role to be played by the intellectuals in building the Four Modernizations, . . . our cause will suffer, and even the fate of the Party and of the country will be endangered.[45]

But discrimination against intellectuals was not simply a prob-

[42]*ibid*, p. 24.
[43]*Renmin Ribao*, 13 April 1983.
[44]*Renmin Ribao*, 13 March 1983.
[45]*ibid*.

lem of ideological inclination. It had been to a great extent institutionalized in the Maoist era. Despite great changes in policy towards intellectuals since 1978, some old rules and regulations still prevented intellectuals from playing a more constructive role in economic reform. In early 1983, the reformers made a new breakthrough in this regard by exposing such institutionalized injustice in the mass media. The widely-publicized case of Mr. Han Kun was an example. As a technician of a state-owned research institute, Han fulfilled his own work on the weekdays, while moonlighting as a technical consultant for a rural enterprise on sunday in the suburbs of Shanghai. Han's work helped create a profit of over 400,000 yuan for the enterprise. Han, sensitive to the ideological constraint, received a monthly pay of 88 yuan under his wife's name, but in early 1981 he accepted a lump sum bonus of 1,200 yuan. The officials in his institute immediately claimed, 'since Han has accepted money, the (political) nature of his question is now different,' which meant that it was acceptable if he worked for nothing, but if he received pay for his extra-work he was money-worshipping and practicing extreme individualism. As a result he was sent to labour in a workshop of the institute and he was formally charged with 'economic crime.' The controversy arose when the workers and staff of the factory he had helped protested. This case lasted for over one year until March 1983 when the court ruled him innocent.[46]

The reformer-controlled press went further to expose cases of continued ideological bias against intellectuals. For instance, the requests of many intellectuals for job swap or moonlighting were viewed as 'lacking a sense of organizational discipline' and 'displaying extreme individualism.' Some officials even considered the requests of intellectuals for readjusting their professional titles, which had long been suspended during the Maoist period and revived again after 1979, as 'seeking power.' Some complained that the present policy towards intellectuals 'praised intellectuals excessively' (peng de taigao). Professionals were criticized as 'self-important' and having a 'lack of experience.'[47] *Renmin Ribao* attributed the ideological cause of such problem to the fact that many cadres from worker-peasant famil-

[46]*Jiefang Ribao*, 4 June 1983.
[47]*Liaowang*, No. 1, 1983, p. 25.

ies had developed a bias against intellectuals under the prolonged leftist influence.[48]

However, despite opposition, the drive to promote intellectuals and knowledge yielded positive results. In 1983, reformers succeeded in ensuring that almost all newly-promoted cadres at the level of the county leadership and above were university educated. During this process of promoting intellectuals, sustained media attention to the existing issues helped shape the new convention in favour of intellectuals. The reformers successfully made use of the discussion on humanism and their controlled media to highlight the inhuman treatment of intellectuals. They significantly reformulated the discursive framework on intellectuals, thus contributing to a greater sympathy towards professionals and contempt for the 'red' cadres who had no expertise. As a result, more intellectuals were promoted to leading positions and became the new and most important constituency for the reform programme.

2 Market *versus* planning

While Hu Yaobang was praising Marx as an intellectual devoted to searching a nondogmatic understanding of complicated and evolving social and economic conditions, he was encouraging Party officials to explore new issues and new ideas. Hu stressed the need to readjust

> those areas (huanjie) in the superstructure that cannot meet the needs of economic base . . . , and those areas in the relations of production that are not suited to the development of productive force.[49]

This was a call for theoretical innovations to adapt the doctrine to the reality.

The pro-reform ideological discourse set the stage for a series of economic reform initiatives. In agriculture, Central Directive No.1 for 1983 urged peasants to seek wealth as quickly as possible. Notable progress was achieved in an ideologically sensitive area of private economy. Reformers again adopted an incremental approach on the issue by moving one step forward towards allowing more hired workers in the private economy. The new

[48] *Renmin Ribao*, 11 May 1983.
[49] *Renmin Ribao*, 14 March 1983.

directive now allowed specialized households to hire more than seven people, the maximum number originally permitted in the 'Certain Policy Provisions Relating to the Non-Agricultural Individual Economy in Cities and Townships' promulgated on July 7, 1981. This had allowed individual businessman to engage up to two 'assistants' and five 'apprentices,' thus diluting the ideologically sensitive issue of hiring outside labour. The notion of seven people was said to come from one of Marx's articles which mentioned the free association of workers up to seven people.

The position of individual business was officially designated in Article 11 of the 1982 Constitution as lawful 'individual economy' (geti jingji) and 'its lawful interests' would be protected. Private economy, which began to emerge in 1981, was accelerated in 1983 thanks to the pro-market ideological climate and clear official position on greater liberalization of capital, labour and markets. The term 'private economy' was used more frequently, in addition to 'individual economy,' to designate those firms which employ at least eight outside workers, a natural development out of the expansive individual household business.

Adopting the strategy of incrementalism and linkage, reformers began to prepare public opinion for an extension of reform from rural to urban areas. Zhao Ziyang declared in a speech in February 1983 on the occasion of the Chinese New Year that 'the success of rural reform further clarifies the orientation of reform in urban industry and commerce and other fields.'[50] This statement was followed by a slight discursive change in the sequence of 'readjustment, reform, consolidation and improvement' with reform preceding readjustment in an editorial of *Renmin Ribao* on 3 March 1983. The tone of the article was also tilted towards reform and called for speeding up the pace of reform while further implementing the policy of readjustment.[51]

However, whether China's economic reform should be market-oriented or not was still a sensitive issue. In his memoir, Xu Jiatun, the ex-governor of Jiangsu Province, recalled his private meeting with Deng Xiaoping on market economy in Jiangsu in the spring of 1983. Jiangsu was known for its vigorous devel-

[50]*Renmin Ribao*, 24 February 1983.
[51]*Renmin Ribao*, 3 March 1983.

opment of township enterprises, which were in most cases collectively owned but responsive to market signals. Xu confessed that he was uneasy before he briefed Deng on Jiangsu's market economy, an expected mind-set shaped by China's prolonged anti-market political culture, and he first made a self-criticism in front of Deng that 'we availed ourselves of the loopholes in state policies.' This implied that Jiangsu's excessive (by the prevailing ideological standards) collective economy, which paid 51% of their profits to the state and kept the rest, often competed with the state sector for raw materials and disrupted the overall state planning.

Xu then mustered the courage to tell Deng frankly that 'the Party Central Committee affirmed market economy before, but later the notion was changed into "the primacy of planning supplemented by market regulation." Only in public can we use this notion, but in reality it is impossible (for us) to retreat (from market economy).' Xu told Deng the aggregate ratio between planned economy and market economy in Jiangsu Province: 'at provincial level, about 50% to 50%; at city and country level, about 40% to 60% or even 30% to 70%. In certain areas of southern Jiangsu, it is already 20% to 80% or even 10% to 90%... As a result, Jiangsu's economic output is doubled within six years.' Deng seemed impressed, observing that 'it seems that market economy is very important.'[52] However, aware that market economy was still ideologically controversial and deviated from the prevailing conventions, Deng did not further elaborate on this issue, and his remark was not made public.

Despite the prevailing conventions, reformers were able to adopt two moderate but significant steps: First, they protected and even encouraged various local experiments of market economy to continue; and second, they took initiatives to reform those areas of planning which ideological consensus had permitted. For instance, steps were taken to restructure the central planning system in a hope to invigorate the role of major cities in regional economic development. In February 1983, Chongqing, a city of over 2 million people, was enlisted as the first large city for a planning reform experiment. It was allowed to carry out planning under direct national guidance rather than

[52]Xue Jiatun, *Xue Jiatun xianggang huiyilu* (Xue Jiatun's Memoir of Hong Kong), Hong Kong, Lianhebao Press, 1993, pp. 8–9.

under provincial control. This decentralization of planning power was also accompanied by other urban reform experiments: expansion of the collective and individual sectors, commercialization of housing, greater decision-making power for enterprises. Wuhan, a city of nearly 3 million people, shortly followed suit. Cities expanded their power over planning and their jurisdictions over surrounding counties to encourage closer economic networks. Both Deng and Zhao Ziyang also started experimentation in economic cooperation between regions and hoped that the Yangtze delta, led by Shanghai, would be a pioneer in comprehensive reform and spur the whole Yangtze delta's economic take-off.

The campaign against spiritual pollution from mid-1983 to the end of the year, however, was widely perceived as a change of the overarching ideology and exposed the vulnerability of many reform policies to a conservative ideological attack. By mid-1983 the contract responsibility system practiced in the countryside and in the cities and the policy of stressing material incentives had led to a substantial differentiation in income and uneven living standards. The decentralization and diversification of economic power since 1978 had in some areas led to a transfer of decision-making power from party officials to the managers of enterprises. Many factories had been leased to aspiring and reform-minded individuals. This redistribution of wealth and power made those less favoured groups eager to express their dissatisfaction and perhaps their 'feeling of moral superiority,' as Schram noted,[53] over those who were steeped in material gains. The campaign obviously provided such an opportunity as well as a discursive framework and could easily find a 'ready-made clientele' against economic reforms and its ensuing ideological change.

As soon as the campaign started, Mao Zhiyong, the Party secretary of Hunan province, emphasized that eliminating spiritual pollution should not be confined only to the Party's ideological institutions. One should guard against 'burying one's head in economic work in neglect of ideology.'[54] Deng's 'socialism with Chinese characteristics' began to be interpreted in such a way that socialism was more important than Chinese characteristics. For example, *Jingji Ribao* (Economic Daily) carried an article

[53]Schram, 1984, p. 48.
[54]*Hunan Ribao*, 3 November 1983.

entitled 'What is Socialism with Chinese Characteristics?' which defined socialism in China as composed of six elements: (1) public ownership; (2) people's democratic dictatorship; (3) the communist ideal as the core of ideology; (4) production aimed at meeting people's material and cultural needs; (5) the practice of planned economy, which contains a commodity economy; and (6) the idea of 'to each according to his work.'[55] Planned economy was also reaffirmed as the most important principle of the Chinese economy. Chinese media once again stressed the importance of Chen Yun's 'bird-cage theory.'

Jingji Ribao also published another article entitled 'It Is Necessary to Adhere to the Planned Economy,' which argued that reform must adhere to socialist orientation, and could not 'weaken the planned economy.' The article further claimed that 'certain comrades' had been advocating 'the market economy and free competition which reflect the ideology of bourgeois liberalization.'[56] A *Guangming Ribao* article entitled 'Guiding Reform with Communist Ideology' stressed that economic reform must serve to develop a socialist public sector and that 'adhering to socialism means adhering to the planned economy.'[57] In the following days, *Jingji Ribao* published a series of 'questions and answers' which were meant to clear up the confusion arising from the ideological campaign. The list of questions would suffice to illustrate the ideological and discursive confusions associated with the campaign: 'Does the implementation of the current policy mean that we are farther away from communism?'[58] 'Is the existence of multi-type ownership a political retrogression?'[59] 'Does economic reform run contrary to socialism?'[60] 'Will the policy of letting some people get rich first lead to polarization?'[61] 'Will the open-door policy infringe upon state sovereignty?'[62] 'Will the appropriate development of private economy restore capitalism?'[63]

The leftist discourse and possible extension of the campaign

[55] *Jingji Ribao*, 8 October 1983.
[56] *Jingji Ribao*, 10 November 1983.
[57] *Guangming Ribao*, 21 November 1983.
[58] *Jingji Ribao*, 11 October 1983
[59] *ibid.*, 12 October 1983
[60] *ibid.*, 13 October 1983
[61] *ibid.*, 14 October 1983
[62] *ibid.*, 18 October 1983
[63] *ibid.*, 20 October 1983

to economic reform policies obviously triggered reformers to set a limit to this ideological drive, as discussed in the first part of this chapter. The discussion sponsored by the reformers on the new technological revolution soon changed the ideological tone of the mass media and provided an entirely different discursive framework for political discussion and a new impetus to economic reforms. While no breakthrough was achieved in the theory of planning vs. market, the reformers succeeded through their prompt administrative and ideological intervention in ensuring that the campaign against the spiritual pollution could not significantly affect economic reforms at the grass-roots level. But they failed to pursue more radical reforms and greater opening as they had desired partly due to the ideological constraints which culminated in the campaign.

3 The expansion of the SEZs

Despite the ideological dispute over the nature and future of the SEZs in 1982, the pro-reform ideological discourse in early 1983 induced more liberal policies in opening up China. The new discursive framework stressed the primacy of productive forces and a non-dogmatic interpretation of Marxism. In this spirit, reformers took clear steps towards expanding the open-door policy since the beginning of 1983. In January 1983, Zhao Ziyang visited Hainan Island, China's second largest island, and soon more flexible policies in foreign trade and investment, previously enjoyed only by the SEZs were granted to Hainan. The idea of Hainan as a SEZ was being seriously considered. In February, Hu Yaobang visited Shenzhen, Shekou and Hainan, urging the local officials to pursue a high growth rate and attract more foreign capital and expand the open-door policy. The fact that two top leaders visited the SEZs in a matter of one month highlighted the importance the top echelon reformers attached to the SEZs. They wanted to launch a new reform drive from the SEZs, and their discourse on bolder reform policies served to encourage reformers across the country.

Despite reformist discourse, ideological constraints were such that many market-oriented methods such as stock holding companies and bankruptcy were still not feasible even in the SEZs. As a result, one important new step taken by reformers was to conduct more experiments on economic reforms in the SEZs.

For instance, Hu Yaobang initiated more experiments in the 'directors' responsibility system' as pilot projects for the rest of the country. This approach based on experimentation constituted one important style of China's economic reforms. But the role of models has always been a trade mark of Chinese communism since the pre-1949 years. The difference between Mao's models and Deng's is that Mao's criterion was principally value-oriented while Deng's was economic performance-oriented. In May 1983 the result of the initial experiment on the 'director's responsibility system' in Shenzhen was considered as successful. The new experiment gave unprecedented decision-making power to the director or manager rather than the Party secretary of an enterprise and was later introduced across the nation as a way-out for state enterprises. A *Renmin Ribao* article observed that 'the factory managers almost unanimously pointed out that the possession of autonomous power is an indispensable condition in managing enterprises well, particularly those engaged in the international market.'[64]

The relatively liberal climate also permitted economists to put forward more original strategies for economic reforms. For instance, Tong Dalin, Vice Chairman of the State Economic Structural Reform Commission, put forward, drawing on the trickle-down theory, the strategy of 'relying on the east and moving to the west,' which gave priority to economic development on the east coast. The benefits would then trickle down to the hinterland.

The 'spiritual pollution' campaign launched in mid-1983 renewed a conservative discourse, which generated an unfavourable climate for the open-door policy in general and the SEZs in particular. Chen Yun criticized the tendency of neglecting the influence of 'the negative things' from the West in pursuing an open-door policy, observing that 'we already talked about the need to pay special attention to the negative things in the process of opening up to the outside world. Judging from the present situation, we have not done enough in preventing the negative consequences (of opening up to the outside world).' Chen was also concerned with the 'corrosive' influence of capitalism on the population and with the possible loss of popular confidence in socialism. 'Some people saw high-rises and expressways, etc, in foreign countries; thus, they

[64]*Renmin Ribao*, 15 May 1983.

believed that China was inferior to the foreign countries and that socialism did not work.' Chen argued that 'in capitalist countries there are millionaires, but their wealth comes from the exploitation of the working people.'[65] However, a serious problem with the conservatives was that they were not able to advance to the population any credible alternatives or programmes more attractive than the apparent market-led prosperity programmes. Many ideologues still believed in the magic power of ideological propaganda over the people and in socialist superiority over capitalism.

The campaign also subjected the SEZs to implicit criticism. SEZ officials became defensive about their policies and efforts, and they were made to prove that they had been engaged in a struggle against spiritual pollution all along. Some supporters of the SEZs were reported to have been criticized. A Hong Kong political journal reported that Ren Zhongyi, the First Party Secretary of Guangdong province, was accused of 'restoring capitalism.'[66] The old arguments about self-reliance, sovereignty and Western cultural influence were revived. The reformers' frustration with the conservative attack on the open-door policy was revealed in an article by Huan Xiang and Dai Lunzhang in defence of the policy. They wrote:

> As a major strategic principle . . . the open-door policy has become our unswerving national policy . . . In the course of implementing this policy we are bound to encounter many new circumstances and problems. What we need is the pioneering spirit and the attitude of seeking truth from facts. We must not try to make petty reforms or stick to old ways and conventions; still less must we backtrack. . . . [67]

Referring to the conservative attack on the SEZs, they commented:

> We must not set the principle of adhering to self-reliance against the open-door policy . . . Even if we let foreign businessmen run a number of enterprises on a sole proprietary

[65]Chen Yun, 'Speech at the Second Plenary Session of the 12th CPC Central Committee,' (12 October 1972), JSFZ, p. 277.
[66]Crane, George, op. cit., p. 93.
[67]Huan Xiang and Dai Lunzhang, 'Unswervingly Implement the Open-door Policy,' *Shijie Jingji* (World Economics), 2 (10 February 1984), pp. 1–8. Quoted in Hamrin, C. L., op. cit., p. 76.

> basis, it will not change the socialist economic nature of China ... We cannot set the development of foreign trade against protecting the national industry.... We should not regard advanced science and technologies and scientific management methods as capitalist things and discard them.... Decadent capitalist things have no intrinsic connection with the open-door policy.[68]

During the campaign Deng again demonstrated his preference for the middle road. Deng severely criticized the 'erosive influence of capitalism' but distanced himself from Chen Yun's view, which tended to lump together all things Western. Deng made a clear distinction between economics and culture. Deng affirmed the open-door policy carried out so far in the economic field by stating that China 'has adopted a selective approach' in importing whatever was economically useful to China. But Deng condemned the allegedly non-selective approach in the cultural field and the importation of 'harmful elements in bourgeois culture.'[69] Deng's clear commitment to this dualism perhaps could explain in part why the SEZs were less affected by this campaign and why the reformers were more straightforward than before in defending the SEZs.

This new attempt was a clear indication that reformers led by Deng began to deviate sharply from the original convention based on Chen Yun's 'bird-cage theory.' The relative success of rural reform and the SEZ policy seemed to begin to convince Deng that he could build up his own authority in the economic field on the basis of reforms and an open-door policy. Primacy given to the market and external contact is definitely the trade mark of his developmentalism. Without running the risk of openly challenging the conservative conventions, Deng's interpretation of the success of reform experiments in the SEZs went a long way in shaping a new political climate favourable to more economic reforms and greater openness to the outside. But a lack of a clear-cut pro-market theoretical discourse still made the reformers vulnerable to conservative attacks as shown in the years to come.

[68]*ibid.*

[69]Deng Xiaoping, 'Speech at the Second Plenary Session of the 12th CPC Central Committee,' 12 October 1983, JSFZ, p. 272

Chapter Four

THE THIRD CYCLE: FROM THE PLANNED COMMODITY ECONOMY TO THE SECOND CAMPAIGN AGAINST BOURGEOIS LIBERALIZATION (1984–1987)

The momentum for reform since the drive for the new technological revolution culminated in the Party's decision on urban economic reform in late 1984. The decision seemed to mark the beginning of a new cycle of reforms by evoking the power of inducing and legitimizing many market-oriented policies. But the new initiatives also caused economic tensions and ideological controversy in 1985. Yet controversy was not strong enough to prevent Deng from initiating a limited political reform in 1986 with the aim of improving the Party's efficiency and removing obstacles to his economic reform programme. Deng's call for political restructuring, however, triggered a radical intellectual attempt to transcend the official discourse and a rising demand for democracy and freedoms. Enraged by the seemingly run-away liberal discourse, the more conservative wing of the Party leadership initiated another campaign against bourgeois liberalization which, with the downfall of Hu Yaobang, began to spill over to economic reforms. Zhao Ziyang, with Deng's backing, prompted a halt to the campaign and effectively checked the ideological offensive against reform and opening to the outside world.

Two major themes are particularly important in this cycle: First, in the process of reforms, radical discursive departures from the prevailing convention tend to make reformers extremely vulnerable to conservative attacks as shown in the downfall of Hu Yaobang. As a result, many ideological innovations have to be presented as part of the accepted conventions, and gradual ideological revision is the norm rather than the exception. Second, conservative resistance to radical economic reforms has caused much confusion and many lost opportunities, but adversity is not always detrimental to reforms. The process of reform seems to suggest that a moderate degree of ideological opposition could sometimes contribute to a more realistic approach to economic reform. In fact, China's now much-praised gradual reform is partly attributable to the presence of a moderate degree of ideological adversary.

A Major ideological trends

1 The planned commodity economy

1984 was a very important year for China's economic reform. Several factors led to a favourable climate for reforms: ideologically, Deng put forward a number of inspiring new ideas as discussed in the previous chapter. In the economic field, the rural reform's success enhanced the confidence of reformers in their ability to extend similar reforms into urban areas; the 6th Five-Year Plan targets had been completed two years ahead of schedule; economic structure became more balanced; and foreign policy scored new successes as shown by the official visit of U.S. President Ronald Reagan, who had been regarded with suspicion for his pro-Taiwan and anti-communist stand, and the signing of the Sino-British Declaration on Hong Kong, which reconfirmed China's enhanced international status and international acceptance of Deng's innovative concept of 'one country, two systems.'

Reformers seized the opportunity that the encouraging climate provided to extend reforms from rural areas to cities, which inevitably entailed the reassessment of many prevailing ideological conventions on socialist economy. Urban reform was officially declared in the CPC Central Committee's Decision on Economic Structural Reform adopted in October 1984 (hereinafter 'Decision'). The Decision was more a pro-reform ideological declaration than a concrete plan, as reformers understood that there must be ideological revisions before more market-oriented policies could be adopted in China's ideological political system. Furthermore, it was still unrealistic to map out specific plans for urban reforms, given that the ultimate goal of the reform was still ambiguous and controversial. The main common denominator shared by the top leadership was the understanding that the current economic system was inefficient and that urban reforms must improve China's economic efficiency and productivity.

By socialist ideological standards, the Decision constituted a fairly important theoretical breakthrough and a significant deviation from the widely accepted conventions. First, the Decision defined the essence of the socialist economy as 'planned commodity economy' by stating in cautious terms that 'Ours is on the whole a planned economy, that is, a planned commodity economy, not a market economy that is entirely subject to market regulation.'[1] The concept of commodity economy originated in 1979, as discussed above but was shelved by the first campaign against bourgeois liberalization in 1981. The concept rejected the classic Marxist view that commodity market and money exchange ultimately come to an end under socialism, as well as the Stalinist theme that socialism only adopts central planning. According to Stalin, only the collective sector contained commodity exchange and it only constituted a very small portion of the socialist economy. The state sector operate on behalf of the 'whole people' and therefore did not need commodity exchange.[2] But according to the new theoretical formula, the whole economy of China should be a planned commodity economy, and the state, collective and private sectors should all engage in commodity exchanges despite their inherent differences. For instance, circulations of capital goods among the state enterprises, as well as marketing of products across economic sectors, all confirmed the existence of a commodity relationship in the Chinese economy. Commodity exchange was therefore perceived as the base of the Chinese socialist economy.

Second, this new idea deviated from the convention based on

[1]*The Decision of the CPC Central Committee on the Reform of Economic System*, in JGKG, p. 239.

[2]J. Stalin, *Sidalin xuanji* (Selected Works of Stalin) Vol. 2 Beijing, People's Press, 1952, pp. 548–550.

the classical socialist 'law of planned and proportionate development,' which is the core of Chen Yun's 'bird-cage theory.' The Decision now gave priority to the law of values, according to which, the price of the commodity must reflect its value. The Chinese economy, claimed the Decision, 'is a planned commodity economy with public ownership as its base, consciously following and applying the law of value.'[3] According to Ma Hong, a commodity economy should 'bring into full play the role of the market and its regulation.'[4]

Third, the Decision redefined the relationship between mandatory and guidance planning. It also established the market orientation of China's economic reforms by making it clear that the objective of the planning reform was to step-by-step 'reduce the scope of mandatory planning and appropriately expand that of guidance planning.' It refuted the convention that put planned economy and commodity economy opposite each other by declaring that 'the full development of a commodity economy is an indispensable stage in the growth of society and a prerequisite for our economic modernization.'[5]

The document also reaffirmed the socialist nature of China's rural reform, and the contract responsibility system was now officially accepted as a necessary step towards the goal of communism rather than as an unavoidable retreat from socialism, as in 1981. It also defended other ideologically sensitive but economically useful practices. For instance, inequalities of income were interpreted by a 'trickle-down' theory and by the concept of a performance-based demonstration effect expected of wage differentials; domestic competition was encouraged as the most effective way to promote modernization; and international interdependence was used to justify the policy of opening to the outside world. The Decision reaffirmed Deng's idea of 'whether a policy that facilitates the development of productive forces should be regarded as the most important criterion for assessing the success or failure of a policy.' In addition to this Decision, two other documents relating to reforming the management of science and technology and of education were adopted in March and May 1985 respectively.

[3]JGKG, p. 239.
[4]Ma Hong (ed.), *Modern China's Economy and Management*, Beijing, Foreign Languages Press, 1992, p. 8.
[5]JGKG, p. 238.

The Decision did not come easily. In fact, the whole drafting process was beset with ideological controversies. Critics of the reform programme were concerned that the expansion of the non-state sector would regress the economy back to the pre-1949 era which was predominated by a semi-capitalist economy and foreign capital. There were also disputes over what stage of political development China had reached if China returned to the supposedly less advanced stage of a commodity economy. The administrative way of managing the economy was still held by many as an important socialist principle.[6] But the reformers capitalized on the favourable political climate and the impressive economic gains achieved in the market-oriented rural reform to press for urban reform. The Chinese media gave wide publicity to the new convention while competing intellectual efforts for theoretical legitimation and transcendence were also taking place.

The new official discourse was perceived as something capable of absorbing a variety of new ideas and blending socialism with capitalism. For instance, Ma Hong spoke out on borrowing economic concepts from capitalist countries since they 'reflect some common laws of commodity economy which cannot be indiscriminately negated.' Some other scholars argued that commodity exchange is a base shared by both capitalism and socialism. It was argued that a commodity economy is 'constantly changing, flexible, capable of incorporating elements of other systems.'[7]

However, constrained by the prevailing convention on the political nature of the market economy, the Decision was not able to use the concept of market economy, although the theme of the document was the gradual commercialization of the Chinese economy. The document used the seemingly confusing concept of 'planned commodity economy' rather than 'market economy' or 'commodity economy.' As proved later, reformers tended to stress the 'commodity' dimension of the economy and conservatives the 'planned' dimension. For instance, the word 'planned' was claimed by some as defining the essence of the Chinese economy. More controversy occurred about the phrase in the Decision that a planned commodity economy was 'not a market economy that is entirely subject to market regulation.'

[6]Wu Jincai, *Zhongguo chensi lu 1979–1992* (Reflections on China 1979–1992), Chendu, Sichuan People's Press, 1992, p. 58.
[7]Guanyu jingji tizhi gaige de taolun (Discussions on Restructuring China's Economic System) in *Wenzhai Bao* (Abstracts), 27 January 1985.

Pro-market reformers claimed that the Chinese economy was another type of market economy, implying its qualitative distinction from the centrally planned economy, while their opponents asserted that this phrase could not give rise to 'another type' of market economy, indicating a qualitative difference from the market economy.[8]

The dispute over the concept of 'planned commodity economy' resurfaced in 1985 when decentralization and market-driven reform led to more strains on the Chinese economy. More conservative leaders refused to accept the emerging convention on the nature of the Chinese economy as a commodity economy. At the Party conference in September 1985, without using the concept of 'planned commodity economy,' Chen Yun claimed that:

> A socialist economy should still adhere to the principle of planned and proportionate development . . . Taken the country as a whole, the statement about primacy of the planned economy supplemented by market regulation is still valid.[9]

He acknowledged the concept of 'guidance planning,' but clearly claimed that 'guidance planning was not equal to market regulation.' He defined market regulation as 'reacting only to market supply and demand' and 'regulation with blindness' (mangmuxing de tiaojie).[10]

In contrast, Deng highly commended the Decision and described it as 'a draft of new political economics that has combined basic Marxist principles and China's socialist practice.'[11] Deng attributed the Decision to a pragmatically induced ideology and indicated that the experience of reform had enhanced the theoretical position of the reformers in their dispute with the conservatives. 'Without the (reform) practice over the past few years,' Deng asserted, 'it would have been impossible to produce this kind of document. Even if it had been produced, it could hardly have been adopted.'[12] In October 1985, Deng told a group of visiting American entrepreneurs that there

[8] *Jingji Ribao*, 14 November 1992.
[9] Chen Yun, 'Speech at the CPC National Conference,' 23 September 1985, JSFZ, p. 316.
[10] *ibid*.
[11] This comment is reported in a number of articles in Chinese newspapers. For instance, *Wenhui Bao*, 23 June 1993.
[12] See *Jingji Ribao*, 4 November 1992.

was no fundamental contradiction between socialism and market economy.

> We used to have a planned economy, but our experience over the years has proved that having a totally planned economy hampers the development of the productive forces to a certain extent. If we combine a planned economy with a market economy, we shall be in a better position to liberate the productive forces and speed up economic growth.[13]

As a pragmatist, Deng was suggesting that market economy and planned economy did not define the difference between capitalism and socialism. The concept of market economy should be regarded as methods for economic development and therefore neutral in value.

This point was further elaborated by Deng himself in later years. It revealed an important approach adopted by the Chinese reformers in ideological innovations: depoliticizing those ideologically sensitive concepts and neutralizing their content in such a way that they could be used for China's market-oriented economic reforms. Many Western concepts were presented in a value-free discursive framework and projected as favourable to China's national interests as in the case of discussing the new technological revolution. Consequently, many Western concepts were gradually incorporated into the reformist doctrine.

2 Socialist orientation of modernization

After the Decision on Economic Structural Reform was adopted in October 1984, a series of articles were published on eliminating leftism in *Renmin Ribao*. The reformers held that the leftist convention had constituted the major obstacle to the implementation of the Decision. The first of the series, entitled 'To Change Old Concepts,' suggested that resistance to reforms did not come from the ordinary people but from some 'leading cadres who have not yet been emancipated from the shackles of old concepts.'[14] The second article published on 5 December sharply criticized propaganda departments for being seriously influenced by leftist ideology and claimed:

[13]Deng Xiaoping, 'There is No Fundamental Contradiction between Socialism and a Market Economy,' (October 23, 1985), Vol. 3, p. 151.
[14]*Renmin Ribao*, 30 November 1984.

> Taking the class struggle as the key link has become a habit within the Party and its influence should not be underestimated. Comrades working on the ideological front in particular must never underestimate the leftist influence.[15]

The publication of the third article, entitled 'Theory and Practice,' which was based on Hu Yaobang's speech at a meeting of the heads of propaganda departments across the nation on 4 December, became a widely-reported international event, as it asserted:

> Marx passed away 101 years ago. His works were written more than 100 years ago. Some of his assumptions were based on conditions of that time. Great changes have taken place and some of those assumptions are not necessarily appropriate today. There are many things which Marx, Engels and Lenin never experienced, things which they never encountered. We cannot expect the writings of Marx and Lenin of that time to solve our current problems.[16]

This immediately led to reports in the Western media that China had abandoned Marxism. Reacting to this, *Renmin Ribao* published a correction the following day, modifying the last remark into 'we cannot expect the writings of Marx and Lenin to solve *all* our current problems,' a clear indication of the top-level ideological dispute concerning the relevance of Marxism to China's reality. Hu Yaobang's departure from the formalized political discourse seemed to be too radical for the conservatives. As Marxism was still the official discursive framework, Hu's deviation was perceived as betraying the conventions; thus, Hu's position was made extremely vulnerable, and his opponents were given a pretext to criticize him for having violated generally accepted conventions. Some of Hu's opponents had developed a doctrinal perception of everything, while others might have feared the political consequence of Hu's remarks on the centrality of Marxism in the Chinese political system; still others seized this opportunity in their power struggle with Hu. All of these, in the end, joined forces to compel Hu to resign in early 1987.

Hu's radical deviation from the conventions also encouraged, perhaps prematurely, a show-down between the reformers and

[15] *Renmin Ribao*, 5 December 1984.
[16] *Renmin Ribao*, 7 December 1984.

conservatives in ideological discourse. For instance, Hu claimed in September, 'a spectre of Leftism is loafing around us.'[17] On 20 December, in his message to the Fourth National Conference of the Chinese Writers' Association, Hu Qili, Hu Yaobang's protégé, spoke out that socialist literature should be 'genuinely free' literature.[18] This radical departure from the prevailing conventions immediately caused a counter offensive from more conservative leaders. Hu Qiaomu and Deng Liqun, who were supposed to oversee ideological and cultural work, were conspicuously absent from this Conference. Chen Yun criticized Hu Qili's formula as going 'against the Party's traditions.'[19] On 12 December, an article in *Jiefangjun Bao* discussed at length the Party's discipline and work style and criticized many problems associated with economic reforms. It also questioned an unequivocal commitment to reforms by arguing:

> Reform is an exploratory and pioneering undertaking, in which many unexpected events can take place. We must not jump to conclusions over things that for the moment we still cannot see clearly or of which we cannot get an accurate grasp. Instead, we must conduct more investigation and study.[20]

This statement represented an implicit criticism of favourable assessments made by reformers on many on-going pro-market reforms.

Furthermore, the conservative ideological trend was strengthened in mid-1985 due to an increase of economic crimes and social dislocations which were associated with economic reforms and the SEZs. This was exemplified by the exposure of the Hainan scandal, in which local cadres in Hainan helped traffic illegal vehicles and made huge profits. Mid-1985 also saw a sharp decline in foreign exchange reserves and criticism of Shenzhen's developmental experiment. Loss of faith in socialism and communism among the youth was widely reported in the Chinese media. All this sent alarms to Chinese communist leaders. A drive to study Marxist theories was thus initiated.

[17]Quoted in Mu Fu, Maixiang ziyou de zuojia dahui (The Writers' Congress that Marches towards Freedom), *the Nineties*, February 1985, p. 52.
[18]*ibid*.
[19]Su Shaozhi, op. cit., p. 345.
[20]'Party's Discipline must not be Relaxed,' *Jiefangjun Bao*, 12 December 1984.

On 7 June 1985, Peng Zhen, Chairman of the National People's Congress, called upon Party cadres to study Marxism:

> To uphold the four cardinal principles, we must advocate, in particular, the study of basic Marxist-Leninist theories, which is a very pressing task.[21]

Deng Xiaoping and Chen Yun also perceived a danger of losing the socialist orientation of modernization. They gave several speeches on the need to study Marxism, adhere to socialism and hold communist ideals. Deng said in March:

> We ourselves are imbued with communist ideals and convictions. We must make a point of fostering those ideals and convictions in the next generation or the next two generations. We must see to it that our young people do not fall captive to decadent capitalist ideas. We must make absolutely sure of that.[22]

Hu Yaobao's radical departure from the Marxist conventions and the crisis of belief in the Chinese society prompted Chen Yun to once again highlight the socialist orientation of modernization. He observed in June 1985:

> It is necessary to make all Party members understand that our cause is socialist with an ultimate goal of communism . . . our economic reform is also socialist economic reform.[23]

He called for building two civilizations (material and spiritual) simultaneously:

> If we do not simultaneously engage ourselves in building spiritual civilization, . . . our material civilization may deviate from correct orientation.[24]

Chen severely criticized some Party members for their 'forgetting socialist and communist ideals and abandoning the principle of serving the people.' At the CPC National Conference held in September 1985, Chen Yun proposed that cadres,

[21]*Renmin Ribao*, 16 August 1985.
[22]Deng Xiaoping, 'Unity Depends on Ideals and Discipline,' (March 7, 1985), Vol. 3, p. 117.
[23]Chen Yun, 'The Two Civilizations should be Achieved Simultaneously,' (June 29, 1985), JSFZ, p. 301.
[24]*ibid*.

especially leading cadres, must study Marxist theories. Chen blamed the present rise of corruption on the present leadership for their 'loosening political and ideological work, and weakening the function and authority of political and ideological departments,'[25] a clear sign of his dissatisfaction with Hu Yaobang who, as the General Secretary of the Party, was officially responsible for ideology. This renewed drive for ideological purity reflected the concern of many Party veterans over changing values and moral standards, which were a result of fast economic reforms and the opening to the outside world.

To protect economic reforms from excessive ideological attack, Deng defended his reform programme as Marxist and socialist. But Deng was also quick to note that some people blurred the ideological direction of reform. He claimed:

> We are trying to achieve modernization in industry, agriculture, national defence and science and technology. But in front of the word 'modernization' is a modifier, 'socialist,' making it the 'four socialist modernizations'.[26]

The goal of Deng's modernization programme can perhaps be analyzed by reference to the Weberian concept of modernization as a changing relationship between 'substantive (value-orientating) rationality and purposive (means appropriate to given ends) rationality.'[27] It is widely assumed that Deng's economic reforms redefined China's future from a value-orientating substantive goal, as during the Maoist period, to purposive rationality; from caring about 'what ought to be' to 'what is.' But this is only partly true.

Deng's renewed emphasis on 'socialist modernization' revealed the often neglected substantive rational goal that Deng set forth for China's economic reforms. Deng's attempt was to strike a balance between the two goals with a value system supporting the goal of economic development so as to achieve a more balanced modern society, as he explained in the Suzhou

[25]Chen Yun, 'Speech at the CPC National Conference,' 23 September 1985, JSFZ, p. 318.
[26]Deng Xiaoping, 'Reform is the Only Way for China to Develop its Productive Forces,' August 28, 1985, Vol. 3, p. 142.
[27]Max Weber, *Economy and Society*, Berkeley, University of California Press, 1969, pp. 809–838 and *On Charisma and Institution Building, Selected Papers*, University of Chicago Press, 1968, Chapter III, pp. 81–94.

model and his later call for learning from the Singaporean experience.

While affirming that the Party's 'highest goal' was communism, Deng was more concerned with the immediate goal of development. He claimed:

> In each historical stage, we have a different programme of struggle that represents the interests of the overwhelming majority of the people in that particular period.[28]

But at the present stage of development, the value issue was also a concern to Deng, who was disturbed about the young generation's loss of faith in socialism and alienation from his modernization programme. He observed:

> Without ideals and discipline it would be impossible for us to modernize. Many of our young people worship the Western countries for their so-called freedom, when they don't really understand what freedom is. So we have to make clear to them the relation between freedom and discipline.[29]

Deng has repeatedly asserted that in economic modernization, the Chinese people should possess ideals, morality, culture and discipline.

But Deng's substantive goal of modernization was not as coherent and specific as his goal of development. His normative requirements reflect a mixture of different values. For instance, Deng defined ideals primarily as communist ones, morality as traditional, culture as educational and discipline as Leninist. But Deng did not explain the possible tensions between these values and pro-market values. Entrepreneurship could conflict with Leninist discipline; communist ideals as defined in the ideological conventions could collide with pro-business values and practice. The absence of clearly defined and coherent values has highlighted one weakness of Deng's ideological discourse. Reforms have created social dislocations characterized by the seeming prevalence of confusing societal and official values and competing norms of behaviour. But Deng's moral norms are insufficient to cope with the changing values. This is perhaps normal for a country undergoing fast social and generational

[28]Deng Xiaoping, 'We must Unite the People on the Basis of Firm Convictions,' (November 9, 1986), Vol. 3, p. 190.
[29]*ibid.*

changes, but unusual for a 'Confucian' state or a 'Leninist' state, where official ideological discourse is supposed to set forth an unified value system.

Deng's substantive goal as embodied in the concept of 'socialist modernization' was further elaborated in his September 1985 statement, in which he stated that socialism had two main features. First, China's economy must be dominated by public ownership. Second, there must be common prosperity. Deng claimed that China is a socialist country because

> the publicly owned sector of our economy accounts for more than 90 per cent of the total. At the same time, we allow a small private sector to develop, we absorb foreign capital and introduce advanced technology, we encourage Chinese and foreign enterprises to establish joint and cooperative ventures and we even encourage foreigners to set up wholly owned factories in China. All that will serve as a supplement to the socialist economy.[30]

But Deng left open the definition of public ownership. As later experience of reform showed, the concept of public ownership became more elastic and began to embrace many non-socialist elements. But Deng's concern about the primacy of public ownership revealed his constant fear of possible excessive polarization arising from his economic reforms.

In discussing common prosperity, Deng took care to distinguish between the ultimate target of common prosperity of all Chinese people and the immediate need to encourage some people and regions to become prosperous first to serve as exemplary models for other people and regions to emulate. Obviously, Deng believed in a dialectic relationship between the ultimate and the immediate targets. This substantive goal was essentially concerned with ownership and distribution, Deng still did not substantiate what kind of coherent cultural values China could realistically embrace in its modernization drive.

3 Political reform

In the Leninist tradition of Party elitism, Deng attempted to improve the Party's efficacy to lead the reform. Paradoxically,

[30]Deng Xiaoping, 'Reform is the Only Way for China to Develop its Productive Forces,' (August 28, 1985), Vol. 3, p. 142.

Deng held that to enhance the role of the Party was to reduce it in a certain manner. Deng perceived as a major threat to his reform programme the Party's pervasive involvement in economic activities and excessive bureaucratic control, which was stifling the initiatives of economic actors. Deng Xiaoping had attempted to initiate a limited political reform as early as 1980, but his famous speech on political reform was not implemented and his plan for such reform was shelved due primarily to his own concern over political stability in the shadow of the Polish crisis. The rapid expansion of reform experiments since 1980, however, rendered it clear that any deferral of political reform would entail ever greater social and economic costs. In May 1986, almost two years after the urban reform was initiated, Deng revived the call for political reform.

Deng's 1980 statement on political reform was republished as a general guide for political reform. Deng expressed that his goal was

> to reform and perfect, in a practical way, the Party and state systems, and to ensure, on the basis of these systems, the democratization of the political life of the Party and the state, the democratization of economic management, and the democratization of the life of society as a whole,[31]

but he also made it clear that the purpose of political reform was 'not to weaken or relax' Party leadership but to 'maintain and further strengthen' it. Deng further claimed that in a country of China's size and population, it was essential to have the Party as the leading core 'whose members have a spirit of sacrifice and a high level of political awareness and discipline.'[32]

Although these general goals were republished, Deng emphasized that the present political reform was aimed at facilitating economic reform. More specifically, Deng intended to eliminate political obstacles to decentralization in the economic reform and to better implement the 7th Five-Year Plan which had been adopted in March 1986.

With no intention to abolish the monopoly of the Party, Deng was, however, afraid of the Party increasingly becoming a developmental liability with its expanding bureaucracy. In June 1986

[31]Deng Xiaoping, 'On the Reform of the System of Party and State Leadership,' in JGKG, pp. 48–69 and Deng Xiaoping (1984), pp. 302–324.
[32]*ibid.*

Deng criticized the mushrooming of official-run companies which constituted an obstacle to decentralization. Deng commented:

> Many companies have been established that are actually government organs. Through these companies people at higher levels have taken back the powers already delegated to lower levels.[33]

Deng believed in decentralization and encouraged local and individual initiatives in economic matters as in the case of rural reform. He also highlighted a number of other political structural problems that were hampering economic reform:

> Organizational overlapping, overstaffing, bureaucratism, sluggishness, endless disputes over trifles and the repossession of powers devolved to lower levels will retard economic restructuring and economic growth.[34]

However, aware of possible political repercussions and intellectual liberalism, Deng displayed his characteristic cautious style by urging for 'prudence' and 'good planning' in this attempt. Political repercussion could be triggered by large-scale social dislocation that had taken place. The reduction of the economic responsibilities of Party officials may have threatened their power and privileges and their resistance could be expected. Deng therefore suggested first to define the scope of political reform and then 'start with one or two reforms.' In September 1986, Deng admitted:

> The content of the political reform is still under discussion, because this is a very difficult question. Since every reform measure will involve a wide range of people, have profound repercussions in many areas and affect the interests of countless individuals, we are bound to run into obstacles, so it is important for us to proceed with caution. . . . we must be very cautious about setting policies and make no decision until we are quite sure it is the right one.[35]

Pro-reform officials and intellectuals more broadly interpreted

[33]Deng Xiaoping, 'Remarks on the Domestic Economic Situation,' (June 10, 1986), Vol. 3, p. 163.
[34]*ibid.*
[35]Deng Xiaoping, 'On Reform of the Political Structure,' (September-November 1986), Vol. 3, p. 178.

Deng's call for political reform. Deng's call for enhancing government efficiency was interpreted to mean institutionalizing the 'scientific decision-making process.' Some argued that decision-making must be based on science and democracy. In July 1986 Vice Premier Wan Li made a key-note speech on the scientific process of decision-making. Wan Li reaffirmed the reformist discourse that academic research should be free from political interference and the need to use soft science to reform the Party's leadership style. Wan's goal of political reform was to create a new type of party which promoted specialists to leadership positions and adapted modern science and technology in formulating reform policies.[36]

Hu Yaobang endorsed political reform but he seemed to have changed his cautious approach displayed during the 12th CPC Congress in 1982 and to have continued his style of radical deviation from the conventions as shown in the controversial article in late 1984. Hu stood for a more radical political reform partly out of his concern about the seriousness of the crisis faced by socialism and partly out of his desire to establish his own authority and power base as the Party's General Secretary. Hu's vigorous promotion of cadres from the Communist Youth League was one example of such efforts. A more radical political reform was a rallying point of Hu's followers.

The difference between Hu and Deng seemed to be more than mere tactics. Hu seemed to hold that political reform in its own right had a unique value beyond merely serving economic reforms. While Hu shared Deng's immediate goal of enhancing the administrative efficiency of the Party, he preferred a more fundamental political structural reform. In his talk with Brzezinski in the summer of 1986, Hu stated quite directly:

> The existing political system had to be restructured, . . . in China too much was controlled from the top, that the existing system of central control was too rigid and too stereotyped, and that therefore substantial decentralization was needed.[37]

In his interview with *the Washington Post*, Hu touched upon the

[36]See the report on Wan Li's speech and comments by some leading intellectuals on scientific decision-making. *Liaowang*, No. 32, 11 August 1986, pp. 6–8.

[37]Zbigniew Brzezinski, *Out of Control*, New York, Charles Scribner's Sons, 1992, p. 160.

issue of reform obstacles, and observed that such obstruction came from a small number of narrow-minded people whose perception of the world was conditioned by 'small-scale production and habitual forces.' He compared reform to sports: 'reform is like a (football) match under new rules but the referee is an old one,' indicating his determination to be tough towards those bureaucrats who refuse to endorse political and economic reforms.[38]

Hu was also ready to tolerate more political diversity and dissent, as shown in his Shekou model. Wide publicity was given to the Shekou model in an attempt to reshape a convention more favourable to political reform. The Shekou Industrial Zone in Guangdong Province started a political reform experiment with the support of Hu Yaobang in 1983. The experiment attempted to institutionalize certain democratic procedures and ensure a clean and efficient government. The members of the Shekou management committee (local government) were elected through a secret ballot every two years from the candidates chosen by a congress of 500 representatives from all parts of society. All the candidates had to present their own policy agenda and accept vigorous questioning from voters. Those elected were subject to an annual vote of confidence. It was reported that in Shekou, one could criticize leaders of all levels. Furthermore, there were 22 non-governmental associations (mainly professional and cultural), and the monthly News Saloon sponsored by *Shekou News* offered a relatively free forum for the 'candid, warm, sharp and sometimes even harsh' exchange of views between leaders and participants.[39]

Despite the seemingly radical nature of the model, it is worthwhile to note the care with which the reformers presented the Shekou model so as to avoid offending some prevailing conventions. The Shekou experience was described not as a western-style democracy, but as a continuation of the Chinese communist tradition of comradely equality and fraternity, which was claimed to have taken shape during the war period. Reformers attempted to identify their experiment of political democratization solely with the past revolutionary experience, rather than with the Western political system. This was another example of softening the edge of radical ideological renovation and increasing the political cost of any conservative opposition. Basic fea-

[38]*Liaowang*, No. 42, 20 October 1986, p. 10.
[39]*Liaowang*, No. 36, 8 September 1986, pp. 10–13.

tures of this model were said to be as follows: a cleaner and more responsive government; greater political transparency; an absence of 'rigidly stratified society;' a relaxed and healthy social atmosphere; and better economic performance.

In any case, the model's general applicability in China was, however, arguable for at least two reasons. First, much of what had been achieved in Shekou depended on its charismatic reformist leader Yuan Geng, who was ready to meet anyone who had a complaint and broad-minded enough to award those who singled him out by name for criticism in local newspapers. In this sense, the success of the model still depended upon, in Weberian words, charismatic authority. Second, Shekou was a small town with a well-educated work force of 18,000 people. But the Shekou experience shed light on the type of democratization the Chinese reformers attempted to apply in China, and its experience could be highly relevant for China's future political change. The publicity given to the Shekou experience also helped induce and legitimize other political reform options.

Political reform was, however, very controversial. Hu Yaobang's radical approach and tolerance towards political diversity alarmed many, including Deng Xiaoping, as shown in a leadership dispute in late 1986 over the Party's 'Resolution on the Guiding Principles for Building a Socialist Society with an Advanced Culture and Ideology.'[40] The sharp disagreement occurred on two key issues that had shaped the official discourse on spiritual civilization: (1) the reference to communist ideology as the core of China's socialist spiritual civilization: Hu's people argued that the communist ideal should be the belief system of the Party members rather than ordinary people, while ideologues insisted on the need to educate the ordinary people to believe in communism; and (2) the reference to criticism of bourgeois liberalization: Hu's people stressed the ambiguity of the concept and the Party's need to cultivate a new role as a reform-oriented elite leading society to achieve modernization through sound and rational policies, rather than sticking to its old role as a priest determined to preach an ideology in order to transform the society. Hu's people also cautioned against the possible abuse of the concept by leftists trying to

[40]*Beijing Review*, No. 40, 26 October 1986, Supplement.

attack reforms. But more conservative leaders insisted that anti-bourgeois liberalization was an essential task for the Party.

Fearing that Hu was too soft towards political liberalism, which in Deng's perception, was a dangerously destablilizing force, Deng once again expressed his support for the more conservative line and implicitly criticized Hu Yaobang. Deng recalled in March 1987,

> (At that time,) some comrades did not agree that the document should include a reference to the need to struggle against bourgeois liberalization. Actually, Comrade Hu Yaobang shared their view. I made a speech at the session. I said that we would have to combat bourgeois liberalization not only now but for the next 10 to 20 years. Today, I add 50 more years to that estimate. If we don't struggle against it, there will be disorder everywhere, with no political stability or unity.[41]

In the end, the document adopted by the Sixth Plenum had considerably watered down the content of the political restructuring that Hu had planned. Premier Zhao Ziyang, a more cautious reformer than Hu Yaobang, was appointed as the head of a new political reform leading group, a clear sign that Hu had lost Deng's trust and his battle with his opponents in the leadership struggle.

4 The second campaign against bourgeois liberalization

Hu and his followers adopted a more liberal attitude towards intellectuals, as shown in Hu's preference for a climate of 'relaxation, tolerance and generosity.'[42] Intellectuals were also seizing the opportunity to both interpret and transcend the official discourse. Eight years of reform and opening up led to a dramatic increase of what Daniel Lerner called 'psychic mobility' towards Western values, especially that of democracy and individual freedom. For instance, the Chinese Social Sciences Academy sponsored a symposium in May 1986 on cultural and academic freedom on the occasion of the anniversary of Mao's One

[41]Deng Xiaoping, 'We Must Carry out Socialist Construction in an Orderly Way under the Leadership of the Party,' (March 8, 1987), Vol. 3, p. 211.

[42]This was a reformist slogan concerning intellectuals and appeared frequently in the media in mid-1986. For instance, *Liaowang*, No. 24, 16 June 1986, p. 4.

Hundred Flowers speech. Shanghai also held a forum to discuss Shanghai's cultural development strategy. Both conferences highlighted the relations between modernization and culture, the importance of freedom of expression and legal protection of such basic freedoms. Both conferences were indirectly suggesting a radical reform of China's present political system.[43] Intellectuals even openly opposed the prerogatives enjoyed by Marxism as the official doctrine in China and concluded that Marxism should be just one branch of the social sciences on an equal footing with others.[44]

The themes of speeches and articles by liberal intellectuals went beyond mere expression of support for Deng's limited political reform to cover freedom of expression, human rights and other apparently sensitive subjects. This radical trend of liberalism was closely identified with several outspoken intellectuals. Among them, Fang Lizhi, a renowned astrophysicist, advocated Western-style democracy and human rights. He gave many lectures across the nation on the rule of law, free elections, free speech and political pluralism. He stressed the revival of the spirit of the May Fourth Movement – science and democracy – and he was best known for his call for 'complete Westernization.' He considered Marxism to be obsolete and held it responsible for China's backwardness. He challenged the Party's rule which, according to Fang, was based on its past military victory, not its economic record. The Party's post-1949 overall performance could be considered a failure.

The other two leading liberal intellectuals were Liu Bingyan, a vice-chairman of the Chinese Writers Association, and Wang Ruowang, a well-known writer from Shanghai. Liu was known for his investigative reporting on the dark side of the Chinese officialdom and his open ridicule of the Four Cardinal Principles. Wang was also a critic of corruption and those principles.[45]

The Party's reaction to the pro-Western trend was mixed. General Secretary Hu Yaobang took a more tolerant attitude,

[43] *Liaowang*, No. 23, 9 June 1986, pp. 9–11.
[44] Su Shaozhi, op. cit. p. 345.
[45] A collection of speeches by Fang Lizhi, Liu Bingyan and Wang Ruowang was published and circulated in China in 1987 as 'internal materials' for criticism. Hong Kong's Shuguang Publishing House republished it together with a number of official articles critical of the three intellectuals. See *Fang Lizhi, Liu Bingyan, Wang Ruowang yanlun zhaibian* (Selected Speeches of Fang Lizhi, Liu Bingyan and Wang Ruowang), Hong Kong, Shuguang Publishing House, 1988.

perhaps out of his perception that with the new technological revolution, China should open itself further to the outside world and to new ideas. Also important were his close ties with Chinese intellectuals, which could suffer from the Party's wilful interventions. But conservatives were deeply disturbed by the trend that marked an invasion of Western liberalism. They believed that such a tendency encouraged a disregard for the Party and communist ideology. Hu Yaobang, the supposedly ideological leader of the Party, was considered as too tolerant of this trend and the liberal intellectuals. Thus, his close ties with intellectuals became a liability.

Anhui student protests in December 1986, triggered in part by the prevailing liberal intellectual atmosphere, led to demonstrations in over 15 cities. Such expressions of political dissidence and the rejection of the prevailing conventions caused alarm to Party leaders, many of whom were just looking for a pretext for a vengeful attack on Hu Yaobang. They regarded the demonstrations as evidence of the unchecked influence of bourgeois ideology, which was threatening China's socialist cause and stability. Having lost confidence in Hu, Deng held that Hu was too closely associated with liberalism and that Hu's political reform plan had deviated too much from Deng's cautious approach. In addition, Hu's plan perhaps cut too deeply into the interests of the Party elders, including Deng himself, by urging them to retire early. Under a joint attack from the Party veterans, Hu had to resign from his post as the General Secretary of the Party, and Premier Zhao Ziyang was named Acting General Secretary despite his own preference for the premiership.

But more conservative leaders wanted not only to dismiss Hu but also rollback many political and economic reforms Hu stood for. They took the opportunity of Hu's resignation to launch the second ideological campaign against 'bourgeois liberalization' and seemed to be more determined than ever before to carry it through. For instance, Bo Yibo drew lessons from the aborted 1983 campaign against spiritual pollution, claiming that the 'struggle to oppose spiritual pollution was cut short soon after the beginning of Party rectification by the leading comrade (Hu Yaobang),' who 'protected and connived with' those who advocated bourgeois liberalization which led ultimately to student demonstrations in late 1986 and early 1987.[46] The dismissal of Hu Yaobang and the subsequent expulsion of the three outspoken intellectuals Fang Lizhi, Wang Ruowang, Liu Bingyan from the Party reversed the liberal trend at least in the first four months of 1987.

Deng endorsed a limited campaign to reverse the liberal trend and reaffirmed the four cardinal principles by explaining more clearly his centrist position in the following statements: Over the past few years the Party 'paid too more attention to interference from the 'Left' to the neglect of that from the Right.' The student demonstrations, Deng claimed, 'has reminded us that we should be more on guard against the latter.'[47] Deng argued that his centrist handling of Hu Yaobang and student demonstrations could ultimately, in Mao's words, 'turn something negative into something positive and help clarify the thinking of both the leaders and the people.'[48]

To Deng, 'bourgeois liberalization' was not only an unacceptable ideological discourse but also more importantly a political destabilizing force, which could undermine what he perceived as China's stability and his plan to achieve the goal of China's modernization by the next century.[49] Deng's approach relates his every step with his long-term goals. His authoritarianism drove him to remove whatever he perceived as political obstacles to the achievement of his goals. Deng emphatically repeated his argument on an authoritarian, top-down process of social change which would ensure economic reform yet permit no challenge to the rule of the Party. Deng stated bluntly:

> We cannot do without dictatorship. We must not only reaffirm the need for it but exercise it when necessary. Of course, we must be cautious about resorting to dictatorial means and make as few arrests as possible. But if some people are bent on provoking bloodshed, what are we going to do about it?[50]

Deng stressed that China's eonomic reform could only be con-

[46]Personal notes.
[47]Deng Xiaoping, 'We have to Clear Away Obstacles and Continue to Advance,' (January 13, 1987), Vol. 3, p. 199.
[48]*ibid.*
[49]*ibid.*, pp. 199–200.
[50]Deng Xiaoping, 'Take a Clear-cut Stand Against Bourgeois Liberalization,' (December 30, 1986), Vol. 3, pp. 195–196.

ducted in 'a state of stability and unity' and 'in a guided and orderly manner.'[51]

Deng chose to play up the assumed horrible consequences of any apparently radical actions and Western liberalism. 'Bourgeois liberalization would plunge the country into turmoil once more,' Deng claimed that if Party leadership were abolished, 'there would be no centre around which to unite our one billion people, and the Party itself would lose all power to fight.' and China would be 'reduced to a heap of loose sand.' Again recalling China's humiliating experience with the Western powers and stressing his nationalist theme, Deng claimed, 'the reason the imperialists were able to bully us in the past was precisely that we were a heap of loose sand.'[52]

However, Deng's discourse was immediately embraced by conservative forces, who also attempted to interpret and transcend it according to their beliefs. For instance, many articles were published to criticize learning from the West. One article noted that some people wanted to 'implement the so-called all-round capitalist reforms. . . . Some people wanted to guide reforms and opening to the outside world onto the path of capitalism.'[53] The changed tone of the overarching ideology soon began to influence the localized ideological atmosphere and affect economic reforms across the country as it raised the political cost of carrying out reform experiments.

Both Deng and Zhao were concerned with the campaign's spillover effect on economic reforms and opening up. With Deng's backing, Zhao Ziyang supported setting a limit to the campaign and took the initiative to roll back ideological attacks on reform. Zhao adopted similar tactics as in the case of resisting anti-spiritual pollution: first, he tried to constrain it by declaring the rural reform free from any ideological criticism and assured the peasants that the rural reforms, especially the household responsibility system, would remain. Zhao set a clear-cut scope of the campaign: the campaign should be strictly confined to the Party and to ideological education.[54] Second, Zhao tried to redefine the campaign in a manner conducive to reforms. Zhao's new idea was to

[51] *ibid.*
[52] *ibid.*, pp. 196–197.
[53] *Liaowang*, No. 5, 19 January 1987, p. 3.
[54] Zhao Ziyang, 'On the Two Basics of the Party Line,' Nos.5 & 6, 9 February 1987, *Beijing Review*, p. 26 and p. 28.

equally blame the leftist offensive for contributing to bourgeois liberalization. Zhao argued that leftist ideas could undermine economic reforms and lower people's living standards, thus facilitating the spread of popular distrust of 'socialism with Chinese characteristics.' Leftism, like the student demonstrations, was also perceived as a source of political unrest. Zhao's supporters argued intelligently that economic reforms and the policy of opening up could effectively improve China's national strength and improve people's living standards, thus constituting one effective way of 'adhering to the four cardinal principles.'[55] Third, Zhao endeavored to downplay the campaign. Zhao stressed that the elimination of 'bourgeois liberalization' was a 'long and sustained' process; therefore, the methods of mass mobilization and political movement, reminiscent of the Cultural Revolution, would not be useful. Only through patient and gradual education, can 'bourgeois liberalization' be checked.[56]

Deng's authoritarian theme concerning China's primacy of stability was shared by Zhao, and they both associated student demonstrations with political instability. For instance, Zhao challenged the students by asking rhetorically:

> Could our reform continue for one day if the political situation were in chaos and social order in turmoil? Everyone is eager to see a take-off of the Chinese economy, but who can achieve it if amidst an earthquake? Only political and economic stability can bring hope to China. We have all suffered during the 'cultural revolution.'[57]

He disagreed with the students' demand for Western-style democracy and offered a classic authoritarian and utilitarian explanation on the issue of democracy. From Zhao's perspective, the students and intellectuals attempted to embrace only the 'formalities' of democracy, which could bring more harm than good to China. Zhao claimed:

> When and where conditions are immature, . . . it will only

[55]'Correctly Understand the Relationship between the Four Cardinal Principles and the Policy of Reform, Opening Up and Invigorating the National Economy,' *Xuanchuan Tongxun* (Propaganda Newsletter, published by the Propaganda Department of the CPC Shanghai Municipal Committee), March 1987, pp. 36–39.
[56]Zhao Ziyang, op. cit., p. 28 and 'the CPC Central Committee's Circular on Several Issues Relating to Opposing Bourgeois Liberalization,' 28 January 1987, JSFZ, pp. 383–389.
[57]Zhao Ziyang, op. cit., p. 27.

be a waste of money and manpower and divert people's attention from the current construction and reform.[58]

In a masterful display of political skill, in May 1987, Zhao declared the campaign victorious and brought it to an end. Zhao stated that building socialism with Chinese characteristics included efforts to combat bourgeois liberalization, and he added that 'great changes have taken place in the ideological field' and the previously 'widespread ideological trend of bourgeois liberalization' had been checked.[59] The reformers's attempt to scale down the campaign reflected partly their concern about its possible impact on economic reform and partly their immediate need for preparing the 13th Party Congress which was scheduled for late 1987. A pro-reform ideological climate would favour their agenda-setting and personnel reshuffling at the Congress.

B Ideology and reform policies

1 Decentralization and re-centralization

The new ideological convention based on the 'planned commodity economy' was not only an ideological statement but also a policy directive which, though not as detailed as desired, entailed a number of pro-market policies relating to price structure, greater enterprise autonomy, adoption of Western managerial skills, and reform of macroeconomic control (from a direct administrative approach to indirect market signals such as taxation, pricing and credit policies).

Continued decentralization to mobilize local and individual initiatives was an issue of ideological dispute. The 'planned commodity economy,' as interpreted by reformers, presupposed an enhanced identification of economic interests among economic agents before they could engage in commodity exchanges in a fair and competitive environment. But reformers' policy preference was conditioned by the concept of 'planned commodity economy' which itself was an ideological and policy compromise. Since public ownership was accepted as the basis of 'planned commodity economy,' the reformers' attention was

[58] *ibid.*
[59] *JGKG*, p. 416.

naturally confined to increasing the efficiency of state enterprises by encouraging them to have independent interests through decentralization, as privatization had been ruled out by the ideological convention. Local authorities and enterprises were thus encouraged to retain more profits and acquire greater decision-making power. This effort effectively boosted local interests and facilitated the growth of rural enterprises and the private economy.

But as a half-way reform of the economic system, decentralization also generated its own problems. For instance, the absence of clearly defined property rights and a soft budget encouraged state enterprises to use their newly acquired power to first consider raising wages and bonuses without necessarily increasing their productivity, thus inflating a consumption drive. Local governments also had a tendency, with newly acquired power, to make investment in those enterprises under their direct control and in those projects that produced quick money. Consequently, decentralization in fact triggered high local spending, too fast a growth rate, and inflation and tension in the supply of energy and transportation.

Such an economic imbalance provided opportunity for the conservatives to question the need for further decentralization. At the level of ideology, a question was raised as to whether central planning and administrative 're-centralization' should be exercised. At the Party conference held in September 1985, the speeches made by Deng Xiaoping and Chen Yun apparently publicized their differences over how to assess the current reforms and the future direction of the reform programme. Deng's speech emphasized the achievements of reforms and the need for further market-orientation. He claimed that the past seven years since 1978 represented one of the best periods since 1949, and he encouraged the population to

> seize the opportunity of the moment and vigorously explore new possibilities, striving to complete the reform before too long.[60]

Chen Yun, however, in his characteristic prudence, focused on the problems the reform had caused and explicitly called once again for the predominant role of central planning in the

[60]Deng Xiaoping, 'Speech at the National Conference of the Communist Party of China,' (September 23, 1985), Vol. 3, p. 145.

economy. In a Marxist discursive framework, Chen held that central planning was an inherent feature in socialism, and observed:

> We are the communist party, and the communist party engages in building socialism. . . . (Socialism) should continue to practise planned and proportionate development . . . [61]

Disturbed by the slowdown in grain production in 1985, Chen defended the importance of central planning in maintaining grain output and criticized market-led rural industry growth at the expense of grain production. He urged for a halt to the commercial trend that had induced peasants into non-agricultural activities by quoting Mao's warning of grave social disorder if the flight from farms was not arrested. Chen also warned against an excessive high growth rate, which meant 'more haste, less speed.'

Moreover, Chen saw a linkage between economic 're-centralization' and ideological education by severely criticizing the insufficient attention given to the Party's ideological and propagandist work and arguing that 'socialist economic construction and economic structural reform require all the more the sense of devotion to the cause of communism.' Chen specifically stated that in the process of reform, one cannot

> weaken the function and authority of the ideological institutions, . . . (the Party bodies at all levels) should actively maintain the authority of ideological institutions. . . . Communist education should not be weakened even slightly. On the contrary, it should be vigorously strengthened.[62]

Chen also supported Hu Qiaomu and Deng Liqun, two conservative theoreticians, in their bid for posts in the Politburo and Secretariat. All this seemed to reveal one major difference between Deng and Chen: Deng preferred to neutralize competing goals and reduce the tasks of socialism into one; namely, economic development and everything else, including ideological education and propaganda, should serve the primacy of

[61]Chen Yun, 'Speech at the CPC National Conference,' 23 September 1985, JSFZ, p. 316.
[62]*ibid.*

economic development. Chen, on the other hand, still adhered to the equal weight of ideological indoctrination, which had its own values like economic development.

Deng and Zhao did not completely embrace Chen's policy of 're-centralization.' Both Deng and Zhao stressed that more market-oriented reforms were the only solution to the current problems. The reformers referred to the lessons of East European countries and warned of the prospect of the vicious cycle, which had been experienced by many socialist countries in their reforms: from an economy stifled by centralization to decentralization, which encouraged pent-up demand for investment and consumption under the soft budget to another round of 're-centralization' which once again stifled the economy.

But Chen's authority in economic affairs and the seemingly run-away consumption demand convinced many top-level leaders of the need for proper 're-centralization.' Deng and Zhao in the end also accepted this policy option upon the advice of some leading economists, but they endeavoured to work out a more clearly defined temporary 're-centralization' as a compromise.

In this ideologically tainted policy dispute in 1985, a prominent feature was the increasingly visible role played by Chinese intellectuals, especially economists who demonstrated a clear preference for market-oriented reforms. To support the reforms, many economists used their expertise to influence decision making in a direction favourable to economic reforms. For instance, a group of economists from the Chinese Academy of Social Sciences headed by Liu Guoguang made an evaluation on the economic situation from 1981 to 1985 and concluded on a very positive note.[63] Some young researchers carried out large-scale surveys in the cities on people's attitude towards reform. One study by the Institute for Research on the Restructuring of the Economic System, based on surveys held respectively in February and July 1985, drew a comparison of people's attitudes towards reforms: the number of those in favour of all prices to be fixed by the state was reduced from 61.8% in February to 34.7% in July; and those who supported partial price reform rose from 30.8% to 58.2%. Furthermore, the study revealed that

[63]Liu Guoguang, Lunliangzhong moshi zhuanhuan (On the Transformation from One Model to Another Model), *World Economic Herald*, Special supplement, October 1985.

93.7% supported 'a comprehensive rather than a partial reform' of the present economic system. 92% of grass-roots cadres held that 'the country will be hopeless without reform.' The study concluded that people's psychological 'absorptive capacity' towards reform had been enhanced.[64]

But this kind of seemingly scientific and objective studies was clearly motivated from the political needs of the reformers, and the questionnaires designed for the surveys tended to expect the desired response. Yet this did not minimize the significance of much of the research carried out by Chinese think tanks and the enhanced role of social scientists in the decision-making process.

As in the discussion on the new technological revolution, reformers relied on foreign sources to support faster economic reform and to oppose prolonged 're-centralization.' For instance, the World Bank's China report and the US Congress report on China facing the year 2000 were both used to justify and defend more market-oriented reforms. One influential journal used the title of 'Reform Will Bring China into the Rank of (World) Powers' to report an interview with the Editor-in-Chief of the US Congress report. The article also highlighted the 'opinions of Western experts' on the need for earlier and bolder price reform.[65] The political manipulation of pro-reform information and the scientific expertise from both China and abroad enhanced the reformers' arguments in favour of market-oriented reform.

It is worth noting the role of economists in decision-making. In contrast to ideologues who tended to turn every issue into an ideological one, Chinese economists attempted to turn ideologically sensitive issues into technical and value-neutral policy discussions, and they initiated a new mode of discourse and transcendence in Chinese political life. Most economists embraced the market orientation of economic reform and some of them served in think tanks as senior advisors for Chinese leading reformers. Reform-minded economists put forward policy proposals for solving the current dispute over 're-centralization' and decentralization. The proposal by Wu Jinglian, a senior economist at the State Council and Fudan University, was extremely influential. Wu suggested that reform required a

[64]*Liaowang*, No. 33, 18 August 1986, pp. 15–16.
[65]*Liaowang*, No. 31, 4 August 1986, pp. 30–31.

'relaxed environment' characterized by aggregate supply exceeding aggregate demand. Wu concluded that it was necessary to combine both economic and administrative means to lower the speed of growth and to ensure sufficient funds for reforms. The compromise and incremental solution adopted by the decision-makers was largely based on Wu's proposal to temporarily reintroduce administrative controls on money supply, wages, foreign exchange, imports and credits until a relatively more relaxed economic environment took shape. After this temporary 're-centralization,' there would be a new round of market-oriented economic reform.[66]

2 Revision of the SEZ strategy

The 1984 Decision on urban reform called for China's further opening to the outside world and making use of the international market. It stated that 'we must make full use of both domestic and foreign resources, both domestic and foreign markets and both skills of organizing domestic construction and of developing external economic relations.'[67] However, the performance of the SEZs as an experiment for opening China to the outside world was not as successful as expected. Mounting economic costs, foreign exchange imbalances, absence of high-tech industries and excessive infrastructure spending indicated that the SEZs did not achieve their planned targets of attracting advanced foreign technology and their export-oriented strategy. Vice Premier Yao Yilin was to certain degree accurate when he criticized Shenzhen for profiteering from sales to the interior instead of earning hard currency through expanding its exports. Yao argued that Shenzhen had been maintained only through continual 'blood transfusions' of domestic investment.[68]

Together with the critical assessment of the SEZs' economic performance was the mounting ideological criticism of the SEZs in 1985. The increasing inequality of income between the

[66]Wu's view was summarized in Wu Jinglian, Hu Ji and Li Jiange, Lun kongzhi xuqiu he gaishan gonggi wenti (On Controlling Demand and Improving Supply), *Renmin Ribao*, 10 October 1986. This was also confirmed by my private talks with Wu Jinglian at a symposium on 'Development Prospects in the Pacific and China's Modernization' held in August 1987 in Shanghai.

[67]JGKG, p. 249.

[68]Xu Xin, *Zhongguo jingji gaige de tansuo* (Probing into China's Economic Reform), Hong Kong, Kaituo Publishing House, 1987, p. 279.

SEZs, coastal areas and the poorer inner regions was raised as a serious issue in the Chinese media. Egalitarian values, a theme which found echo in the Chinese cultural tradition, were also revived in the media. What was perceived as the reemergence of exploitation in private enterprises and joint or completely foreign owned ventures in the SEZs was another hot issue raised by the SEZ opponents. In a visit to the southern Fujian delta in February 1985, Hu Qiaomu was disturbed by the various deviations from the conventions to which he was still committed and the many 'unsocialist ways' of getting rich such as speculation and hiring more labour than allowed. He decided to revise the slogan of 'getting rich is glorious' into 'getting rich through honest work is glorious,' implicitly criticizing Hu Yaobang's call for peasants to 'get rich as quickly as possible.' He suggested that political losses in the SEZs surpassed economic gains. To many more conservative leaders, special privileges enjoyed by foreign investors from tax breaks to the leasing of land were tantamount to the nineteenth-century concessions to the Western powers in China's coastal areas. Hu Qiaomu was also concerned with the ineffective role of Party units and trade unions in foreign enterprises. He urged more control over foreign capital to protect the 'national interests.'[69]

The revelation of the Hainan scandal was another blow to reformers. Many Party and government officials on Hainan Island, China's latest economic zone, made windfall profits by abusing relaxed foreign exchange controls to trade foreign commodities, especially Japanese automobiles, with the mainland. Ideologues tried to link the SEZs with corruption so as to limit their development, and to this end wide publicity was given to the scandal as well as unfavourable stories about the SEZs.

In the summer of 1985, as policy debate on the SEZs heated up, even Deng seemed to move away from his previously firm commitment to the SEZs made only a year before. On 29 June 1985, Deng Xiaoping told a visiting Algerian delegation:

> The Shenzhen Special Economic Zone is an experiment. It will be some time before we know whether we are doing the right thing there. It is something new under socialism.

[69]Based on my interviews with a number of cadres in Shenzhen in March 1993. G. Crane also gave an account of the 'retrenchment' of SEZ policy during this period. See G. Crane, pp. 108–116.

> We hope to make it a success, but if it fails, we can learn from the experience.[70]

These remarks immediately triggered more attacks on the SEZs. Realizing that his remarks had been interpreted unfavourably for the SEZ policy, Deng hastened to observe a month later that he did not negate his previous positive assessment on Shenzhen by reaffirming two points:

> First, the policy of establishing special economic zones is correct; and second, the special economic zones are an experiment. There is no contradiction here.[71]

As a seasoned politician, Deng placed himself in a relatively flexible and detached position but his clear support for continued experiment of the SEZs was an impetus to the baffled zone supporters. They made efforts to rebut criticism. They defended the ideological correctness of the open-door policy by stressing Lenin's New Economic Policies and the impressively high growth rate of the SEZs. They blamed the low level of technology or lack of reform in foreign exchange control for the problems in the SEZs and argued that overvalued currency discouraged exports. According to them, greater reform was the only solution to the problems. But the nationwide retrenchment did not favour more dramatic reforms.

Criticism of the SEZs became more complicated in late 1985 in the sense that not only were central planners unhappy with the SEZs and open policy, but so were radical students, who perceived an element of China's excessive concession to the Western powers, especially to Japan in China's open-door policy. This was an indication of a rising trend to disagree with the official conventions based on Deng's call for opening China to the outside world. On the occasion of the anniversary of the 1937 Japanese invasion of China, several thousand students took to the streets in Beijing against the Japanese 'economic invasion.' Hu Yaobang was perceived as pro-Japanese and was implicitly criticized by students. Both the opponents and supporters of the open-door policy were now faced with a delicate situation. Despite their different attitude towards Deng's open-door policy,

[70]Deng Xiaoping, 'Reform and Opening to the Outside World are a Great Experiment,' (June 29, 1985), Vol. 3, p. 134.

[71]Deng Xiaoping, 'Special Economic Zones should Shift their Economy from a Domestic Orientation to an External Orientation,' (August 1, 1985), Vol. 3, p. 137.

they were both afraid of the rising radical tendency, which rejected the authority of the Party or that of the official conventions. The opponents found that their continued criticism of the open-door policy might appear to encourage the political dissidence always associated with the student demonstrations in post-Mao era. The supporters were afraid that the students' radical patriotism might play into the hands of the opponents of the open-door policy and thus undermine the reformers' predominant position in pursuing the policy.

Such apprehension was reflected in a pause of criticism of the SEZs in the Chinese media. Reformers used the media to influence public opinion in the hope to guide the population in a direction favourable to the conventions based on Deng's open-door policy. An article carried in *Zhongguo Qingnian Bao* (China Youth Daily) on the theme of patriotism and open-door policy referred to the reformers' tortuous experience in contemporary Chinese history. All reformers had suffered setbacks and thus highly praised the courage of those who were determined to learn from foreign culture and carry out reforms in China. The article suggested that students should understand the complexity of the situation and throw their support behind the open-door policy. The article stated:

> putting forward the policy of opening up to the outside world and adhering to it require extremely great courage (Yongqi) and resourcefulness (Danlue).[72]

The student demonstrations and the official response to it revealed the complex political context of Deng's open-door policy.

Reformers also seemed to realize that their original strategy for the SEZs was too ambitious and radical to be operational. As a result, ideologues and central planners were given an opportunity to discredit the SEZs for not producing the desired results. The best way to confront the zone opponents and sceptics was perhaps not through ideological discourse but policy revision, and reformers were now under strong pressure to explore other policy alternatives for SEZ development that could produce fast and visible results. The old strategy stressed the so-called 'four primaries:' foreign investment was to be the primary source of construction funds; joint venture and wholly foreign-

[72]*Zhonggguo Qingnian Bao* (China Youth Daily), 26 October 1985.

owned enterprises the primary form of zone enterprises; zone-made products primarily exported overseas and the market forces primary means of macroeconomic management. The problem with this over-ambitious plan was that it defined the present tasks of the SEZs in terms of its end-goal. This approach only made the SEZs more vulnerable to the challenge of their critics for failing to achieve the goal.

By late 1985, a new and more realistic strategy was emerging. The reformers' new plan asked what could be done realistically first. The answer was based on a cool assessment of present possibilities and requirements, rather than a vision of an end-point that could only be achieved in a more distant future. It was called a 'two-way' model or 'double fan' strategy, according to which, zones were designed to use foreign investment and technology transfer to build an industrial capacity to compete in the international export market. Domestic resources and the domestic market were also to be used for the development of an export-oriented economy. According to this strategy, there would be a selective opening of the home market to zone-based foreign enterprises if they used advanced technology ('exchange market for technology'). Consequently, the SEZs would not only bring China into the world market but also bring world market forces into China. The reformers also agreed that the export-orientation of the SEZs would remain unchanged, but a more realistic goal was set out to promote small and medium enterprises that focused on light industry and higher-quality manufacturing.[73]

By mid-1987, the new strategy seemed to have produced results, and the SEZs became export-oriented and earned hard currency, and foreign investment increased dramatically. The reformers declared that the old problems in the SEZs were solved. And by June 1987, seizing the opportunity of preparing a more vigorous reform agenda for the coming 13th CPC Congress, Deng Xiaoping demonstrated his enhanced authority in economics and stressed not only the economic success of the SEZs but also the political significance of the SEZs in facilitating the unification of Hong Kong, Macau and Taiwan and in promoting the integration of the Chinese economy with the outside world. Deng proclaimed:

[73]G. Crane, op. cit., pp. 118–119.

> I am now in a position to say with certainty that our decision to establish special economic zones was a good one and has proved successful. All scepticism should by now have vanished.[74]

Deng further claimed that 'our open policy will certainly continue; the problems is that we have not yet opened wide enough.'[75] Deng's approach to the SEZs was clearly different from Chen Yun's moderate Leninist approach: Deng encouraged the market-orientation of the SEZs and their integration with the world capitalist market, because he held that this was the only way to develop an internationally competitive economy.

The 1985–87 dispute over the SEZs seemed to offer two useful lessons: first, criticism of new policies and ideological controversy do make things more difficult for reformers, but as in a democracy, a moderate amount of adversary may be a useful pressure on reformers to make their reform programmes more realistic and operational, as shown in the case of the revision of the SEZ strategy. Second, the relative success of the SEZs convinced Deng of the validity of his ideological values in the market-orientation of economic reform and in the integration of China with capitalist economies through participation in international market competition. This further substantiated his search for a new and efficient model for China's modernization.

Such success went a long way in establishing Deng's self-confidence and authority in economic matters, where Chen Yun used to predominate. This newly acquired authority enabled Deng to deviate more openly from the established conventions, as illustrated by one of Deng's talks on the relationship between the economy and the market in February 1987 when the campaign against bourgeois liberalization was still alive. Deng clearly expressed his purposive (means-ends) and pragmatic interpretation of the market as something value-neutral and conducive to Chinese-style socialism:

> Why do some people always insist that the market is capitalist and only planning is socialist? Actually they are both means of developing the productive forces. So long as they

[74]Deng Xiaoping, 'We shall Speed up Reform,' (June 12, 1987), Vol. 3, p. 237.
[75]Deng Xiaoping, 'Speech at a Meeting with the Members of the Committee for Drafting the Basic Law of the Hong Kong Special Administrative Region,' (April 16, 1987), Vol. 3, 217.

> serve that purpose, we should make use of them. If they serve socialism they are socialist; if they serve capitalism they are capitalist.[76]

Deng also challenged the accepted convention based on Chen Yun's doctrine, which confined socialism to the primacy of central planning:

> It is not correct to say that planning is only socialist, because there is a planning department in Japan and there is also planning in the United States. At one time we copied the Soviet model of economic development and had a planned economy. Later we said that in a socialist economy planning was primary. We should not say that any longer.[77]

This pro-market theme underlined the reformist tone of the 13th CPC Congress.

3 Urban reform options

The ideological innovation represented by the 1984 Decision on urban reform provided a new favourable legitimizing power for bold and fresh reform measures. This situation can be described by adapting a well-known phrase of Marx: While other philosophies are concerned with interpreting the world, the most important role of the new reformist doctrine is to change it. Reformers wanted to reshape the state-economy relationship so as to transform the highly-centralized planned economy into a commodity economy. But what would be the principal features of a 'planned commodity economy'? Liu Guoguang outlined in 1986 some major features of new policy alternatives as follows:

(1) Economic decision-making power should be delegated from an excessively centralized central state to a multi-layered decision structure in which the state is mainly responsible for macro-economic control, while the micro-economic activities should be the business of enterprises, households, and individuals.

(2) Direct economic regulations in which the vertical administrative control predominates should be replaced by indirect

[76] Deng Xiaoping, 'Planning and the Market are both Means of Developing the Productive Forces,' (February 6, 1987), Vol. 3, p. 203.
[77] *ibid.*

regulations characterized by various economic means ranging from taxes to interest rates; in other words, a market economy under the planned guidance of the state.

(3) The egalitarian system of distribution should be abolished, and a new one based on a combination of both material incentive and social justice should be established.

(4) A clear distinction should be made between the functions of the state and enterprises. A vertical administrative relationship between the state and enterprises and between enterprises should be replaced by a horizontal network of links between enterprises based on economic interests rather than political considerations.[78]

Substantiating the concept of 'planned commodity economy,' Liu's views marked a clear step forward towards a more market-oriented economy. These new policies also stressed pro-business values such as individual initiative, differentiation in income and autonomy of enterprises. In terms of ideological implications, they seemed to suggest a more radical deviation from the accepted conventions based on the primacy of planning. The 1984 Decision represented important ideological innovations which were, however, presented as part of orthodoxy under the notion of combining Marxism with Chinese reality.

The Decision sanctioned a new mode of experiment in economic reform, which called for expert advice and gave stimulus to the intellectuals to participate more actively in the process of economic reform decision making. In 1986, policy debate among economists illustrated a decisive shift on the part of Chinese economists further away from their former substantive rational goal for a classless society to a seemingly value-neutral purposive goal of modernization; from discussing the political nature of economic policies to the technical operation of policy alternatives. However, ideological factors continued to play a conditioning role in many policy options. A heated policy debate occurred between two schools of reformist thought around 1986. The first one was represented by Wu Jinglian. According to Wu, various problems of reform all originated from the incomplete nature of China's economic reform and its lack of operational strategy. The present reform was described by this school as ad hoc reformism. According to Wu, the most serious problem was

[78]*Beijing Review*, Liu Guoguang, 'Major Changes in China's Economy,' No. 49, 8 December 1986, p. 17.

the prolonged irrational price structure which encouraged unfair competition.

Price reform had been so controversial that before 1984 most Chinese economists dared not confirm openly the basic idea in economics that supply and demand determine price because socialist planning, rather than the market, was assumed to be able to determine the price.[79] During 1984, especially after the pro-market Decision was adopted in October 1984, there was an immediate change of discursive tone and content relating to price. A lively debate occurred about the need for price reform and what strategy in price reform should be adopted. The more radical scholars advocated a policy of price adjustment followed by price liberalization (xiantiao houfang), while more conservative economists, suspicious of the market economy, stood for continued price readjustment and opposed the view of subjecting most products to market prices. In 1985 a compromise was reached and the dual price system was thus adopted under which a product could have both a state-fixed price and a market price. As a half-way reform of price structure, this school represented an incremental approach characteristic of China's economic reforms. The dual price system confined and gradually reduced the scope of the state-fixed price and expanded the share of the market price.

But the system also triggered strong complaints about official corruption as it enabled officials with access to goods at the low state price to make profits at the market price. Wu Jinglian held that the dual price structure, introduced as a partial reform, bred corruption and should be changed. Wu's solution was to initiate comprehensive and coordinated reforms in several key areas including pricing, taxation, and interest rates so as to create an appropriate environment for fair competition.

The second school was represented by Li Yining, an economics professor at Beijing University. Li argued that the issue of ownership rather than price should be tackled first, and that state enterprises could not operate efficiently under a 'soft budget' and a social welfare scheme. The solution was to create an incentive mechanism (liyi jizhi) within enterprises and workers and staff would own certain well-defined portions of assets of their enterprises. Supporters of this school tended to stress cer-

[79]Shan Ren, Zhongguo de jingji gaige yu jingji xuejia (China's Economic Reform and Economists), *Intellectuals*, Winter 1987, p. 24.

tain steps in political reform and legal reform in order to overcome the ideologically sensitive issue of reforming ownership and cutting the administrative ties between the enterprises and governmental organs. Since enterprise ownership had an important bearing on incentive, responsibility and the performance of enterprises, Li advocated the establishment of more stockholding companies and cooperative enterprises. He interpreted such type of enterprises in the socialist discursive framework as a new type of socialist public ownership in which workers were genuine masters of their own means of production. Li believed that the stockholding system would serve to expand the public sector. His bold plan outlined five types of ownership for the Chinese economy:

(1) State-owned enterprise including banks, railways, and post offices, which would not adopt the shareholding system but would undergo substantial management reform.

(2) Existing small state-owned repair, catering and retail enterprises which should be leased, contracted or sold to collectives. No state-owned enterprises of this type should be established in the future.

(3) Existing small state-owned factories, which should be gradually turned into cooperative factories and should not be established in the future.

(4) Existing larger state-owned enterprises involving less vital business, which should be gradually turned into joint stock companies with limited liability. Newly-founded larger enterprises should adopt the shareholding system from the very beginning.

(5) All Sino-foreign joint ventures, which should adopt the shareholding system with limited liability.[80]

The concept of stocks in a socialist country caused controversy. Some supporters claimed that there were two types of stockholding companies: capitalist and socialist; socialist ones were made up of the 'properties of united producers' based on public ownership, while capitalist ones were based on private ownership.[81] Other supporters attempted to neutralize the stock-

[80]*Beijing Review,* Li Yining, 'Possibilities for China's Ownership Reform,' No. 52, 29 December 1986, pp. 17–19.

[81]See *Guangming Ribao*, 24 January 1986 and Liu Shibai, Shilun shehuizhuyi gufenzhi (On Socialist Stockholding System), *Jingji Yanjiu*, (Economic Research), No. 12, 1986.

holding system as an inevitable form of large-scale economic development associated with a commodity economy and both socialism and capitalism could make use of it.[82] Opponents held that stocks constituted a privatization of public enterprises and a big step backward, which would generate a new bourgeois class.[83] The compromise view, both on economic and ideological grounds, held that it may not be appropriate for large and medium-sized enterprises, but it could be an effective way for raising the efficiency of small ones.[84] The argument for ownership reform was supported by a broad spectrum of intellectuals, who were to transcend the deep-rooted convention that equated socialism with public ownership and who regarded inefficient public ownership as a most serious bottleneck in China's economic development. 'Without an independent property rights system,' an article in *Liaowang* stated:

> It would be impossible to realize the benign change in property rights . . . Hence, the acceleration of the reform of the property rights system and the establishment of a legitimate and independent new property rights system, based on a socialist commodity economy have become the necessary prerequisites for setting up a market order and realizing the fair competition. . . . [85]

Fearing the possibility of politicizing the economic reform by inducing ideologically sensitive changes of ownership, Wu Jinglian held that price reform was ideologically more acceptable and feasible than ownership reform. Even short of ownership reform, price and other reforms could go a long way in establishing a competitive external environment for state enterprises and would subject them to market forces and heightened competition, both domestic and foreign. Tong Dalin, Vice Chairman of the State Council Commission for Restructuring the Economic System, however, favoured Li's approach by listing a number of advantages of stockholding, the principal of which was that it led to the separation of ownership from management,

[82]Gu Shutang, Gufenzhiwenti taolun pingshu (Comment on the Dispute over Stockholding System), *Jingji Xue Wenzhai* (Economics Abstracts), No. 7, 1987.
[83]Hu Jichuang, Gufenzhi jiujing shi shenmexingzhi (What kind of Nature is the Stockholding System?), *Jingji Xue Dongtai*, (Developments in Economics), No. 5, 1988.
[84]*Jingji Guanli* (Economic Management), No. 3, 1987, pp. 16–18.
[85]*Liaowang*, Overseas edition, No. 27, 3 July 1989.

thus facilitating the separation of government administration from enterprises. Li justified his approach in Marxist discourse as a step towards a genuine public ownership and criticized Wu's approach as 'unrealistic' with 'high social cost' and even warned that an ill-prepared price reform could terminate the cause of reforms.

Premier Zhao Ziyang at first apparently favoured Wu's approach, perhaps due to his concern with the ideologically sensitive ownership reform and its possible social consequences. While allowing for more experiments in ownership reform, Zhao's people made efforts to draft a plan of comprehensive reform covering price, tax, the fiscal system and bankruptcy largely in line with Wu's ideas. Despite the fact that price reform was considered as the core of the urban reform programme in the 1984 Decision and was supported by economists led by Wu, this reform was in the end indefinitely suspended due to several reasons: first, the existing inflationary environment did not favour a reform centering on price liberalization; second, the state revenues continued to decline; and third, reformers feared the loss of popular support for reform, which could tilt the top-level power balance in favour of the conservatives, who were now complaining about reform and wanted to slow down its pace, as shown in the State Council directive issued on 14 January 1987 at the height of the campaign against bourgeois liberalization. The directive claimed that the main task for 1987 was to stabilize prices. In 1987 there would be no increase in the number of goods whose prices were to be subject to market forces, a further indication of political sensitivity of the price reform.[86]

In the reform process, Chinese reformers were often faced with a dilemma between what was practical, given various political, social and economic constraints, and what was desirable according to a rational plan. The reformers like Zhao Ziyang were generally pragmatic enough to put what was practical before what was desirable if the two could not be achieved simultaneously, but they also constantly attempted to make sure that what was practical be in line with what was desirable so that the former became a step towards the latter, as shown in the concessions they made on price reform and in their attitude towards Li's proposal.

[86]'Price to be Kept Stable,' Nos. 5 & 6, 9 February 1987, *Beijing Review*, p. 3.

Zhao's refusal to adopt the proposal on drastic ownership reform was in part due to his fear of ideological opposition and political resistance. Conservatives had equated ownership reform with privatization, which was totally ruled out in the prevailing ideological convention, and even Deng had repeatedly stressed the primacy of public ownership as a characteristic of socialism. It was true that the 1984 Decision already challenged the old ideological convention that economic ownership should undergo an inevitable transition from 'lower' (private, co-operative and collective) to 'higher' (state or 'whole people') levels of ownership. The Decision argued that this violated the basic Marxist principle that the relations of production must conform to the level of productive forces.

But the discursive convention on ownership did not change dramatically as the Decision still considered public ownership as the foundation of China's planned commodity economy. A privatization plan could hardly be conceived, as it could become too radical a deviation from even the new ideological convention based on the Decision. There were also important economic and social reasons for deferring ownership reform: short of market prices, it was difficult to evaluate the assets of the state enterprise; conditions were not ripe for large-scale privatization due to the limited purchasing power of the population; and the state enterprise in China, as embodied in the 'danwei' system, was what sociologists call a 'total institution,' not only responsible for production but also for social services. Drastic and across-the-board ownership reform would also entail the reorganization of social services ranging from health, and education to pension schemes.

Zhao, in the end, opted for what could be called a microeconomic reform focused on improving enterprise management. Pursuant to the ideologically important distinction made in the 1984 Decision between ownership of an enterprise and its management, Zhao introduced a number of reform measures. During 1986, more experiments were carried out in enterprise management in the experimental cities. Directors were allowed to employ workers on a contractual basis. Enterprises were given greater decision-making power over production, marketing, personnel and tax arrangements, thus reducing the scope of interference from the superior administrative organs. Many state-owned enterprises were turned over to collective management.

A limited number of enterprises were allowed to experiment with Li's approach by dividing shares among the state, the enterprises and the individual workers.

Zhao's option for enterprise management reform once again illustrated the reformers' incremental approach to economic reform. They first adopted those measures which were to encounter the least resistance, while allowing experiments in many reforms to unfold. Under the circumstances, Zhao held that changing property relations were less important and feasible than increasing the efficiency of state enterprises by lowering costs of production, and improving management, quality, marketing and services. In other words, from Zhao's perspective, the old system still had potentials and values in the transitional stage. If conditions were not ripe for a major price or ownership reform, then the only feasible approach was to continue with ad hoc reforms and to tap the remaining potentials of the old system. Any step in the direction of market-oriented economy was better than an absence of reform, given the prevailing ideological and political constraints.

4 Ad hoc reforms and setbacks

The ideological manoeuvre represented by the 1984 Decision was novel in its evocation of the power of legitimizing a number of policy changes. But as discussed previously, a significant reform of ownership and price was still not feasible due partly to ideological reasons. Furthermore, the 1986/1987 campaign against bourgeois liberalization triggered a leftist revival, which affected economic reforms. For instance, the ratification of the Enterprise Law was delayed as the campaign did not encourage further erosion of the power of the Party secretaries. The Law was designed to establish the authority of directors and managers of state enterprises in order to prevent Party secretaries from interfering in the operations of the enterprise. The Law had been originally planned to be discussed and ratified by the National People's Congress in March 1987. But the Standing Committee of the NPC, presided over by Chairman Peng Zhen, decided to defer considering this Law.

Most reform policies adopted by reformers were still ad hoc in nature, as in the early 1980s they did not constitute elements of a well-conceived reform strategy. Nonetheless, these ad hoc reforms also represented remarkable progress towards a market economy, and ideology was still a conditioning factor in them. A survey of major ad hoc reforms adopted could clarify this point.

In May 1987, Zhao criticized those who 'describe things proven conducive to the emancipation of productive forces as capitalist and things restraining productive forces as socialist.' He made it clear that the main criterion of progress or regression is 'whether it is conducive to the emancipation of productive forces.'[87] The fact that the reformers had to adopt large numbers of ad hoc reforms indicated that there were still many obstacles to large-scale and comprehensive reforms and that only ad hoc and gradual policies could reduce political risks and raise the political cost of resistance by the conservatives.

First, some small state enterprises were chosen for ownership reform pilot projects in 1985. Ideologically, the new concept of planned commodity economy favoured more private ownership and market regulation, but public ownership was still to be predominant. Furthermore, the conventions held that large state enterprises constituted the 'backbone of the socialist economy.' By choosing small enterprises for ownership-reform experiments, more conservative leaders were assured that such experiments would not dramatically affect the 'backbone of socialist economy' whether the experiment succeeded or failed. It was also in the interest of reformers to be able to boldly experiment with their projects. Beginning from 1985, the state started to lease or contract some state-owned small enterprises to collectives or individuals. By the end of 1986, more than 10,000 enterprises practiced this new approach.

The initial results were encouraging. An official study claimed four advantages from such practice: (1) separating management from ownership; (2) implementing the principle of full responsibility for losses and profits; (3) the emergence of capable and innovative entrepreneurs; and (4) improved productivity. Consequently, this practice promoted the productive forces, implemented the principle of 'to each according to his work' and retained public ownership. It was therefore considered 'socialist.'[88]

But even these moderate deviations from the orthodox con-

[87]JGKG, p. 425.
[88]Liu Zaokuan, Zhenque renshi zulin qiye de shiyufei (Correctly Understand the Right and Wrong of Leasing Enterprises), *Jingji Xue Zhoubao*, (Economics Weekly), 12 July 1987.

ventions caused ideological controversy. The widely publicized case of Guan Guangmei was an example. Guan was originally the manager of a state-owned grocery store in Benxi of Liaoning Province. In April 1985, she resigned from her job to lease, through public bidding, eight state-owned stores in Benxi. She became the general manager of the newly formed the Dongming Commercial Group with over 1,000 employees. In 1987, the business revenue of this successfully managed business chain accounted for one-half of the total profits for the city's 36 grocery stores. During this period, both her employees and her personal income increased drastically in proportion to the after-tax profits of the store. Guan's annual income exceeded 40,000 yuan.

Her case incurred a dispute regarding her way of management and her huge income difference (20 times) with her employees, despite the fact that she donated most of her income to her company or to her assistants. She was ridiculed as a 'landlady who reaps others' profits,' 'a capitalist without capital,' and 'engaging in bourgeois liberalization.' The reformers seemed to realize the need to seize this opportunity to push pro-business values and reform policies. Premier Zhao personally intervened in her support and the Party Committee of Benxi formally declared Guan 'was not a figure engaged in bourgeois liberalization.' Competition was praised as conducive to socialist modernization and income difference as necessary at that stage of development.[89] The publicity given to Guan's case by the reformers was a carefully designed educational campaign to sensitize the public with market concepts, so as to influence the prevailing conventions towards greater tolerance for economic reforms and their ensuing results.

Second, the ad hoc approach was also shown in the limited experiment of stock-holding companies and stock exchanges in certain cities like Shenyang, Shanghai, Beijing, Tianjin and Wuhan. For instance, Beijing's Tianqiao Department Store was allowed to experiment with the share-holding system. The General Manager of the Store confessed that in 1984 their practice had been criticized by some as a 'capitalist thing' and they were so politically uncertain that they 'felt like they were walking on thin ice.' The government office did not know how to register their company, because the business license procedure in China

[89]For Guan's case, see *Jingji Ribao*, 13 June 1987, and *Wide Angle*, May 1987, p. 46.

involved a designation of ownership. As the Store's shares were divided by the state, the collective and individuals, it was in the end registered as 'an economic entity of state, collective and individual ownerships.' Of the total shares to the value of 3 million Yuan, over 70% belonged to government institutions, 20% to enterprises, and the rest to individuals. No trading of individual shares was permitted. The established convention in 1986 still held that the nature of such enterprises hinged upon the percentage of different ownerships. As 'quantitative change could lead to a qualitative change,' the General Manager still considered that his Store did not reach a qualitative change, and therefore it was 'basically public' and 'predominated by public ownership' and politically correct. Reformers highly praised such experiments and held that this kind of incremental approach had created independent interests of enterprises and effectively checked the unwanted interference from government officials. Again, publicity given to this experiment cautiously described it as 'an experiment in the form of public ownership.'[90]

In Shenyang, the first stock exchange opened in August 1986, which allowed the state, the enterprise and individuals to purchase the shares of companies as an investor. By March 1987, some 130 firms in Shenyang had been turned into stockholding companies. But only a small proportion of private shares (less than 10 percent of total shares) was permitted and private shares were not allowed for free trading for fear of speculation.

The second campaign against bourgeois liberalization was a blow to the experiment of the shareholding system, which had been favoured by many reformers as a way-out for unprofitable state enterprises. Deng's meeting in the autumn of 1986 with John J. Pheleon, Jr. the Chairman of the New York Stock Exchange could have been an indication that shareholding system would be practiced in China's urban economic reform. Yet with the dismissal of Hu Yaobang, the State Council announced in April 1987 that no state firms could issue stock to the public, although some collectives could continue this experiment under stricter control.[91]

Third, one important reform was to introduce bankruptcy into Chinese enterprises. Under the existing socialist economic

[90] *Liaowang*, No. 40, 6 October 1986, p. 29.
[91] N. Kristof, 'A Debate in China over Stock Trading,' *New York Times*, 27 April 1987.

system, no firm had been allowed to go bankrupt because bankruptcy was theoretically inconceivable for enterprises whose ownership belonged to 'the whole people.' The firms which suffered losses could rely on state subsidies. In early 1985, the city of Shenyang decided to experiment with bankruptcy on a limited scale: if an enterprise's debts exceeded total assets, and if accumulated losses surpassed 80 per cent of fixed assets, it could be declared bankrupt. When learning that this criterion meant that over 40 out of the city's 3,700 collective factories could go bankrupt, the city government decided to handle the experiment with greater caution. A period of time was granted for these factories to improve their performance. In August 1985, three factories were given warning notices, and one of them was declared bankrupt in August 1986.

Heated debate occurred about the Bankruptcy Law. The Chinese media gave fairly extensive coverage to the debate in 1986. Those who argued against the Law raised many ideological issues. For instance, one view held that the state should continue to give subsidies to enterprises on the brink of bankruptcy because even a small number of bankrupt enterprises constituted a violation of the socialist principle of full employment. Another view suggested that those workers unemployed because of bankruptcy should receive an income no lower than those still employed. Only by this way, could one ensure fairness and protect the interests of the workers. Reformers refuted such views by arguing that if the state continued such subsidies, it would be tantamount to wasting the 'money of the whole people,' and if these workers received the same pay as normal workers, then none of them would ever be concerned with their own performance or that of their enterprises. Reformers related such 'Left' thinking to the effect of 'social opium derived from the "iron rice bowl" – a system of lifetime job security. One could be addicted to it.'[92] Towards the end of 1986, the Bankruptcy Law was finally adopted by the National People's Congress following a heated debate, but its implementation record was poor.

Fourth, another ad hoc reform was the contract labour system. It was introduced to many state-owned enterprises in 1986 aimed at breaking the 'iron rice bowl.' While earlier thinking about the role of the market was still confined to the product market,

[92]*Liaowang*, No. 47, 24 November 1986, p. 34.

the new formula of 'planned commodity economy' dramatically expanded the scope of the market in China by extending it to labour, capital, capital goods and other previously forbidden areas. The labour market began to take shape through the contract labour system, gradually terminating the previous system of allocating permanent jobs to workers. The new system required recruits to sign a contract for a given period of time and the management had the right to recruit and fire workers. The new system took effect on 1 October 1986. By the end of 1986, the number of contracted workers in the state sector totalled 5.24 million. The approach adopted was incremental, based on a political compromise that the new system, in principle, did not affect the workers employed before the new rule was adopted. As a result, the vested interest of most workers currently employed was protected and consequently reduced resistance to the new policy (at the expense of efficiency). This compromise, however, also marked the beginning of a reform with great significance and put a gradual end to lifelong job security.

Fifth, the 'factory director responsibility system' (FDRS), formally endorsed by the Second Plenary Session of the Sixth National People's Congress in May 1984, also served to illustrate the complicated politics of China's economic reform. In the new system, the Party was no longer supposed to serve as the 'leading core' of the enterprise. The director or manager assumed 'unified leadership, command, and all-round responsibility for factory production, operations and administration.' The power of the Party secretary was severely curtailed. The Party committee's role was now restricted to the area of 'Party construction' and political and ideological work, concerned mainly with motivating membership throughout the enterprise, inspiring other staff members and workers through its own exemplary behaviour. The Party committee was no longer to have the final say on enterprise policy-making but to offer 'advice and suggestions.' Yet, it was also stated in the FDRS regulations that the Party committee was to 'guarantee' (baozheng) that the factory maintain a socialist course and to 'supervise' (jiandu) enterprise operations, and to correct any deviations from the Party's principles and policies.[93]

The impact of the FDRS was first of all psychological, as the

[93]*Jingji Guanli*, (Economic Management), No. 27– 28, December 1985, pp. 23–27.

system accelerated the demoralization process of many Party cadres, who increasingly found their 'profession' irrelevant. Furthermore, there was indeed a relaxation of the Party's control over the workers' behaviour and thought. Rewards were now offered more on performance, rather than professed political loyalty. But the ambiguity of the system still created confusion, and according to H. B. Chamberlain, there were still three structural levers at the disposal of the Party: its power to 'supervise' enterprise operations; its decisive role in personnel management; and its disciplinary authority over all members of the Party organization.[94] As a result, much expectation could only be placed on 'enlightened' Party secretaries who willingly gave up any administrative interventions. In early 1987 when the Second Campaign against Bourgeois Liberalization was launched, many conservatives still claimed that Party secretaries should 'guarantee' and 'supervise' not only during and after major enterprise decisions were taken, but also before. 'It is important to anticipate major problems' and 'take preventive action.'[95] Consequently, despite the official operation of the FDRS in 1984, few enterprises had really put it into operation. The dispute regarding the Party secretaries' function erupted time and again in the years to come.

[94]H. Chamberlain, 'Party-Management Relations in Chinese Industries: Some Political Dimensions of Economic Reform,' *China Quarterly*, No. 112, December 1987, pp. 631–661.
[95]*ibid.*, p. 652.

Chapter Five

THE FOURTH CYCLE: FROM THE PRIMARY STAGE OF SOCIALISM TO SOCIALIST MARKET ECONOMY (1987–1992)

Having successfully put an end to the second campaign against bourgeois liberalization, Zhao Ziyang officially announced the concept of the 'primary stage of socialism' in his report to the 13th Congress of the CPC held in late 1987 in an attempt to justify market approaches adopted or to be adopted in the reform process. Chapter Five will start with this concept, which can be considered as the beginning of a new cycle of ideological trends. Pro-reform ideology led to fresh steps towards opening China's coastal areas to the outside world as shown in Zhao's 'coastal development strategy.' But the reform momentum ran into a crisis in 1988 with the failure of the abrupt price reform. The discussion on neo-authoritarianism reflected the dilemma faced by Chinese reformers, who had to cope with the decline of their authority and the need for tougher economic reforms. Profoundly shaking the Chinese political system, the 1989 democratic movement marked, to a significant extent, an attempt of Chinese intellectuals to radically transcend the scope of economic and political reforms that Deng had prescribed for China. The fight against peaceful evolution in the aftermath of the 1989 event once again revealed the depth of ideological controversy over China's economic reforms. This conservative discourse lasted until 1991 when the reformers began to launch a counter-attack culminating in Deng's widely publicized tour of south China during which Deng singled out the Left as the prime target of his criticism.

A Major ideological trends

1 The 13th CPC Congress: Political reform and the primary stage of socialism

The 13th Congress of the Communist Party of China was held in late October and early November 1987, marking an important milestone in the process of reform. With Deng's support, reformers effectively limited the consequence of political setbacks, resulting from Hu's downfall in the early months of the year, and began a new wave of reforms. The Congress was noted for two themes: first, the revival of political reform; and second, the concept of the 'primary stage of socialism.'

With greater self-confidence, partly derived from his adroit handling of the 1986/1987 ideological campaign, Zhao began to deviate from the conservative convention which viewed the Chinese society as a monolithic entity in which people only had common interests, as economic reforms over the years had created a greater diversity of social interests and interest groups. To keep a more diversified society in support of reforms, Zhao seemed to recognize the need to transform the Party's traditional role as administrative arbitrator in everything into a new role of mediating between the Party and different sectors of society, without abandoning the power of final judgment. Consequently, in his report to the Congress, Zhao acknowledged that there now emerged a kind of de facto economic and political pluralism under the one-party system. He stated:

> To correctly handle contradictions and reconcile various social interests is an important task in a socialist society. . . . Different groups of people may have different interests and views, and they too need opportunities and channels for the exchange of ideas.[1]

It was clear that on the one hand, the Chinese political system had difficulty in coping with an increasingly decentralized economic system and more diversified society. On the other hand, the Party would not repeat the 1986 experiment in which politi-

[1]Zhao Ziyang, 'Advance Along the Road of Socialism with Chinese Characteristics – Report Delivered to the 13th National Congress of the Communist Party of China on October 25, 1987,' *Beijing Review*, No. 45, 9–15 November 1987, Centrefold. p. XIX.

cal reform was to go beyond what the conventions could tolerate and thus undercut Deng's overriding belief in a controlled and gradual political reform.

This delicate situation conditioned Zhao's proposed approach to political reform. Zhao put forward three methods to reform the Party-society relations: (1) the Party should recruit more from different social groups, especially groups such as newly-emerging entrepreneurs and intellectuals; (2) the Party should encourage people, especially those from new social groups, to associate themselves more actively with institutions dependent upon the Party such as those 'democratic parties' and trade unions so as to provide them with a mechanism of participation in Party-dependent institutions. The Party would also tolerate a degree of autonomy of these institutions within a broadly defined ideological framework so long as they did not oppose the leading role of the Party; and (3) there should be more dialogues between the Party and different social groups to solicit views and opinions and reconcile possible disputes among them.

Zhao's concern had its own political imperatives. The reform process had already caused a redistribution of power and interests and it was therefore useful to channel possible frustrations and solicit constructive suggestions through officially sanctioned channels. Furthermore, increasingly market-oriented economic reforms also required greater expertise from intellectuals and more sacrifices from different social groups. Therefore, the Party should be more flexible in handling its relations with society and cultivate a new image, and solicit greater public support.

As in 1986, the efficiency of the Party was still the major concern of reformers. Zhao once again called for a separation of functions between the Party, the state and the enterprises. He compared the Party's excessive intervention in others' business to 'tilling land of others while leaving one's own land barren.' He warned that this approach could turn the Party into an interest group that would leave no room to maneuver in resolving conflicting interests and that would be blamed for all failures. Consequently, Zhao proposed to abolish all CPC work departments that carried out overlapping functions with those of state departments. Zhao urged the Party to extricate itself from direct administration while retaining its political leadership over the country and economy.[2]

Another important theme of the Congress was the notion of the 'primary stage of socialism,' which had originally been put forward by Su Shaozhi as early as 1979 to explain why China should readjust its relations of production to suit its actual stage of development. But Su's view had been criticized as being too radical of a departure from the accepted conventions. Zhao's people now revived the concept based on the belief that China was suffering from what Marx called 'the incompleteness of its (capitalist) development.'[3] Compared with Lenin's Russia, the same issue of whether a society emerging from feudalism could pass straight to socialism emerged. Like Lenin, Deng found the pressing need to speed up economic development after the Party gained power. In early 1987, Deng even admitted that China was, strictly speaking, 'not qualified to engage in socialism,' which caused alarm in the top leadership. Deng was cautious enough not to publicize his comment, but it proved a stimulus for his followers to elaborate on a new convention of socialism. When the draft of Zhao's report centering on the theme of the primary stage of socialism was presented to Deng, he immediately accepted it, observing, 'it is a good design.'[4]

As the result of the reformers' new theoretical endeavour, this concept consisted of four elements. First, socialism was an evolving process which neither Marx nor Lenin was able to foresee so concretely in their lifetime. Zhao asserted:

> We are not in the situation envisaged by the founders of Marxism, in which socialism is built on the basis of highly developed capitalism, nor are we in exactly the same situation as other socialist countries. So we cannot blindly follow what the books say, nor can we mechanically imitate the examples of other countries.[5]

Second, China was still in the primary stage of socialism. Zhao stated that China's present stage of economic development

[2] *ibid.* p. XVI.

[3] Quoted in D. Lane, *Leninism as an Ideology of Soviet Development*, in Emanuel de Kadt and G. Williams (ed.), *Sociology and Development*, Tavistock Publications, 1972, p. 26.

[4] *Renmin Ribao*, 23 June 1993.

[5] Zhao Ziyang, op. cit. p. IV.

was still marked by a number of factors such as low per capita GNP, a large rural population, and a high illiteracy and semi-illiteracy rate. All this pointed to the fact that China was still in a primary stage of socialism.[6]

Third, during this stage, economic development was of overriding importance for the Party. Zhao highlighed the issue of removing poverty and backwardness as the 'fundamental task' of this stage for the Party and defended Deng's thesis of primacy of economic development, claiming:

> Helping to expand the productive forces should become the point of departure in our consideration of all problems, and the basic criterion for judging all our work should be whether it serves that end.[7]

And fourth, this stage was not short. It started in the 1950s and would continue to the middle of the next century, corresponding to Deng's grand goal of making China approach the level of the developed countries by 2049, the one hundredth anniversary of the PRC.[8]

This economically-determined notion of socialism was more instrumental in rationalizing the quest for economic growth and opening to the outside world than the more orthodox notion of socialism as a process of transforming the relations of production. The development of the forces of production was now defined as the criterion of all the Party's work, an indication that the Party formalized its position on legitimizing its rule by delivering tangible economic results. In this context, the role of the Party was also redefined. The primary role of the Party was no longer that of attaining a classless society but promoting economic development, which was identified as in the fundamental and long-term interests of the proletariat. This performance-oriented interpretation of socialism was another step towards Deng's market socialism in which the quest for 'optimal resource allocation' was also to be the principal concern of the Party.

The concept of the 'primary stage of socialism' was innovative and bold even to the degree of being cynical as it created the

[6]*ibid.*
[7]*ibid.*, p. V.
[8]*ibid.*

impression that Marxism could be manipulated to suit any political and economic needs. This indicated a shift on the part of reformers from incremental ideological innovations to more radical ones, thanks to their increased power in the central leadership and localities. But the new theory was still elaborated in a strict Marxist discursive framework. The theory was explained as another effort in combining Marxism with Chinese reality. It was an innovation which was presented as orthodoxy, a return to Marxist basics. While perhaps raw power in favour of reformers enabled them to impose their theory on the Party, the discursive manner in which the reformers' ideological discourse was conducted also raised political costs of overt opposition. However, the theory was such that on the one hand, it served to induce and legitimize many reform policies, and on the other its arbitrarily defined stages of socialism revealed a similar arbitrary behaviour in international communist history, such as Stalin's 'basic achievement' of socialism in 1936 and Brezhnev's 'advanced socialism.' This, therefore, contributed to increased public cynicism about the authority of the official doctrine.

Reformers used this theory to promote their reforms. According to the new formula, China should engage in the following tasks during the primary stage of socialism: (1) vigorously develop commodity economy and raise labour productivity; (2) adhere to the policy of opening to the outside world and adopt more flexible measures to attract foreign capital and technology; and (3) reform the relationship between the economic base and the political superstructure that was incompatible with the development of the productive forces. More specifically, the strategic objective of economic reforms during the primary stage of socialism was to achieve what was described as 'the state regulates the market and the market guides enterprises.'

Three interrelated sub-objectives were: (1) changing the economic functions of government; (2) distinguishing the management from the ownership, reforming the managerial system and initiating the experiments of ownership reform; and (3) using price reform to ensure competitive market prices in the economy.

At the Congress, the Party line was officially described as 'one centre (central task)' and 'two basic points' (Yige zhongxin, liangge jibendian), which meant that the central task for the Party was economic development, and this centre should be achieved on the basis of 'two points,' one being reform and opening up, while the other the four cardinal principles.[9] In fact, 'one centre and two basic points' had already appeared in the 1984 Decision. But it was now identified as the Party's basic line in the new era. This formula constituted a key idea of Deng's doctrine in the sense that economic development was placed as the centre of everything; even the ideological campaign under the four cardinal principles was to serve the purpose of economic development.

2 Neo-authoritarianism

Economic reforms began to run into difficulty in 1988. At the spring session of the National People's Congress, deputies openly complained about the high inflation rate of over 20%, insufficient investment in agriculture and education, and rampant official corruption. The emerging consensus was that the dual-track price system was primarily responsible for breeding official corruption, but it was not easy to find a solution. Zhao's report to the 13th CPC Congress did not include an immediate plan for price reform because a radical price reform to introduce market price could be politically risky and unpopular. Deng, however, was much more determined than any other leaders to usher in a drastic price reform, arguing that it was better to endure short-term pains than long-term ones.

Deng decided to introduce a major price reform to do away with the dual-track price system and create market prices. Aware of possible repercussions, Deng spoke on a number of occasions about bravery in the face of difficulties and risks, and he expected people's support. Deng's proposal was given wide publicity in the Chinese media. Most likely under Deng's insistence, Zhao changed his cautious position on price reform and began to speak out for a quick price reform. One interpretation of Zhao's change of attitude held that Zhao found it politically necessary to complete the toughest reform when the charismatic Deng was still alive.[10] In the summer of 1988, Zhao, against many odds, initiated a price reform programme and had it adopted by the Politburo. The plan concluded that the economy

[9] *ibid.*, p. VI.

[10] Interview with Wang Xiaoqiang on 27 November 1991 at Cambridge University, U.K.

was in good shape to sustain drastic reform and called for the decontrolling of the prices of most commodities in five years. But within two weeks after the decision was published, the plan had to be shelved due to hectic bank withdrawals and panic-buying.

Consequently, Zhao was forced to admit policy mistakes, and Li Peng and Yao Yilin began to assume more responsibility for managing economic affairs. The reputation of the reformers like Deng and Zhao was severely tarnished by this aborted price reform. Rampant inflation, failed price reform and rising official corruption put people in doubt about the competence of the reformers and even the legitimacy of the reform programme. Cynicism was widespread among the people. All this coincided with the increasingly liberal trends in the Soviet Union under Mikhail Gorbachev and his policy of *glasnost* which seemed to contrast so sharply with China's elderly leadership and relatively uninspiring ideological rigidity.

Against this backdrop, radical intellectuals began to advocate a more fundamental change of the political and economic system, a Chinese *glasnost*, as a way-out of China's present crisis. The radical school held the Chinese culture responsible for its failure to appreciate and support more radical reforms. In contrast to the radical school, there was another school that advocated stronger authority of reformers in the present crisis so that the reformers would be able to enforce some unpopular changes. Two major ideological events in 1988 symbolized this period of intellectual transcendence, both having a long-term impact on the orientation of reform and Chinese society in general.

The first event was a six-part TV documentary entitled *Heshang* (River Elegy), shown in China in the late summer of 1988. It sparked a heated debate in the form of a cultural discourse, with focus on the cultural roots of China's economic and political problems and the justifications for the open-door policy. The other was discussions in late 1988 and early 1989 on the neo-authoritarianism, which stressed the need for a strong reform-oriented government and enlightened leadership at a time of economic and political crisis.

The TV series *Heshang* was written by a group of intellectuals in their 20s and 30s, including Su Xiaokang, a 39-year-old writer; Wang Luxiang, a 32-year-old lecturer in Chinese literature and

Yuan Zhiming, a Ph.D candidate in philosophy at the People's University. They challenged the most treasured ideological convention in Chinese politics: patriotism based on the splendors of Chinese traditional culture and the Party's task as protector and promoter of all past glories. Su wrote:

> there is a blindspot in our national psyche: it is a vague belief that all of the shame of the past century is the result of a break in our glorious history. Ever since 1840, there have been people who have used the splendours and greatness of the past to conceal the feebleness and backwardness of our present state. It is as though we crave this ancient and time-worn poultice to salve the painful realities of the past century. We seem to find great solace in every archaeological discovery. Yet the fact remains, our civilization is moribund.[11]

The authors questioned the wisdom of mystifying China's cultural symbols such as the Yellow River, which gave birth to Chinese civilization but also caused countless flood victims; and the Great Wall, which was nothing but a 'massive monument to tragedy, . . . a symbol of confinement, conservatism, impotent defence and timidity in the face of invasion.' The most important theme of the TV series was that China still lived by the yellow earth, not the blue ocean, turning inward rather than outward, as did the Europeans of the Renaissance and the privateers of Queen Elizabeth I. Therefore China should courageously open her door widely, as the prosperous Tang Dynasty did.

Referring to the Cultural Revolution, the series declared, 'one can only hope that history will not make fools of Chinese intellectuals yet again!' Although the criticism was supposedly about the Cultural Revolution, it contained a bitter criticism of the cyclical ideological campaigns during the Deng era. Although the screenwriter advocated more radical reforms under the stronger authority of reformers, its theme of cultural nihilism also encouraged a rising call for learning from the West, especially its private ownership and competitive political system. Both issues had been raised in different forms many times in the process of reform, and the recent reform crisis once

[11]The text of *Heshang* is contained in *Xinhua Wenzhai* (Xinhua Abstracts), September 1988, pp. 104–119.

again highlighted the fact that economic reform in a communist country frequently was more political and ideological than economic.

The retrenchment policy adopted by Premier Li Peng, which depended heavily on administrative means, was widely perceived as an attempt to suspend the reform programme. One popular saying went that 'it takes a whole decade to carry out reforms and opening up; but it takes only one night to terminate them through administrative control.' Fierce ideological opposition to ownership reform as evident in the Chinese media could be a major reason why the reformers opted for price reform, a customary tactic used by Chinese reformers to tackle the relatively easier task between the two difficult ones, but the failure of price reform only highlighted the fact that China's economic reform had reached a critical moment when some remaining ideological hurdles had to be removed. Consequently, there was an increasingly strong call on the part of intellectuals for democratization and political reform.

Shanghai's influential *World Economic Herald* launched a discussion on the issue of 'qiuji,' or China's qualification as a nation in the world, and many contributors called for 'new enlightenment' and democracy. The central theme of the discussion was to revive 'youhuan yishi,' or consciousness of anxiety for the fate of China. Many liberal intellectuals urged making up for the lessons missed since the May 4th movement by presenting China's pressing problems as feudalism and dogmatism. Ruan Ming, a former researcher at the Central Party School, discussed the 'feudalization of Marxism in China.' Hu Jiwei, former editor-in-chief of *Renmin Ribao*, claimed:

> The reality of reform and of opening to the outside world is urgently calling for the earlier birth of the theory on democracy and the accelerated progress of practice of democracy.[12]

Fang Lizhi expressed his disagreement with Deng's 'socialist modernization with Chinese characteristics,' arguing that modernization had universally agreed standards, that is, Western

[12]These views were cited for criticism by ideologues in 1990. For example, Chen Yan, 'What have they propagated?' *Qiushi* (Seeking Truth), No. 7, 1990, pp. 24–27.

standards, and he claimed that 'modernization knows no boundary.'[13]

Parallel with the rising demand for democracy was an apparent reverse discursive trend that emphasized the political authority of the government and called for a gradual approach to democratization through a period of neo-authoritarianism. The discussion on neo-authoritarianism occurred in China between late 1988 and early 1989, which interestingly took the form of a political science discourse involving not only political scientists but also economists and officials. The debate had originated as early as 1986 when a group of Shanghai intellectuals began to discuss the role of individual leaders and centralized powers in the process of modernization. Wang Huning, a political scientist at Fudan University, presented a position paper on the 'necessary concentration of power in the process of reform'[14] if China were to effectively utilize its scarce resources and overcome the problems of an imperfect market and a low educational level. Many considered Wang's view as anti-democratic.[15] The political developments following the fall of Hu Yaobang in early 1987 made it impossible to discuss this politically sensitive issue. It was the economic reform crisis in 1988 and the prevailing pessimistic atmosphere towards economic reform that revived the debate.

The neo-authoritarian school had three major arguments. First, it styled itself as political realism. Aware that China's stability was an essential condition for economic reforms and foreign investment, the school hoped to introduce economic liberalization in a controlled manner and carry out reforms step-by-step in order to avoid any possible political chaos, which could jeopardize the reform programme. This school argued that at such a time of crisis, when much of the reform programme virtually stopped, it was all the more necessary to prevent irrational thinking and hasty behaviour which, rather than serving the reform, could only play into the hands of anti-reformers. By adhering to a cautious economic reform policy, it was quite

[13]Quoted in *Renmin Ribao*, 25 July 1989.

[14]Liu Jun and Li Lin (ed.), *Xinquanweizhuyi* (Neo-authoritarianism – dispute over the programme of reform), Beijing, Jingji Xueyuan Publishing House, 1989, p. 34.

[15]My talks with Wang Huning at Fudan University, Shanghai, on 24 April 1994.

possible to regain the momentum for reform and gradually introduce it into the political field.

Second, the rule of an 'enlightened authority' was an inevitable transitional stage for China. It argued that economic liberalization in a country of China's size, tradition and resources should be achieved through a period of enlightened and centralized political power. Wu Jiaxiang, a deputy director of the Investigation and Research Department of the General Office of the CPC Central Committee, argued that two issues had seriously hindered the reform and could only be solved through a strong centralized power capable of enforcing unpopular reformist measures: (1) individuals tended to escape from the unfamiliar market force, because it was in human nature that 'people hope to gain as much as possible with as little effort as possible.' For instance, the existing job-security was always preferred to the reformist experiment of short-term or fixed term contracts; government-subsidized raw materials to those on the market; and government loans to commercial loans; and (2) as the Chinese economy was still a blend of economics and politics, and enterprises were still not independent, decentralization as practiced in the process of reform had resulted in the retention of power by the 'intermediate social stratum.' At this stage, a new authority must emerge to break this old structure and take the power away from the intermediate stratum to ensure the development of economic freedoms and avoid the present 'civil wars' at the intermediate level between different governmental departments and between different regions.[16]

Wu argued further that neo-authoritarianism was a universal transitional stage from traditional to modern society, while some others like Xiao Gongqin asserted that it only represented a special political stage associated with the third world countries during the early period of modernization.[17] Wu cautioned against the call for democratization and stated that after all, Hitler had been elected and that immature democratization could only slow down or even put an end to economic reform. As an example, he asserted that the British monarch had initiated and promoted the modernization process during the

[16]Wu Jiaxiang, Xinquanwei: tongxiang shichang hua kaiwang minzhu hua de tebie quaiche (Neo-Authoritarianism: Express Train Leading to Marketization and Democratization) in Liu Jun and Li Lin, op. cit. p. 43.
[17]*ibid.*, pp. 34–38.

Industrial Revolution by 'pulling down 100 castles a night' and he argued metaphorically that a flirtation between autocracy and freedom should precede the marriage of democracy and freedom in the process of modernization.[18]

This view was shared by many reform-minded officials. Chen Yizi, director of the Institute for Research on the Restructuring of the Economic System, and Wang Xiaoqiang and Li Jun, both vice directors of the Institute, presented their position on the issue in an interview with *World Economic Herald*, in which they classified the process of modernization into four models: hard governments and hard economies (the Soviet model); soft governments and hard economies (India, etc.); hard governments and soft economies (the Four Little Dragons); and soft governments and soft economies (the developed countries). They concluded that the third system (hard governments and soft economies) had yielded better results than the first and second, while post-war experience did not show that any developing countries could succeed with the fourth model. Obviously, they considered the development experience of Asia's 'little dragons' as models in which there was a combination of vigorous market economy and a temporary period of benign autocracy.[19]

The third argument of this school was a separation of economics and politics, and the belief that market-oriented economic reform should precede political freedom and democratization. Zhang Bingjiu, a doctorate candidate at Beijing University, argued that at this stage of China's economic reform, the most important task was to separate economics from politics, remove Party cells from factories, and establish property rights and enterprise autonomy and a financial and labour market. Zhang asserted that the 'factory director responsibility system' as advocated by reformers was not operational given the existence of the Party committees for supervision. According to Zhang, the semi-centralized system 'could become a decisive force in further eliminating the old system.' This school argued that the premature efforts for establishing democracy could only hinder economic development and the construction of a full-fledged market. Zhang further advanced the concept of a semi-

[18]*ibid.*, p. 35.
[19]*World Economic Herald*, 30 January 1989.

centralized system commensurate with the development of its commodity economy, in contrast to the old centralized system associated with the planned economy or a future system based on the separation of power and compatible with developed market economy. According to Zhang, this theoretical distinction would enable people to know what should be done at the present stage and what can only be achieved in the future.[20]

As the discussion was widely covered in the Chinese media, it was also reported in the Hong Kong press that Zhao Ziyang and Deng Xiaoping were tacitly supportive of the neo-authoritarian theme. On 6 March 1989, Zhao was said to tell Deng:

> There is a theory about neo-authoritarianism in foreign countries, and domestic theoretical circles are now discussing this theory. The main point of this theory is that there should be a certain stage in the modernization process of a backward country wherein the driving force should come from strongman politics with authority and western-style democracy should not be adopted.[21]

Deng then purportedly commented: 'This is also my idea. But the specific wording of this notion (of neo-authoritarianism) should be reconsidered.'[22]

This was not officially confirmed, but in the recently published 'Selected Works of Deng Xiaoping,' Deng told 'leading members of the CPC Central Committee' on 4 March 1989:

> We have to send out a signal that China will tolerate no disturbances. . . . Taiwan's concentrated attack on the Four Cardinal Principles shows precisely that we cannot discard them. Without them, China would be in turmoil.[23]

Deng suggested economic rationality behind authoritarianism:

> China cannot allow people to demonstrate whenever they please, because if there were a demonstration 365 days a year, nothing could be accomplished, and no foreign

[20]Zhang Binjiu, *Jingji tizhi gaige he zhengzhi tizhi gaige de jincheng yu xietiao* (The Progress and Coordination of Economic Systemic Reform and Political Systemic Reform) in Liu Jun and Li Lin, op. cit. pp. 13–14.
[21]*the Mirror*, Hong Kong, April 1989, p. 8.
[22]*ibid*.
[23]Deng Xiaoping, 'China will Tolerate no Disturbances,' (March 4, 1989), Vol. 3, p. 279.

investment would come into the country. Tightening our control in this area will not deter foreign businessmen from investing in China; on the contrary, it will reassure them.[24]

Deng's remarks did not suggest that Deng shared the ultimate goal of the neo-authoritarian advocates, but Deng apparently found their basic arguments useful for the operation of China's economic and political reforms. The advocates also drew inspirations from the authoritarian theme in Deng's 'socialism with Chinese characteristics' and attempted to interpret and transcend the conventions sanctioned by Deng through advocating the ultimate goal of Western style democracy and the full-fledged market economy based on private ownership.

Leading reformers gave tacit consent to this debate, perhaps due to their affinity with the functional role played by these arguments at a time of crisis. This revealed their own anxiety over the prospects for China's economic reform and over the possible post-Deng crisis at a time when General Secretary Zhao Ziyang's political fate seemed to be in danger due to the setback of the price reform and the upsurge of conservative ideology, which stood for a return to the old approach of central planning.

This school of thought was, however, opposed by both radical reformers and ideological conservatives. The major argument put forward by the former was that economic modernization must be accompanied by political modernization characterized by rule of law, rather than by rule of man. Yu Haocheng, a well-known legal expert, wrote in the *World Economic Herald* in early 1989,

What comparison can be drawn between the little dragons – all free, externally oriented economies, tightly constrained by the international market . . . and China's vast economy, which still remains under tight and powerful political control?[25]

Yu further argued against a flirtation between autocracy and freedom because this 'honeymoon' occurred in Europe only when the rising bourgeoisie found the power and the need for

[24]*ibid.*
[25]*World Economic Herald*, 6 February 1989.

the monarchy to pull down regional barriers in order to achieve national unity and a market economy.

However, Yu argued, China had long been a 'centralized, totalitarian, and feudalistic country' since its unification under Qinshihuang in 221 B.C. who was not interested in vigorously developing a market economy. Yu stressed that economic reform required democratization of the Party and the government. Yu raised a rhetorical question:

> Should the development of a commodity economy necessarily be achieved at the expense of democracy and freedom?[26]

His answer was negative. Yu asserted that neo-authoritarianism expressed the 'needs and thinking of small-holding peasants living in a state of natural economy' and the influence of the 'feudalistic legacy.' Yu went further to criticize the criterion of productive forces, a reformers' favoured theme, arguing:

> One needs freedom just as one needs air, the sun and water; and an imprisoned man, no matter how good his food is, will find life hard to bear.[27]

This debate marked a significant new trend in China's ideological discourse. In the early 1980s, Marxism was the only sanctioned language of discourse in China's intellectual and political life. Different values were either derived from Marxism or presented in such a way so as to acquire a degree of legitimacy. Since mid-1985, increasing autonomy was observed in China's intellectual and ideological discourse. Discussion on Chinese culture and neo-authoritarianism were the first major ideological discourses carried out in a non-Marxist discursive framework. As Barry Sautman rightly observed, both the opponents and supporters of neo-authoritarianism expressed a clear 'commitment to privatizing the Chinese economy and – sooner or later – introducing a competitive political system.'[28]

The fact that such a debate could be permitted and even tacitly encouraged by the top leadership revealed a much broadened scope of ideological resources to be used for their doctrinal revision and policy formulation. Such resources already went

[26] *ibid.*
[27] *ibid.*
[28] Sautman, op. cit., p. 99.

beyond classic Marxism and Leninism and reached the Western social sciences and capitalist experience, especially that of the East Asian NIEs. In this process, pro-reform intellectuals working in the think tanks played an important role. It could also be an indication that at least some top-level reformers may have permitted such discussions as an ideological trial balloon to test how far they could deviate from the more conservative official conventions without causing a strong uproar of opposition. From reformers' rationalized framework, many elements in this school of thought could be eventually incorporated into the new conventions that they intended to shape. But this tolerance of radical deviation carried with it political risks for the reformers and one of the major mistakes allegedly committed by Zhao after his downfall was his abandoning of a Marxist ideological front and letting bourgeois ideologies 'run amuck.'[29]

3 The struggle against peaceful evolution

In 1989, the Chinese Communist Party confronted its worst crisis since the Cultural Revolution (1966–1976). Believing that political reform was the means forward for China's half-reformed economic and political system, Chinese students and intellectuals held demonstrations that caused an even greater divide within the top leadership at a time of a succession struggle and an economic crisis. The 1989 democracy movement itself revealed the political ramifications of China's large-scale economic reform and opening up, as well as of the tremendous increase of 'psychic mobility' towards Western ideas and Gorbachev's *glasnost*. Ideologically, the demonstration embodied a complicated mix of a vague call for democracy, fragmented liberalism, cultural nihilism and the residuals of Maoism. Disaffection with Deng's style of leadership was partly triggered by his abrupt decision to push price reform, the failure of which raised people's doubt about the competence of the reformers.

Chinese radical intellectuals shared the Weberian view that legal-rational forms of development were preferred to the charismatic domination of the power structure, which generated a tendency of arbitrariness. Moreover, official corruption and inflation further deepened the population's frustration and

[29]This criticism of Zhao was contained in almost all the articles critical of Zhao published in late 1989 in China.

resentment which drew workers and people of many other social strata to the students' side.

The Chinese political system was obviously not ready to handle this complicated situation and unprecedented open challenge to the official convention based on the four cardinal principles. Most demonstrators did not call for overthrowing the Party, but they urged a high degree of societal and intellectual autonomy from the Party, as well as the Party's apology for all the ideological campaigns carried out under Deng. The top-level leadership was also divided on how to handle the crisis. Zhao Ziyang stood for a more reconciliatory attitude towards and a more sincere dialogue with the demonstrators; while Deng urged for a quick and firm termination of the seemingly runaway situation, displaying his authoritarian position.

Similar to the cases of previous student demonstrations, Deng made it clear that no concession could be made to students or workers. Deng asserted that once a concession was made, demand for more concessions would become inevitable, and he claimed that the demonstrators were instigated by 'a small group of bad elements,' who wanted to 'overthrow the Communist Party and socialist system,' and that these people only represented a destructive force, which tended to usurp the power from the Party and bring about institutional paralysis.[30] Deng mustered all of his influence with the army and suppressed this campaign at a tremendous political cost, suggesting the extreme importance he attached to power. His desire to retain power was also connected with his conviction that he had the right answer to China's basic problems. He held that the Party's role in maintaining China's stability must be protected at all costs and that his developmental strategy represented the interest of the overwhelming majority of the population.

In studying communist politics, issues are often simplified into a dispute between ordinary people, who are oriented towards a purposive (means-ends) goal, and the Party, who is oriented towards substantive (value) one. This could be the case between ordinary people and Party ideologues. However, Party reformers, as in the case of China, seem to demonstrate also a strong commitment to the purposive goal as well as its associ-

[30]Deng Xiaoping, 'Address to Officers at the Rank of General and Above in Command of the Troops Enforcing Martial Law in Beijing,' (June 9, 1989), Vol. 3, p. 295.

ated substantive goal. For instance, the Tiananmen Crisis illustrated that both the demonstrators and Deng Xiaoping acted rationally and according to their own values. It was rational for students and workers to protest because inflation and corruption endangered their interests, and authoritarianism curtailed their freedom of expression, given their pro-Western liberal values. It was rational for Deng to suppress the protest because he felt not only his own power, but also his whole reform programme and clearly-defined GNP targets being threatened by the prospect of political disorder, given his belief in elitist authoritarianism and developmental primacy.

Deng's basic authoritarian theme was to place economic reform and political stability before everything else and establish the rule of the Party on the basis of performance legitimacy. But the Tiananmen Crisis was illustrative of an apparent vulnerability of this approach: political gains from economic performance might be dramatically devalued once there emerged serious economic and social problems or perceived problems, such as spiral inflation, high unemployment or widespread corruption.

In the aftermath of the Tiananmen Crisis in June 1989, the Chinese leadership was compelled to confront a set of problems and found itself in a highly unstable situation. Internally, it was faced with maintaining political stability at every level of urban society, which had not yet recovered from the shock of the crackdown. Externally, China had to redefine its relations with the major Western powers which applied sanctions against China. Under the circumstances, what should constitute the main tasks for the Party became a pressing issue dividing the top leadership. Deng advocated more ideological education of the population on the importance of the four cardinal principles, but he held that economic development should still be given priority, and that market-oriented reforms and the open-door policy should continue. He reaffirmed the formula of 'one centre (economic development) and two basic points (reform and opening up on the one hand and the four cardinal principles on the other).'

However, more conservative leaders clearly opted for reindoctrination. They held that there should be a large-scale campaign against 'peaceful evolution,' a phrase attributed to a remark made in the 1950s by John Foster Dulles, ex-Secretary of State of the United States, that Western powers should encourage the peaceful evolution of socialist countries from socialism to capitalism and place this hope on the youth of these countries. In the aftermath of the Tiananmen Crisis, this ideological campaign which Deng shared partially, became the predominant political theme until mid-1991, mainly because the Tiananmen 'unrest' gave orthodox leaders much enhanced leverage in the leadership struggle. They now had an opportunity to place the substantive goal ahead of the purposive goal.

In one of his major policy statements reflecting a consensus based on the authority of Marxist orthodoxy, General Secretary Jiang Zemin stated:

> the ideological sphere is a major arena of struggle between people trying to effect peaceful evolution in China and people working against it. Bourgeois liberalization is the antithesis of the four cardinal principles and the struggle between these two is, in essence, a political struggle over whether or not the leadership of the Communist Party is to be upheld and whether or not we are to adhere to the socialist road. By and large, this struggle is usually manifest in ideological and theoretical struggle. If socialist ideology does not prevail on the ideological front and in the media, bourgeois ideology will. Party committees at all levels should attach great importance to ideological work.[31]

In his report to the National People's Congress in March 1990, Premier Li Peng also called for 'vigorously strengthening and improving ideological and political work.' Li urged

> an extensive education in patriotism, collectivism, socialism, communism, self-reliance and hard struggle as well as in revolutionary traditions and professional ethics.[32]

During the campaign against 'peaceful evolution,' there were three constant themes, respectively, reflecting the ground lost by the conservatives over the past decade of reform. First, the leading role of the Party in all areas of work was reaffirmed.

[31]Jiang Zemin, 'Building Socialism the Chinese way,' (Speech delivered on July 1, 1991 at a meeting marking the 70th anniversary of the founding of the CPC), *Beijing Review*, 34, No. 27, (July 8–14, 1991), p. 25.
[32]Li Peng, 'Continue to Work for Stable Political, Economic and Social Development in China' (Report delivered at the Third Session of the Seventh NPC), *China Report*, 26 No. 4 (1990), p. 45.

The previous attempts at separating the functions between the Party, the state and the enterprise were implicitly criticized in the media. Luo Zhenkai, a Party scholar from the People's University, presented a typical view against the erosion of the Party's role when he criticized Zhao Ziyang for his position on separating the function of the Party from that of the government. According to Luo, Zhao had attempted to

> completely separate the Party from the government, confine the Party to managing its own affairs and replace the Party with the government under the pretext of separating the function of the Party from that of the government.

Luo further argued that if Zhao's plan were fully implemented,

> the role of the Party cells as the political core of the grassroots units would be completely undermined, . . . and (the role of party cells) as a fortress of the socialist cause would no longer exist, and the Party would become 'a general commander without soldiers' (kongtou siling).[33]

The second theme was to condemn Western countries for allegedly plotting to undermine China's socialist system. Many books and articles were published about how the West had attempted to undermine the socialist countries through 'peaceful evolution.' The Tiananmen Crisis was described as a deliberate attempt by a small group of bad elements in collusion with the West. At a certain point, even some well-established policies of opening-up were questioned. For instance, learning from Western managerial experience was challenged when a conservative noted that Western managerial experience, 'on the one hand, reflects the objective demand of socialized large-scale production' and 'on the other, serves the capitalists in exploiting workers' and was 'used to extract surplus-values from workers.' If not properly handled, learning from Western managerial

[33]Luo Zhenkai, *Gongchandang de lingdao zhineng jiaqiang buneng xueruo* (The Leadership of the Party Can only be Strengthened Rather than Weakened) in the Propaganda Department, CPC Beijing Municipal Committee (ed.) *Jianchi sixiang jiben yuanze fandui zichanjieji ziyouhua ganbuduben* (Adhering to the Four Cardinal Principles and Opposing Bourgeois Liberalization – a Reader for Cadres), Beijing, Beijing Press, 1990, p. 165.

experience could result in the 'peaceful evolution' of the Chinese political system.[34]

The third was to blame market-oriented reform for China's socio-political problems and to question the orientation of the past reforms. This view held that market-oriented reform was the root cause of bourgeois liberalization. Wang Rengzhi, the newly appointed conservative editor-in-chief of *Renmin Ribao*, called for a study on the economic cause of bourgeois liberalization. He singled out several pro-reform intellectuals for criticism and refuted their view on the emergence of a middle class to become a basis for democracy as 'encouraging bourgeois liberalization.' According to Marx and Engels, Wang noted, 'the middle class meant the bourgeois class.' His prescription for checking bourgeois liberalization was to check the development of the private economy so as to prevent it from serving as a basis for bourgeois liberalization.[35]

Another article claimed that private enterprise and joint ventures were

> not a component part of socialist economy. . . . If some of our specific policies and measures were inappropriate (shi dang), (these sectors could produce) some economic and social forces which were anti-socialist and constitute the economic basis of bourgeois liberalization.[36]

The issue of reform being socialist or capitalist was once again revived, as shown in a key-note editorial in *Renmin Ribao*:

> The reform and opening up that we speak of are reform and opening up on the basis of adhering to the four cardinal principles. . . . However, in the past few years certain people have looked at reform and opening up from the viewpoint of bourgeois liberalization and opposed adhering to the four cardinal principles. The 'reforms' they speak of actually mean changing the course of socialism to that of capitalism;

[34]Sha Jianshen, *Shehuizhuyi fangxiang burong gaibian* (Socialist Orientation Must not be Changed), *ibid.*, pp. 68–72.
[35]*Renmin Ribao*, 23 September 1990.
[36]Huang Meilai, *Jianjue dizi xifang sixiang wenhua shentou* (Firmly Resisting Western Ideological and Cultural Penetration), Propaganda Department, CPC Beijing Municipal Committee, op. cit., pp. 295–296.

> the 'opening up' they speak of actually means turning China into an appendage of imperialism.[37]

The political reform planned at the 13th CPC Congress was shelved. The scheduled dismantling of the Party core groups in governmental institutions was abandoned. The media once again focused on strengthening Party leadership in all areas of Chinese society.

Deng, as before, supported a limited ideological campaign to check the pro-Western liberalism. But Deng's approach seemed to be both nationalistic and ideological. Deng's conclusion that the objective of the West was to change China's political system dictated Deng's discourse, which emphasized socialism with Chinese characteristics, state sovereignty and China's independent status. Deng remarked that by applying sanctions on China, the G-7 'assume they have supreme power and can apply sanctions on countries and peoples who do not listen to them.' Referring to Western criticisms of China's human rights record, Deng recalled the dismembering of China's territory since the Opium War and claimed that those countries

> that play power politics are not qualified to talk about human rights. . . . Since the Opium War, when they began to invade China, how many Chinese people's human rights have they violated![38]

Deng reiterated his authoritarian theme to Nixon and Kissinger:

> If China wanted to shake off poverty and modernize, stability was crucial. We can accomplish nothing without a stable environment. . . . If factors that might cause unrest emerge in future, we shall take tough measures to eliminate them as quickly as possible, so as to protect our country from any external interference and to secure our national sovereignty.[39]

The dramatic changes in Eastern Europe and the Soviet Union seemed to have further convinced more conservative leaders

[37] *Renmin Ribao*, 22 September 1989.
[38] Deng Xiaoping, 'First Priority should always be Given to National Sovereignty and Security,' (November 23, 1989), Vol. 3, p. 336.
[39] *ibid*.

about the struggle against 'peaceful evolution.' The CPC Politburo adopted a decision in 1990 calling for 'preventing peaceful evolution,' adherence to Party leadership and opposition to a multi-party system, but also urged further economic reforms and opening up. Some conservatives took the situation more seriously and suggested indirectly that as during the Cultural Revolution, the struggle between the two classes and two roads should be regarded as the main contradiction facing China today.[40] Deng Liqun was reported to have observed that the problems of bourgeois liberalism since 1978 'prove the correctness of Chairman Mao's theory on class struggle, and the dramatic changes in Eastern Europe also vindicate the correctness of this theory.'[41]

The same event, however, seems to have made Deng more determined to rely on economic development as the only way-out for China. Deng argued that the disintegration of the Soviet Union was largely the result of its economic failure. Furthermore, Deng saw an unprecedented opportunity for China to demonstrate to the world the efficacy of its Chinese-style socialism, as he noted:

> If, while these countries are in turmoil, China doubles its GNP in real terms for the second time, according to plan, that will be a success for socialism. . . . if China holds its ground and attains its goals for development, that will demonstrate the superiority of socialism.[42]

Deng's interpretation of the Moscow coup was conveyed to the public by Yang Shangkun, then President of China, in his October statement on the occasion of the 80th anniversary of the 1911 Revolution. Deng was quoted as saying:

> We should firmly stick to economic construction and continue along this path unless there is large scale foreign aggression. We should never divert our attention or allow undermining or interference in this central task.[43]

[40]*Mirror*, February 1991, p. 28.
[41]*ibid.*, p. 29.
[42]Deng Xiaoping, 'With Stable Policies of Reform and Opening to the Outside World, China can Have Great Hopes for the Future,' (September 4, 1989), Vol. 3, p. 310.
[43]*Renmin Ribao*, 9 October 1991.

Concerning the prevailing struggle against 'peaceful evolution,' Deng was reported to have observed:

> So long as the leading bodies uphold Marxism and adhere to the Party's basic line, we should not be afraid of peaceful evolution. This should not be overemphasized among the workers, peasants, and soldiers at the basic levels.[44]

It is worth noting that on ideological issues Deng now made a clearer distinction between the political elite and the masses in terms of the requirement for the degree and intensity of ideological commitment. He further developed the Leninist elitist tradition by emphasizing the top-level leadership in the hands of Marxist reformers committed to the formula of 'one centre and two basic points,' and he apparently rejected an all-out conservative ideological offensive, which emphasized a firm and positive ideological commitment from the masses through indoctrination.

4 Deng's talks in south China

Since late 1990, China began to recover from the political repercussions of the Tiananmen Crisis and return to the pre-1989 conventions on reform and opening to the outside world. The Seventh Plenum of the Thirteenth CPC Central Committee, held at the end of 1990, could be regarded as a major indication of such a change. The conference was known for its discord between central and local authorities and its resolution in favour of the latter. Prior to the Plenum, some local authorities already showed their resistance to pressure from the central government to retrieve the decision-making powers it had delegated to them.

At the Plenum, the local authorities achieved formal concessions from the central government, marking a significant change in the relative strength of the more conservative central and more reform-minded local authorities, thanks to a decade of decentralization which had dramatically expanded local economies and consequently political interests and power. Behind this test of strength was the changed financial relationship between the central and local authorities. Financially speaking, local authorities acquired tremendous autonomy. In 1988 the

[44] *Ching Pao*, 5 March 1992.

total governmental revenue was 262.8 billion yuan, 60% of which belonged to local authorities. In 1990, the total amounted to 432.3 billion yuan, of which 58% was local revenue. Furthermore, local governments have extrabudgetary funds, which were not included in the national figure, comparable to the total national revenue.[45]

The reformist doctrine was also effectively used by the local authorities to resist the pressure from the centre and retain their autonomy. In the aftermath of the Tiananmen Crisis, both conservatives and reformers expressed their commitment to the overarching convention on the need for economic reforms and opening to the outside world thanks to Deng's insistence; however, there was a great difference in terms of sincerity and intensity of such a commitment. Within this broad discursive framework, local authorities were able to highlight decentralization as one of the most important policies of economic reform and justify their resistance to any retrieval of decentralized power in the name of continuing economic reforms and opening to the outside world. This approach legitimated their request for retaining their existing autonomies and increased the political cost of any open opposition from the more conservative leaders in the central government. The Plenum finally adopted the CPC leadership proposal pertaining to a ten-year plan for economic and social development and the Eighth Five-Year Plan. While declaring the continued policy of economic retrenchment, the proposal also stated that the reform policies of the 1980s should be continued. This proposal was adopted by the National People's Congress held in the spring of 1991.

The momentum for reform was gradually strengthening. In March 1991, Shanghai's *Jiefang Ribao* (Liberation Daily) published an article entitled 'Reform and Opening up Requires New Ideas' under the pseudonym Huang Puping, which called for further reforms and opening to the outside world. The article was prepared by Zhu Rongji, then the mayor of Shanghai, with the backing of Deng Xiaoping. The author claimed:

> Both planning and the market are means and forms of resource allocation, rather than a sign for distinguishing socialism from capitalism . . . We cannot equate in a simple

[45]Satoshi Amako, 'China's Reform and Open-Door Policies: the Pace Picks up,' *Japanese Review of International Affairs*, Vol. 6, No. 2, Summer 1992, p. 142.

> manner the planning with development of socialist commodity economy and the market with capitalism... We cannot set the use of foreign capital against self-reliance.[46]

Referring to the prevailing ideological discourse against innovative reforms, the article commented,

> one should not regard specific conclusions in books as dogma to restrain one's action, nor should one regard those initially effective methods as perfect.[47]

As the article deviated dramatically from the prevailing official discourse on the 'peaceful evolution' and the supposedly correct political orientation of reforms, it immediately encountered sharp criticism from the conservatives. Wang Renzhi, Director of the Party Propaganda Department began investigating the background of the article and *Renmin Ribao* and *Guangming Ribao* published articles to criticize Huang Puping and began to debate on whether reforms should be socialist or capitalist. But the trend was moving in favour of reform and opening to the outside world with Deng's increasingly clearer position on the need to speed up reforms. Li Peng published an article in the May 25th edition of *Renmin Ribao* in which he apparently distanced himself from more conservative ideological conventions and policies, stating that although economic readjustments were necessary to cool down an overheated economy and serious inflation, reform could now be accelerated. He stressed price reform as the central issue in restructuring the economic system.

While there were still ideological tensions about reform and opening-up in China, a coup d'etat against Soviet President Mikhail Gorbachev in August 1991 triggered the collapse of the Soviet Union, the world's first Marxist-Leninist country. Deng Xiaoping immediately issued what was known as the 24–character directive, urging dispassionate observation and admonishing against any attempt to make China the leader of the world communist movement, reflecting Deng's determination to focus on China's domestic economic development. As discussed earlier, while the conservative forces believed that the cause

[46]Huang Puping, *Gaige kaifang yaoyou xinsilu* (Reform and Opening up Requires New Ideas), *Jiefang Ribao*, 2 March 1991.
[47]*ibid*.

of the collapse of Soviet communism was ideological, Deng concluded with more self-confidence that the cause was primarily economic: the failure of Soviet economy was the prime cause of the collapse of the USSR and the Soviet Communist Party. This conclusion convinced Deng to hold his long-held position on development as China's top priority and to reverse the present conservative ideological trend which, if unchecked, could undermine his whole reform programme.

In January and February 1992, Deng Xiaoping launched his reformist ideological offensive by giving a number of talks on his Chinese-style socialism during an inspection tour of south China. It resembled Mao's style when he launched his major ideological movements in the 1960s and 1970s. Both Deng and Mao faced opposition in Beijing (in Mao's phrase, Beijing had become an 'impenetrable fortress') and thus undertook unusual trips to south China and launched attacks against their opponents in Beijing. One major purpose of Deng's innovative discourse on reform was to create a pro-reform climate for the 14th CPC Congress scheduled in late 1992, which would influence the policy agenda and personnel arrangement. Tony Saich made the point that Deng intended to 'create a public expectation that will be very difficult for opposing policy tendencies to reject.'[48]

During the trip, Deng made a number of statements clearly indicating his break with the moderate Leninist approach.[49] The central theme of his talks was about seizing opportunities to speed up market-oriented economic reforms and combating the Left. He highly praised reforms in the past 14 years and confessed that the Party would not have survived the trauma of Tiananmen if it had not already started with economic reforms and opening up. To this end, Deng further defined his view on the relationship between the planned economy and the market economy and once again criticized the leftist anti-market attitude, by observing:

> A planned economy is not equivalent to socialism, because there is planning under capitalism too; a market economy

[48]Tony Saich, 'The Fourteenth Party Congress: A Programme for Authoritarian Rule,' *China Quarterly*, No. 132, December 1992, p. 1137.

[49]The text of Deng's talks is circulated in China as the No. 2 Document of the CPC Central Committee. It is carried in *The Nineties*, April 1982, pp. 42–47 and in Vol. 3, pp. 358–370.

> is not capitalism, because there are markets under socialism too. Planning and market forces are both means of controlling economic activity. The essence of socialism is liberation and development of the productive forces, elimination of exploitation and polarization, and the ultimate achievement of prosperity for all.[50]

Deng also summarized his criterion of productive forces when he claimed that excessive cautious and slow progress in reform and opening up, 'in the essence,' is due to the fear of 'introducing too many elements of capitalism' and of 'taking the capitalist road.' He argued that to distinguish socialist road from capitalist one depends on

> whether it promotes the growth of the productive forces in a socialist society, increases the overall strength of the socialist state and raises living standards.[51]

Deng also touched upon the Right/Left conflict and his discourse ushered in a dramatic change of the ideological climate in China from the leftist struggle against 'peaceful evolution' to Deng's primacy of economic development.

> Right tendencies can destroy socialism, but so can 'Left' ones. China should maintain vigilance against the Right but primarily against the 'Left.'[52]

Deng further criticized the conservatives' opposition to economic reform as 'Left' tendency:

> Regarding reform and the open policy as means of introducing capitalism, and seeing the danger of peaceful evolution towards capitalism as coming chiefly from the economic sphere are 'Left' tendencies.[53]

Displaying his pro-business authority, Deng did not mince his words to warn three types of people to step down: those who supported reform in public but opposed it in private; those who did not understand the Party's primacy of economic devel-

[50]Deng Xiaoping, 'Excerpts from Talks Given in Wuchang, Shenzhen, Zhuhai and Shanghai,' (January 18–February 21, 1992), Vol. 3, p. 361.
[51]*ibid.*, p. 360.
[52]*ibid.*, p. 362.
[53]*ibid.*

opment; and those who did not care about the economic performance of the areas under their leadership. Deng also summarized his general approach to ideologically sensitive policy issues when he observed:

> It was my idea to discourage contention, so as to have more time for action. Once disputes begin, they complicate matters and waste a lot of time. . . . Don't argue; try bold experiments and blaze new trails. That's the way it was with rural reform, and that's the way it should be with urban reform.[54]

In fact, Deng himself was engaged in a number of debates in the process of reform, such as the dispute over the role of the market economy and the political nature of the SEZs. But Deng was largely accurate in the sense that on many ideologically controversial issues, Deng and his followers succeeded in keeping reform experiments safe from a major ideological onslaught. These experiments, once successful, proved effective in producing chain reactions and inducing new reforms and new ideas, which were then incorporated by reformers into the new ideological conventions to induce and facilitate more reforms. For instance, the contract responsibility system was allowed to continue as an experiment despite ideological controversy and was then gradually theorized as a Chinese socialist model of rural development. Once the convention on the responsibility system was established, it was introduced into other areas of the economy, and discursive conventions based on it induced and legitimized similar reforms in industry and commerce.

Deng's developmentalism was further substantiated by his idea of maintaining a high growth rate, as he concluded that 'development is the absolute principle.'[55] Maintaining a relatively high growth rate became his urgent call to revive reforms from the prevailing retrenchment. Deng set forth the idea that a period of continued high growth was an effective method of economic development indispensable for a country like China.

> Judging from what we have accomplished in recent years,

[54]*ibid*. p. 362.
[55]*ibid*., p. 365.

> it should be possible for our economy to reach a new stage every few years.[56]

Deng supported a kind of cycle of an accelerated period of development followed by a period of consolidation and then followed by another period of accelerated growth. But Deng did not provide any elaborate intellectual arguments to support his reasoning. He only emphasized China's reform experience and praised rapid economic growth under Zhao Ziyang. Deng claimed:

> The years from 1984 to 1988 witnessed comparatively rapid economic growth. . . . China's wealth expanded considerably and the economy as a whole was raised to a new level. . . . We might call it a leap, but unlike the Great Leap Forward of 1958, it did not damage the structure and mechanisms of economic development as a whole. . . . Had it not been for the leap in those years when the economy rose to a new level, the readjustment of the following three years could not have been carried out so smoothly.[57]

Deng's call for rapid growth also derived from his sense of nationalism by comparing China with its fast-growing neighbouring countries, as he observed in August 1991:

> People are talking about the 'Asia-Pacific century.' Where do we stand? In the past China lagged behind the developed countries but was more advanced than the poor ones. This last is no longer always the case. Some countries in Southeast Asia are full of enthusiasm for development and may move ahead of us. . . . If we don't seize this opportunity to raise the economy to a higher level, other countries will leap ahead of us, leaving us far behind.[58]

Displaying his characteristic pragmatism, he urged new experiments in adopting market mechanisms practiced in the capitalist economies, so long as they could promote the Chinese economy. A notable example was the stock market, a subject of great controversy since the mid-1980s.

[56]*ibid.*, p. 364.
[57]*ibid.*, pp. 364–365.
[58]Deng Xiaoping, 'Review Your Experience and Use Professionally Trained People,' (August 20, 1991), Vol. 3, p. 357.

'Are securities and the stock market good or bad? Do they entail any dangers? Are they peculiar to capitalism? Can socialism make use of them?'

Deng raised these rhetorical questions and pleaded for their experimentation in China. 'We allow people to reserve their judgement, but we must try these things out.'[59]

There was a clear economic rationale behind Deng's pro-market discourse. Economically, a market economy had become a matter of necessity due to 14 years of reform which had created a self-sustained pro-market momentum: markets had been established for many consumer goods; for funds, labour, real estate and technology. Price controls had been relaxed. Compared with 1978, the proportion of government fixed prices in total retail sales dropped from 97% to 20% in 1991, while market prices climbed from 3% to 68.8%, with the remaining 10.2% being determined under the government's guidance. Moreover, further reforms demanded the market expansion into finance, banking and other areas.

If the essentially ideological-determined conclusion that the objective of the West was to change China's political system dictated Deng's emphasis on China's sovereignty, the equally ideological-determined conclusion that Western capitalism is primarily driven by profits dictated Deng's advocacy for attracting more foreign capital and technology to China. Irrespective of the political system, Deng believed that Western capital would come to China if it maintained its stability and engaged in reform and opening-up. However, Western style democracy, according to Deng, could create chaos in China and undermine China's stability on which foreign investment depended.

Therefore, he firmly defended his open-door policy as socialist and refuted the critiques of foreign investment and joint ventures, Deng claimed that the SEZs were socialist because public ownership was still predominant.

> The SEZs bear the surname 'socialism,' not 'capitalism.'. . . . In the case of Shenzhen, public owned sector is the mainstay of the economy, while the foreign-invested sector accounts for only a quarter. . . . We have the large and medium-sized state-owned enterprises and the rural enterprises. More important, political power is in our hands. Some people

[59]Deng Xiaoping, Vol. 3, p. 361.

> argue that the more foreign investment flows in and the more ventures of the three kinds (joint, cooperative and foreign-owned), the more elements of capitalism will be introduced and the more capitalism will expand in China. These people lack basic knowledge.[60]

As a pragmatist, Deng gave a list of advantages obtainable from foreign investment:

> At the current stage, foreign-funded enterprises in China are allowed to make some money in accordance with existing laws and policies. But the government levies taxes on those enterprises, workers get wages from them, and we learn technology and managerial skills. In addition, we can get information from them that will help us open more markets. Therefore, subject to the constraints of China's overall political and economic conditions, foreign-funded enterprises are useful supplements to the socialist economy, and in the final analysis they are good for socialism.[61]

Fearing the political ramification of Deng's statements, the conservative-controlled Beijing media did not report Deng's talks in south China for almost two months, despite the fact that the Shenzhen and Shanghai media already disclosed many of them, which triggered a strong reaction from more conservative leaders. It was reported in the Hong Kong press that 35 senior leaders, including Chen Yun and Li Xiannian, signed a letter to Deng Xiaoping in which they made six requests: (1) upholding firmly the Marxist-Leninist Party line; (2) correcting any deviations from socialism; (3) undertaking a publicity campaign for communist ideas and ethics; (4) conducting education in socialist ideology across the country; (5) conducting a struggle against the decadent Western ideology and its corrosive influence; and (6) continuing reforms and opening up that are socialist in nature. The conservatives also called for 'understanding Deng's talks in a comprehensive way,' the same approach that Deng had adopted in 1978 when criticizing many of Mao's ideas. Dissatisfied with the trend against the Left, Ma Yinbo, Deputy Editor-in-Chief of conservative *Qiushi* (Seeking Truth), commented that 'no one now talks about "vigilance against the

[60] *ibid.*, pp. 360–361. (The first sentence is a literal translation of my own.)
[61] *ibid.*, p. 361.

Right." Deng Xiaoping's remark of "vigilance against the Left" was turned into "combating the Left." '[62]

There was also controversy over Deng's accelerated development strategy. At the annual meeting of the National People's Congress in March 1992, Premier Li Peng cautiously followed the major themes of Deng's talks, but he opted for a more conservative growth rate of 6 per cent, as opposed to Deng's 10 per cent. Nor did Li Peng mention Deng's talks on leftism as a greater danger than rightism. It was upon the deputies' opposition that Li made significant changes in his report.

But Deng's talks were generally well received by the population. Deng's talks were generally perceived as a positive factor contributing to a reconciliation between the regime and the society after the Tiananmen Crisis and the political changes in Eastern Europe and the Soviet Union. They created a kind of new predictability between the regime and the society, in the sense that the regime was now ready to tolerate and even encourage a far wider range of economic and other individual initiatives (short of open challenge to the Party). The society positively embraced such economic and other associated freedoms with a more realistic assessment of the need for the country's stability. Undoubtedly the changes in Eastern Europe and the disintegration of the Soviet Union, on the one hand, prompted Deng to push further his developmentalism; on the other hand, these changes instilled a stronger sense of political realism in the population about the possible political and economic repercussions that could result from a radical political transformation.

B Ideology and reform policies

1 Zhao's coastal development strategy

The doctrine on the primary stage of socialism formulated at the 13th CPC Congress provided a useful ideological framework for legitimizing a number of bold reform initiatives. One initiative was to allow farmers to transfer land-use rights to others. Land could be contracted to various users and such land-use

[62]Fang Weiyi, *Zuojia zhuang de fanpu* (The Counter-offensive of the Left), *Nineties*, January 1993, pp. 47–48.

rights could be further transferred. This practice removed an earlier ideological constraint based on the view that business transaction charges in land-use transfers involved exploitation. In urban areas, the sale of land-use rights was approved in the Shenzhen Special Economic Zone. From late 1987 to the end of 1988, land-use rights for over 90 pieces of land were sold for 11.3 billion Yuan plus 10 million US dollars.[63] This approach encouraged a profitable use of land, yet still honoured the ideological conventions on public ownership of land and thus reduced ideological disputes over land ownership.

Another important development was the revival of the much disputed Enterprise Law, which was first drafted in August 1980 and voted down twice at the more conservative National People's Congress under Peng Zhen in 1985 and 1987, mainly because of the difficulty involved in separating the functions of Party secretaries from those of enterprise directors. Ideologically, the theory on the primary stage of socialism created a new ideological convention on greater autonomy of enterprises and their directors so as to stimulate efficiency and productivity.

Furthermore, Zhao made full use of his newly acquired authority in the Party leadership to facilitate the passage of the Law: contrary to the normal procedure, on 9 January 1988, the draft law was first submitted directly to the Politburo which, presided over by General Secretary Zhao Ziyang, gave its 'approval in principle,' and it was then sent to the National People's Congress for final adoption. This approach seemed to suggest that Zhao was ready to practise a kind of new authoritarianism to enforce China's reform policies. The sixty-nine article Law gave all the key decision-making power to the directors and managers of enterprises and it set limits to the power of Party secretaries and government officials. But as later experience demonstrated, the implementation of the Law proved much more difficult than its adoption. For instance, Article 61 of the Law stipulates that an enterprise can reject any unwanted demands from government, and it can even lodge a complaint against, report, or expose the demands to the relevant departments. However, most enterprises still dared not pursue this course of action, mainly due to the continued confusion about

[63]Liu Zongxiu (ed.), *Baiwei xuezhe dui shenzhen de sikao* (Reflections on Shenzhen by One Hundred Scholars), Shenzhen, Haitian Publishing House, 1991, p. 332.

the relationship between the Party and society and to the lack of a strict and independent juridical system.

The most important reform policy adopted immediately after the 13th CPC Congress was perhaps the new coastal development strategy put forward by Zhao Ziyang in early 1988. The idea had originally been advanced by Wang Jian, a researcher under the State Planning Commission. Zhao redefined Wang's concept and put it in a broader political context. Since the Party Congress, Zhao made three inspection tours of the southeastern coastal region from November 1987 to February 1988. Zhao described the new idea as the 'strategy of great international economic circuit.' Zhao held that with an abundance of labour in her coastal region, China should take advantage of current worldwide changes in the industrial structure, with many countries trying to move from labour-intensive to information-intensive industries, and attract their low-ended manufacturing industries to China's golden coast.

This strategy entailed another concept called 'liangtou zaiwai' (extending both ends of the economy abroad), which meant importing in large scale raw materials to be processed and exporting the end products abroad. This would solve China's huge labour surplus in agriculture, the relative shortage of raw materials, and at the same time promote exports to earn foreign exchange, which in turn would provide funds and technology for the development of industry, service and agriculture. Zhao held that in this way the entire economy could be invigorated.

Deng immediately endorsed Zhao's plan and noted, 'pursue it boldly, speed up the pace and be sure not to forfeit this opportunity.'[64] On another occasion, Deng repeated his famous remark on building 'several more Hong Kongs' on the mainland.[65] One important aim of this strategy was to expand China's market-oriented economic reforms. Under this strategy, Guangdong and Fujian provinces were given the right to experiment with comprehensive reforms, including administrative and social reforms.

The strategy was significant for several ideological reasons. First, it went further in breaking with the moderate Leninist

[64]This comment is contained in Footnote 99, p. 408, of the Chinese version of *Selected Works of Deng Xiaoping*, Vol. 3, Beijing, People's Press, 1993.
[65]Deng Xiaoping, 'We Should Draw on the Experience of Other Countries,' (June 3, 1988), Vol. 262.

approach, which stressed trade rather than investment, with Stalin's notion of two parallel markets, one socialist and the other capitalist, confronting each other in the world economy and with the notion of international capital as a destructive force which had caused the two world wars. The strategy reaffirmed China's intention to attract foreign capital and integrate her most developed regions with the world's capitalist economy. By adopting an export-oriented strategy for a country of China's size, the Chinese reformers indicated their determination to make China's market-oriented economic reforms irreversible.

Second, this strategy, as designed by Zhao, would entail many unprecedented reforms and considerably change China's central planning system and restructure China's industrial management in line with market economy, as practised in capitalist countries. In April, Li Tieying, a new member of the CPC Secretariat, observed that Zhao's strategy was a new approach to economic reform, and any problems encountered in implementing this strategy should be met with more reforms.[66] One example was the disputed issue of hiring foreign managers. Zhao observed:

> One must change the concept that managing enterprises by foreigners was tantamount to losing state sovereignty. In the world today, it is a common practice to hire managers from different countries.[67]

Zhao praised a model enterprise managed by a retired German engineer in Wuhan and stressed that hiring competent foreign managers was an effective reform with many advantages: breaking with China's old managerial system and 'guanxi' (connections); improving the quality of Chinese managers and workers; ensuring higher efficiency; and attracting more foreign investment.[68]

Reformers called for operating enterprises in line with international practice, and relevant experiments were carried out. Reformers began to experiment with 'one enterprise, two systems,' drawing inspiration from Deng's 'one country, two systems.' For instance, a printing and dying mill in Liaoyang

[66] Li Tieying, *Yanhai diqu yao daitou jianli xintizhi* (Coastal Areas Should Take the Lead in Establishing the New System), in *Zhongguo Jingji Tizhi Gaige* (China's Economic Systemic Reform), No. 5, 1988, pp. 88–120.
[67] *Renmin Ribao*, 23 January 1988.
[68] *ibid.*

allowed two workshops to operate as 'special areas' managed entirely by Hong Kong managers according to their managerial methods. The Hong Kong managerial experience was then grafted onto other workshops of the enterprise.[69] It is interesting to note that the model of 'one country, two systems' and 'special economic zones' represented not only an innovative policy framework for their original purposes, but also provided inspiration to other reforms and created new conventions for legitimizing various policy options.

Third, it reconfirmed the correctness of SEZ policy pursued by reformers. If the entire coastal area was allowed to open to the world like the SEZs, then the experience of the original SEZs would be ideologically sound and instrumentally useful for China's economic cooperation with the outside world. Shenzhen officials were upbeat and began to talk about 'today's Shenzhen is tomorrow's China.'[70] The SEZ model and the strategy were both elevated beyond mere economic reforms to the level of promoting political reunification with Hong Kong, Macau and Taiwan. The strategy was to attract overseas Chinese investment into southern China, and Hainan was designated as a pilot zone for attracting Taiwanese investment. Fujian also expected Taiwanese investment. Even the concept of the Chinese Economic Ring or Chinese Economic Community was used to depict the potential cooperation between the mainland and overseas Chinese from Hong Kong, Taiwan, and Southeast Asia.

To further push the coastal strategy, the reformer-controlled media gave wide publicity to it. One effective way of advertizing the new policy was to highlight both its urgency and Chinese nationalism. Many articles were published on how East Asian NIEs had seized the opportunity to attract foreign capital and technology and catch up with the developed countries and how China had missed the opportunities in the 1950s and 1960s and warned the consequence of missing out the present 'worldwide change of industrial structure.'[71]

Another way to push the strategy was to urge emancipating the mind and embracing new ideas. *Renmin Ribao* published a

[69]*Zhongguo Jingji Tizhi Gaige* (China Economic Systemic Reform), No. 8, August 1988, pp. 32–34.
[70]This remark was and is still quite popular in Shenzhen, as confirmed during my trip to the city in March 1993.
[71]See, for example, *Liaowang*, No. 14, 4 April 1988, pp. 32–35.

series of articles and lashed out at those who were sceptical about the strategy. These articles blamed the sceptics for equating the policy of opening up to embracing foreign economic aggression and claimed that these people were still deep-rooted in small-scale peasant economy mentality. They were urged to change their minds and catch up with the changing times. In February 1988, Zhao Ziyang published an article entitled 'Let Us Further Emancipate Our Minds and Productive Forces,' which criticized the conservative discourse of emphasizing stability over reform and opening up. Zhao used the past successes to justify the present need for new ideas by generalizing that over the past nine years, every new reform measure had been the result of emancipating the mind, and that more of such emancipation was necessary if the productive forces were to be further developed. He asserted Deng's theme that 'whatever helps to develop the productive forces and improve people's lives should be accepted, tried, and explored.'[72]

Vigorous impetus to the coastal strategy was also made possible by the fact that despite national austerity, most SEZ indicators were good for the year 1988.[73] Past experience with the SEZs also boosted the reformers' confidence in the strategy, which had been designed after much learning had been acquired in the SEZs and coastal cities.

2 Policy on the private sector economy

The 1987 discourse on the primary stage of socialism was partly aimed at promoting private business in China. Ideologically, the new discourse claimed that during the primary stage of socialism, which was supposed to last one hundred years from the 1950s, the principal contradiction was not the class struggle, but the contradiction between the growing material and cultural needs of the people and China's backward productive forces. Therefore, the doctrine claimed that the principal task of the Party for this stage of development was to develop a planned commodity economy with public ownership playing the dominant role, while actively promoting diverse sectors of the economy, including the private sector.

A thorny issue involved in promoting the private sector econ-

[72] *Renmin Ribao*, 7 February 1988.
[73] *Renmin Ribao*, 11 September 1989.

omy in a socialist country was that of much condemned exploitation. The basic Marxist principles are rooted in the belief that most social evils are derived from private ownership. Marx and Engels declared in 1848 in 'the Communist Manifesto' that the theory of the Communists may be summed up in one single sentence: abolition of private property. However, drawing lessons from the Maoist experience of eliminating private business and its disastrous consequences, Chinese reformers endeavoured to promote the private sector.

To overcome ideological resistance from the conservatives, it was essential to find a discursive framework to legitimize the reformers' policy preference. In this context, Zhao introduced the argument that the advantages of the private sector to socialism overwhelmed its disadvantages, and hence there was a distinction between exploitation in capitalist countries and that in China. Zhao observed that the private sector economy in China did contain a certain degree of exploitation, but it 'promotes production, stimulates the market, provides employment and helps in many ways to meet people's needs.' It is also bound up with the public sector and remains subordinate to it and strongly influenced by it. It is therefore assumed to be different from the private sector in a capitalist country.[74]

In June 1988, *Renmin Ribao* published the 'Provisional Regulations on Private Enterprises' and the corresponding income tax regulations.[75] This was a clear indication of the official attempt to further promote private economy and have it protected by an effective legal framework. The number of households engaged in private business had grown from 100,000 in 1978 to 14.5 million in 1988, employing 23 million people. The years 1988 and early 1989 saw a vigorous promotion of the private sector and a rising demand for ownership reform and privatization.

This effort, however, came to a temporary halt in the aftermath of the Tiananman Crisis. The 1989/90 campaign against 'peaceful evolution' was partly an attempt to redress 'bourgeois liberalization' in the economic field: growing private business, the reduced role of central planning, and greater income disparities between different segments of society and within particular social groupings. The private sector economy was singled out by

[74]See Zhao Ziyang's report at the 13th CPC National Congress in *Renmin Ribao*, 26 October 1987.
[75]*Renmin Ribao*, 30 June 1988.

the ideologues as the root cause of the 'turmoil' and 'bourgeois liberalization,' as well as an element of an overall programme designed to bring China to capitalism. Privatization was considered the hotbed of such corrosive ideas as the 'multiparty system' and 'total westernization.'

As mentioned in the previous chapters, the subject of ownership reform had been heatedly debated in 1987 and 1988. The economist Li Yining argued in favour of such a reform and experiments with stock ownership and stock markets also took place. As the economic crisis deepened, some economists went even further in 1988 to advocate a fundamental reform of China's property system, arguing that state ownership in which no one felt he was an owner was the root cause of the current low productivity of state enterprises. But now such deviation from classical socialism was considered as part of 'bourgeois liberalization' supposedly promoted or at least tolerated by Zhao Ziyang.[76]

The offensive against private business had several political imperatives. First, it was linked with the leadership struggle. Consequently, private business was interpreted as in one way or another linked with the 'turmoil' of 1989 so as to discredit those who sympathized with the students. Private business was considered as an economic manifestation of 'bourgeois liberalism.' As many private businessmen actively supported the students through donations or direct participation, the Chinese press published many articles blaming private business and privatization as one major cause of the Tiananmen Incident. An article in *Renmin Ribao* in September 1989 linked privatization with an organized attempt to undermine socialism. The article described privatization as 'the economic programme of the plotters of turmoil,' citing statements from Fang Lizhi, Liu Xiaobo and Su Shaozhi, three prominent intellectuals associated with the student demonstrations.[77]

In an attempt to oust reformers, conservatives endeavoured to associate the private sector economy or privatization with disgraced Party leader Zhao Ziyang and those members of his

[76]Many articles were published to criticize market-oriented economic reforms, especially ownership reform. For instance, Wu Shuqing, *Gaige kaifang bixu jianchi shehuizhuyi fangxiang* (Reform and Opening up Must Adhere to Socialist Orientation), *Renmin Ribao*, 17 November 1989 and Gao Di, *Ruhe kandai zhongguo de qiong* (How to Perceive China's 'Poverty'?), *Renmin Ribao*, 5 January 1990.
[77]*Renmin Ribao*, 22 September 1989.

think tanks in exile. It served the factional purpose to discredit Zhao and his followers, especially those still in power, although Zhao had never openly advocated privatization. Many reform-minded economists and political scientists had called for privatization or quasi-privatization and Zhao was blamed as 'tacitly supporting' and 'secretly encouraging' privatization and private business. An article critical of the pro-reformer's *World Economic Herald* concluded that the reasons for the spread of this ideology were the corrosive Western influence and 'Zhao Ziyang's indulgence and connivance and his failure to take forceful measures to deal with bourgeois liberalization.'[78] The attempt by the conservatives to discredit Zhao seemed to be part of their broader attempt to remove Zhao's followers in the leadership struggle.

Second, there was the urgent need to find a scapegoat for many economic and social problems, which were partly responsible for the 1989 democracy movement. Although the private sector was far more efficient than the state sector, private business was now blamed for competing with 'large, more efficient' state enterprises for materials and credit and for engaging in tax evasion, bribery, profiteering and cheating. 'Unequal income distribution,' an issue of much controversy and complaints, was singled out in the media as a major social problem largely caused by private sector economy. In an article entitled 'Eliminate Unfair Income Distribution,' published in August 1989, General Secretary Jiang Zemin commented on protecting entrepreneurs' lawful rights and interests, but he gave obviously more attention to punishing their unlawful activities. In his 1989 National Day speech, Jiang pointed out that the Party policy towards the private and individual sectors was to encourage 'their active development within the limits specified by the state,' but also 'to strengthen supervision and guidance over them by economic, administrative and legal means, so as to give full play to their positive role and also restrict their negative aspects harmful to socialist economic development.'[79] The official press gave wide-publicity to stories about private businesses' tax evasion and illicit activities.

[78]Zhou Longbin, *ping siyouhua sichao* (Comment on the Ideological Trend of Privatization), *Renmin Ribao*, 4 September 1989.
[79]Jiang Zemin zongshuji de jianghua (Speech by General Secretary Jiang Zemin) (delivered on 29 September 1989), *Renmin Ribao*, 30 September 1989.

Third, the conservatives wanted to reassert their ideological authority in reshaping discursive conventions on economic matters. Ideologically, private business involve hired labour, exploitation, and private ownership of the means of production. Despite the stunning success of the private sector and its contribution to the Chinese economy, ideologues still had difficulty in accepting a vigorous private sector in a socialist country, and they still insisted on the predominant role of the narrowly defined public sector and the primacy of central planning. In August 1989, in an article entitled 'Uphold the System of Public Ownership' in *Guangming Ribao*, the author claimed that completely wrong were those who held the view that only by scrapping the public ownership system could the productive forces be developed.'[80]

The Fifth Plenum of the 13th Party Central Committee, held in November 1989, reaffirmed the conservative convention that the individual and private sectors were 'a helpful and necessary supplement to the socialist economy,' but 'better supervision and guidance should be provided through economic, administrative and legal means to encourage their development within the scope prescribed by the state;' and also that the 'negative aspects' of the two sectors should be restricted. The November decision reaffirmed the 'role of big and medium-sized state-run industries as the backbone of the national economy' and specifically barred individuals from engaging in certain activities, including the coal business and trade in 'other important wholesale operations in important consumer products.'[81]

As a result of this conservative offensive, a kind of political bias against private business was revived and political and economic policies based on such ideological discrimination were adopted. Politically, according to the new line, 'exploiters,' which had never been clearly defined, should not be permitted to join the Communist Party. In October 1989, a Party internal circular instructed local branches not to admit heads of private enterprises as Party members because 'the actual relationship between the private enterprise owners and their workers is one of the exploiter and the exploited.'[82] This was a change of the

[80]*Guangming Ribao*, 26 August 1989.
[81]*Renmin Ribao*, 17 January 1990.
[82]'Party Ruling Bars Private Businessmen,' *South China Morning Post*, 2 October 1989.

official policy set out by Hu Yaobang, who had urged the Party to attract private entrepreneurs. The Party leadership placed renewed emphasis on industrial workers as the Party's class base.

Economic discrimination against the private sector was also evident. In July 1989, the State Administration for Industry and Commerce demanded a thorough and nationwide rectification and inspection of private and individual businesses. The campaign covered a wide range of illegal activities, including illegally dealing in capital goods and durable goods in short supply, selling false, harmful or poisonous products; compelling others to buy or sell commodities; hiking prices; engaging in selling reactionary or pornographic materials; and engaging in speculation and profiteering. The order also included an investigation of private and individual enterprises registered as collectives or engaged in unregistered business operations. Enterprises found guilty would be punished accordingly. In the second half of 1989, a special programme was implemented to collect taxes from private businesses. As a result, taxes collected from the individual businesses in the first half of 1990 reached 6.65 billion Yuan, 26.5 per cent more than in the same period the year before, despite the fact that business revenue varied little.[83]

But this ideological campaign against private economy met with many difficulties. Many top leaders realized the tremendous benefits the private sector brought to the Chinese economy in terms of tax, production and job opportunity. By the end of 1989, the official press began to take a more moderate and balanced tone in its coverage of private economy. The proposals for the Eighth Five-Year Plan (1991–1995) and the Ten-Year Economic Programme (1991–2000) adopted in December 1990 were still far more conservative than that of the 1984 Decision and Zhao's 1987 Report on matters relating to private business. While the proposals supported an 'ownership structure embracing diverse economic sectors' that could 'bring into play the supplementary role of the individual, private and other economic sectors,' they also mentioned that it would be essential

[83]'Steps Taken to Protect Private Business,' *China Daily*, 11 August 1990 and 'Crackdown Makes Tax Coffer Swell,' *China Daily*, 26 October 1989.

to 'administer and guide them in a better way.'[84] It was not until Deng's discourse during his tour of south China that private business began to regain its full momentum and leap forward.

3 Dispute over the orientation of reform

After the failure of the price reform in 1988, the Chinese press reported an extensive popular 'weariness with reform' and a deteriorating social mood. A lot of discussions in the media on the crisis of reform took place, including the aforementioned debate on Chinese culture and neo-authoritarianism. The austerity programme characterized by strengthened administrative control was widely interpreted as a serious setback for China's economic reform. Zhao admitted that 'some methods' adopted in the course of the austerity programme 'seem to be of a retrogressive nature.' But Zhao insisted that this setback was temporary and did not represent a change of the reform's orientation. He claimed:

> These methods have been introduced because there is no alternative, the purpose being to gain time for solving other problems. This is the price we should pay for the time being.[85]

Deng endorsed a limited austerity programme to control inflation by stressing the authority of the central government. But like Zhao, Deng was still committed to the market orientation of economic reform. Different from the moderate Leninist approach, which stressed central planning and re-centralization, Deng's perception of the austerity programme and enhanced central authority was based on his conviction for a hard state to push bolder reforms. He urged all provinces and governmental departments to implement the policies of the austerity programme, but he made it clear that it was temporary and that China must deviate from the moderate Leninist methods used

[84]Zhonggong zhongyang guanyu zhiding guomin he shehui fazhan shinian guihua he bawu jihua de jianyi (Proposals of the CPC Central Committee Relating to Formulating the Ten-Year Programme and the Eighth Five-Year Plan for National Economic and Social Development), *Renmin Ribao*, 29 January 1991.
[85]*Renmin Ribao*, 12 April 1989.

during the 1960s (in the sense that there must still be a reasonably high growth rate and there must be continued reforms).[86]

In contrast to central planners, Deng seemed to exploit the opportunity provided by the austerity programme to build a pro-business hard state, rather than a central planning hard state. A pro-business hard state was assumed to be relatively autonomous from the pressure of the partisan interests of social groups and to be interested in creating conditions for market-oriented economic development. In contrast to soft states, a hard state was

> ready to place an obligation on people in all social strata, and to require its rigorous enforcement, in which compulsion plays a strategic role.[87]

Drawing inspiration from East Asian NIEs, Deng believed, as was the case in some NIEs, that state intervention was economically necessary and culturally acceptable in China, if the goal was to modernize the country and catch up with the developed countries. Deng held that a hard state led by the pro-reform Party would be essential since the reform programme required both nation-wide coordination and economic participation.

Despite the austerity programme, pro-reform economists continued to interpret and transcend Deng's pro-reform discourse through advocating their own beliefs in more radical reforms. For instance, both Li Yining and Wu Jinglian still held their respective views on the shareholding system and on price reform.[88] But the failure of price reform seemed to convince more economists of the need for ownership reform. Many economists agreed that market-oriented economic reforms would inevitably entail ownership reform and the establishment of the shareholding system. For instance, Wu Jiaxiang and Zhong Pengrong, two young economists, published an article entitled 'the Shareholding System is a Practical Form of Public Ownership.'[89] They argued in a Marxist discursive framework that a shareholding system would genuinely enable the people to acquire the means of production and a sense of ownership;

[86]Deng Xiaoping, Vol. 3, p. 271.

[87]Keun Lee and Hong Yong Lee, 'States, Markets and Economic Development in East Asian Capitalism and Socialism,' *Development Policy Review*, Vol. 10, 1992, p. 109.

[88]*Nineties*, December 1988, pp. 22–24.

[89]*Jingji Ribao*, 17 February 1989.

hence it was more in line with the original Marxist concept of public ownership. The *World Economic Herald* devoted many articles to the so-called 'citizens' ownership (min ying zhi),' a euphemism for privatization in late 1988 and early 1989.

The campaign against 'peaceful evolution' in the aftermath of the Tiananmen Crisis dealt a severe blow to the market orientation of economic reform. The 1990 National People's Congress adopted a cautious attitude towards reform with Premier Li Peng stressing the continued presence of class struggle in certain areas and announcing that the austerity programme would continue. Furthermore, a serious ideological question about the political orientation of economic reform was raised more loudly than ever before; namely, what kind of 'surname' economic reform policies should bear – 'socialist' or 'capitalist.' A number of related questions were raised: Should the growth of the productive forces be the main criterion of the Party's performance? How does one define the nature of a socialist economy? Should a Chinese socialist economy ultimately be a commodity economy or a planned economy? What should be the relationship between the state and the economy? Should the state regulate the economy primarily through economic and legal means or through administrative measures? As far as the concept of 'planned commodity economy' was concerned, more stress was now placed on planning. Deng's slogan of 'encouraging some people to get rich first' was blamed for creating polarization.[90]

In December 1990, Chen Yun was reported to have expressed his view on the orientation of China's economic reform. According to a credible Hong Kong journal, Chen criticized deviations from Marxism in China's economic reforms. 'Economic reforms must be guided by a theory,' Chen observed, 'as this is the case with the capitalist countries. We should take Marxism-Leninism as a guide for our socialist construction rather than merely a decoration. . . . In his 'Capital,' which Chen had read 3 times,[91] 'Marx has developed a number of themes such as socialist public ownership; planned and proportionate development; and "to each according to his work." ' Chen argued, 'all this has become socialist reality. Of course, Marxist theory is not dogma. It will develop, but the essence of Marxism cannot be altered at will or abandoned.' Chen criticized the post-1978 reformers and their

[90]Yuan Shang and Han Zhu, op. cit. p. 196.
[91]Deng Liqun, op. cit., p. 45.

policies by observing that China's present economic problems originated from two types of bad leadership:

> The first type are the self-claimed Marxists who do not act in light of China's actual conditions; the second are those who lack Marxist leadership skills and do not study Marxism and practice the so-called 'all-dimensional opening up' in violation of objective economic laws and national conditions.[92]

The predominance of doctrinal conservatism influenced a number of policies. For instance, more stress was now placed on solving income disparity by 'gradually alleviating the contradiction arising from an unfair distribution of social wealth' and 'strengthening supervision over the incomes of private and individual businessmen, among others.'[93] The 8th Five-Year Plan (1991–1995) called for a modest 6% annual growth rate of GNP, much lower than Deng had expected. The conservative ideological climate produced confusing signals for reforms. Consequently, many reform experiments were left in a stalemate, such as pilot projects in stock markets, shareholding schemes and bankruptcy. The prevailing ideological setting certainly did not favour more actions in these ideologically sensitive areas, and intellectual debates about these experiments came to a halt.

'The factory director responsibility system' was once again challenged, and Party leadership in enterprises was reemphasized. The official line sent confusing signals for enterprise reforms: the director now was urged to become the 'centre' of management, while the Party secretary should be the 'core' of enterprises. Criticism of enterprise reforms also mounted. For instance, one article pointed out, 'as a result of emphasizing "running the factory by capable people" and "running the factory by the elite," Party leadership and ideological and political work have been weakened in enterprises . . .' Zhao Ziyang was singled out for weakening the Party leadership and ideological work in grass-roots units. 'Many Party cadres in enterprises hold that over the past few years, Comrade Zhao Ziyang has only emphasized the legal-person position of enterprise directors and their important position and responsibilities in enter-

[92] *Mirror*, Hong Kong, February 1991, pp. 32–33.

[93] Jin Jian, *Ping siyouzhi xuanyan* (On the Privatization Manifesto), *Renmin Ribao*, 2 December 1989.

prises to the neglect of the position and role of the Party organization. Thus the ideas of "supervision" and "guarantee" (by the Party) have become obscure.'[94]

However, this conservative trend met with widespread opposition from reformers and extensive passive resistance from the population. The institutional framework for ideological indoctrination had been significantly undermined as a result of economic reform, with the dismantling of the commune system and political study sessions in enterprises. Furthermore, conservatives were unable to offer any inspiring ideas or credible policy alternatives. Nevertheless, the ideological atmosphere was repressive and did not contribute to reforms. It was under these circumstances that Deng's discourse in south China was immediately embraced by reformers and many ordinary people, whose individual and collective experience and expectations seemed to accord more with many of Deng's arguments. Deng's priority to development gave reformers the opportunity to recover and strengthen their power and initiate new policies, and it enabled ordinary people to enjoy greater individual freedom and enrich themselves. Snatching the opportunity, reform-minded intellectuals and officials launched a propaganda campaign to give publicity to Deng's discourse. The Chinese media was quickly filled with Deng's catch-phrases, such as 'China should maintain vigilance against the Right but primarily against the "Left."' and 'the Party's basic line should run for one hundred years.'

An illustration of this reformist counter offensive can be found in the three widely reported symposiums on Deng's talks, held within a short one-month span during the spring of 1992.[95] These meetings gave pro-reform economists an opportunity to raise their pent-up complaints against the stifling leftist atmosphere which had prevailed in policy discussions in the past two years, and to reshape ideological conventions in favour of

[94]Gong Zantao, *Gaizao de shizhi shi quxiao sixiang gongzuo* (The Nature of the 'Transformation' is to Eliminate Ideological and Political Work) in the CPC Beijing Municipal Committee, op. cit. p. 286.

[95]The first symposium was sponsored by the pro-reform journal *Gaige* (Reform) on 13–4 March 1992. See *Jingji Ribao* (7 April 1992). The Second was sponsored by the Philosophy Department of the Central Party School. See Shanghai's *Wenhui Bao* (14 April 1992). The third one was initiated by *Wenhui Bao*. See *Wenhui Bao* (18 April 1992). For a summary of the symposiums, see Yuan Shang and Han Zu, '*Deng Xiaoping nanxun hou de zhongguo*' (China after Deng's South Inspection Tour), Chapter VII, Beijing, Gaige Press, 1992.

reforms. In these symposiums, economists and officials stressed that economic reforms should be preceded by the emancipation of the mind because, they argued, leftist theoretical confusions had restrained people's minds and capacity and had cost China many invaluable opportunities. Some suggested that if reforms were always shadowed by the question of 'socialist or capitalist,' it would be like a sword of Damocles over the head of 'cadres and the masses,' who would always have misgivings in the process of reform. Deng's criterion of productive forces was endorsed while other criteria, such as political and moral ones favoured by the conservatives were now silenced. It was stressed that the fundamental criterion of productive forces could not be blurred.

Interpreting Deng's discourse as an effective weapon to deal with leftism, reformers wanted to reshape a convention for implementing their beliefs and justifying the economic and cultural borrowing from capitalism. Yuan Hongbing, a political scientist, attributed all evils to leftism by observing that leftism had 'discredited the ideal of communism,' constituted the force of 'burying the socialist cause; destroying the socialist culture' and was the 'origin of corruption,' 'a most decadent ideology' and 'the hidden peril of unrest.'[96] Dong Furen, a well-known economist, complained about the conservative criticism of innovative reformers. 'If a person who has done one thing wrong out of 100 right things is to be punished, then we can only cultivate a generation of mediocre and incompetent people.' Liu Suinian, a senior official and economist, compared leftists to patients suffering from the 'marketphobia syndrome.' He further claimed that when the day that China established a socialist market economy with Chinese characteristics arrived, it would mark the success of China's economic reforms.[97]

Some economists stressed that the relationship of production should be analyzed at two levels: at the level of 'the fundamental system,' there was the distinction between capitalism and socialism, but at the level of 'the operational mechanism,' there was no such distinction. Wang Guangying, Vice Chairman of the Chinese People's Political Consultative Conference, stated

[96]Yuan Hongbing, *Ranglishi buzhai beiqi* (Don't Let History Shed Tears Again) in *Lishi de chaoliu* (The Historic Trend), Beijing, People's University Press, 1992, pp. 13–28.
[97]Yuan Shang and Han Zu, op. cit., p. 205.

that three ideological claims should be established through studying Deng's talks: (1) the four cardinal principles should also serve and be subordinated (fucong) to the goal of economic development; (2) only economic development could fundamentally consolidate the socialist system and prevent 'peaceful evolution;' and (3) whether productive forces were promoted should be the criterion of socialism and capitalism. Wang stressed Deng's concept of 'seizing the opportunity' and pleaded for a 'sense of urgency, crisis, time and mission' in catching up.[98] Similar efforts continued throughout 1992 and thus altered the conservative ideological trend and ushered in a renewed drive for economic reforms and opening to the outside world.

The object of Deng's talks in south China was not only to prove the validity of his own doctrine and the falsity of that of his opponents, but also to implement his doctrine to achieve the desired economic and social effects. As the new convention confirmed that the market orientation of reform was socialist, a number of dramatic steps were taken to promote economic change which would produce long-term consequences. The first major step was to make state-owned enterprises more independent from government. The State Council issued 'Provisions for the Transformation of the Management Mechanism of State-Owned Industrial Enterprises.'[99] These Provisions grant enterprises fourteen detailed rights of autonomous management and further clarify the legal status of state-owned enterprises so as to end the subordinate relationship between enterprises and government. These rights include the right to manage enterprise property, the right to foreign trade, and the decision-making power over investment and over hiring or firing labour. But the implementation of the Provisions have encountered tremendous difficulties. As a result, the state sector still performs poorly. Nearly half of state companies pose losses today.[100]

Second, a great step was taken towards converting a large share of the state industry into stockholders' companies. In 1992 the state approved 363 more shareholding enterprises, of which 224 were incorporated companies and 139 limited liability companies. Moreover, stocks of 34 enterprises were placed on the

[98]*Renmin Ribao*, 23 June 1992.
[99]*Jingji Cankao Bao* (Economic Reference), 26 June 1992.
[100]'China Says State Sector Is Dragging Economy,' *International Herald Tribune*, 27 April 1994.

two officially sanctioned stock exchanges in Shanghai and Shenzhen. Approximately 10,000 enterprises in China were involved in mergers. Cross-trade, trans-regional and trans-ownership consortiums became a trend.[101] Rather than an all-out programme for privatization which was ideologically unacceptable, Chinese reformers preferred a corporatized structure for Chinese enterprises.[102] The Shanghai and Shenzhen Stock Exchanges both issued B-type stocks to attract foreign investors. Stocks of some well-performing state enterprises are also sold to foreigners. However, such tangled cross ownership has also caused confusion over 'corporate rights' and a new ideological dispute over controlling state assets.[103]

Third, a new price reform was implemented without much fanfare. Reformers seized the opportunity of relative market oversupply (resulting from the austerity programme) to introduce price reform. Another 571 products were freed from state price control in 1992, leaving only 20 per cent of all prices under state control.[104] While this time price reform was relatively more smooth than before, it has caused an increasingly alarming inflation rate. While the Chinese economy grew at 13.4 per cent in 1993, the nationwide inflation ran at 13 per cent and is expected to be 17 per cent for 1994. As a result, the government has to take measures to slow down price reform.[105]

Fourth, a greater opening to the international market dominated China's economic scene: areas open to foreign trade and investment have been dramatically expanded from the coastal regions to the Yangtze River valley, most of the frontier regions and the inland provinces. In this process, Shanghai's Pudong development zone, an area larger than Shanghai proper, is allowed to adopt policies more special than those of the SEZs. Deng hopes that Shanghai will become the driving force of China's modernization endeavour in the 1990s. In coordination with the invigoration of Shanghai, the State Council has decided

[101]*Beijing Review,* Wu Naitao, '1992: From Planned to Market Economy,' No. 2, 11–17 January 1993, p. 14.
[102]Zhou Xiaochuan, 'Why China Refuses All-out Privatization?' in *Chinese Economic Review,* Vol. 4, No. 1, 1993, p. 68.
[103]Kevin Murphy, 'Chinese Firms Slipping into Private Hands,' *International Herald Tribune,* 19 April 1994.
[104]'High Speed Economic Growth Sustainable' in *Beijing Review,* 24–30 May 1993, p. 15.
[105]'China Expects 17% Inflation, Missing Targets,' *International Herald Tribune,* 25 April 1994.

to open cities along the Yangtze River such as Chongqing, Jiujiang and Wuhan. These cities, together with the lower Yangtze River delta centering on Shanghai and Nanjing, have in fact opened to the outside world a region of 1.8 million square kilometres with 380 million people and 40% of China's gross value of industry and agriculture.

All the border regions along China's boundary with Russia, Mongolia, and Korea in the north; with Central Asian republics in the west; and with Vietnam and Laos in the south, are encouraged to develop transport, frontier trade and various forms of economic and technical cooperation. China also revived her momentum to reenter the GATT and accepted the international (or capitalist) norms of business as the goal of her market-oriented economic reforms and as an impetus to speeding up domestic reforms. The slogans of 'pushing Chinese enterprises to compete in international market' and 'making Chinese standards compatible with international standards' embodied this revived pro-market convention. Moreover, China has further widened her areas for absorbing foreign capital. Before 1992, most foreign investment was in labour intensive processing industries and hotels. Now China intentionally directs foreign investment into such areas as energy, transport, real estate, and into the tertiary industries, including retail and financial business. Official figures show that some 44 billion US dollars was invested in China between 1979 and the middle of 1993, almost half of which came after the beginning of 1992.[106]

[106]'China's Diaspora Turns Homeland,' *Economist*, November 27–December 3, 1993, p. 65.

Chapter Six

THE 14TH CPC CONGRESS: THE ESTABLISHMENT OF DENG XIAOPING'S THEORY (1992–1993)

In discussing ideological evolution, Brzezinski has observed:

> The shaping of events necessarily involves situations that are either unforeseen or dictate a logic of their own, even if initially fitting the theoretical assumptions. Doctrine is then 'creatively' extended, new principles are extrapolated from the original set of assumptions, new generalizations crystallize, and, finally, the identity of the ideology emerges.[1]

Since 1980, when he put forward the vague concept of socialism with Chinese characteristics, Deng has been trying to define a clearer and more coherent rationale for his reform programme and to establish his ideological authority. Fourteen years of sweeping reforms have provided the opportunity to significantly substantiate many of Deng's reformist ideas.

Deng's talks in south China in 1992 signaled such an attempt to establish the identity of his most important ideas and values. The 14th Party Congress held in October 1992 represented the same attempt to codify Deng's ideas into an official doctrine called 'Deng Xiaoping's theory on building socialism with Chinese characteristics.' As the paramount leader since 1978, Deng has either initiated or authorized many reformist ideas, which have established the general orientation for reform policies. In this context, it may be legitimate to describe China's post-Maoist mainstream ideology as Deng's theory. The new doctrine is adopted to replace the old orthodoxy, which was under increasing erosion with the diffusion of relative prosperity and the formation of more diversified interest groups.

[1]Brzezinski Z., 1976, pp. 97–98.

The official interpretation of Deng Xiaoping's theory, as formulated at the 14th Party Congress, claims that it contains nine major themes: (i) on the developmental path of socialism, Deng stresses the concept of seeking truth from facts and building Chinese-style socialism, rather than copying foreign experience; (ii) on the developmental stage of socialism, Deng outlines a period of the primary stage of socialism which lasts at least one hundred years; (iii) on the fundamental task of socialism, Deng claims that it is 'to liberate and develop the productive forces, to eliminate exploitation and polarization and ultimately to realize common prosperity;' (iv) on the driving force of socialism, Deng advocates market-oriented economic reforms and prudent political reforms; (v) on the external conditions of socialism, Deng stands for an independent foreign policy and opening China to the outside world for information, capital and technology; (vi) on the political guarantee of socialism, Deng emphasizes the four cardinal principles and the struggle against bourgeois liberalization; (vii) on the strategies of socialist construction, Deng encourages some people and some regions to get rich first and outlines a three-phase developmental plan to enable China to reach the level of the developed countries by the mid-21st century; (viii) on the leading force of socialism, Deng stresses the leadership of the Party and the widest possible united front composed of all patriots; and (ix) on the unification of the country, Deng puts forward the concept of 'one country, two systems.'[2]

The 14th CPC Congress stressed the two most important concepts in Deng's theory: One is what has been conceptualized as 'socialist market economy,' and the other is Deng's redefinition of socialism. Deng's belief in the market force seems to be vindicated by the largely positive results of rural reforms and the experience of the SEZs where market force predominated. Deng has long held that market forces are value-neutral mechanisms that both socialism and capitalism can make use of. But it was not until 1992 that Deng felt confident enough to publicly

[2]Jiang Zemin, Jiakuai gaige kaifang he xiandaihua jianshe bufa duoqu zhongguo tese shehuizhuyi shiye de gengda shengli (Speed up the pace of reform, the openness and modernization in order to strive for even greater victories for the cause of socialism with Chinese characteristics – work report to the 14th CPC Congress), Part One, *Renmin Ribao*, overseas edition, 21 October 1992. pp. 1–2.

declare his clear departure from the moderate Leninist approach. This indicated that his conscious effort in building authority in the economic field through doctrinal renovation and reform experiment has scored a decisive victory. Deng's 'socialist market economy' is perceived as a relatively successful alternative to Chen Yun's moderate Leninist approach. To illustrate Deng's concept of the market, Jiang Zemin claimed:

> In China, practice has proved that where market forces are given fuller play, the economies are vigorous and have developed in a sound way.[3]

The two main features of 'socialist market economy' are interpreted by Vice Premier Zhu Rongji as, first, 'highly efficient resource allocation and productivity of labour' and second, 'social justice and common prosperity.' In the tradition of Deng's pragmatism, Zhu explained why reformers led by Deng decided on a 'socialist market economy:' 'Resource allocation under a market economy is more efficient than that of a planned economy,' Zhu observed, 'This is an important reason why China has opted to incorporate it.' But socialism is also important because 'maintaining a just society and work towards the common prosperity of its people is a socialist ideal. Public ownership of property can better maintain social justice and increase common prosperity than systems which encourage private ownership.' Zhu stressed that Chinese reformers were confident that 'China can establish a market economy while public ownership continues to predominate.'[4] Jiang even claimed that China should be able to establish a market economy under a socialist system, which 'can and should operate better than one under the capitalist system.'[5]

The difference between the capitalist market economy and the socialist one is still somewhat confusing. Pro-reform economists and officials like Liu Guoguang saw more similarity than difference between the two because both economies let market forces serve as the basic means to allocate resources and respond to the changing relations between supply and demand. In addition, free competition will create a more efficient economy. Liu argued that the main difference was that socialism would permit the

[3]*ibid*.
[4]*Beijing Review*, 24–30 May 1993, p. 14.
[5]*International Herald Tribune*, 13 October 1992.

state to play a larger role than in capitalist countries. In relatively specific terms, Jiang Zemin explained how the state should manage the economy under the new ideological convention: macroeconomic tools, rather than administrative means, should be the main instrument of control; the plan should be confined to 'strategic targets;' and the state should endeavour to remove local barriers to an 'integrated national market.' Under the new convention, the concept of planning will also be renewed. The main task of planning will be to set rational strategic targets for national economic and social development, to forecast economic development, to control total supply and total demand, to readjust the geographical distribution of industries, and to master the financial and material resources necessary for the construction of important projects.[6]

In the context of recognizing the primacy of market force, the 14th Congress also more positively confirmed the role of the non-state sector than the 13th Congress had done. Jiang's report provides two important ideas on the subject: (i) diversified economic components can on a voluntary basis practice diversified forms of joint management, which means that the non-state sector can cooperate with the state sector or with foreign partners; and (ii) state enterprises, as well as collective and other enterprises will all enter the marketplace and the state enterprises will play their dominant role through fair competition, which means that the state sector (at least in theory) does not have privileges over the non-state sector in the marketplace.

This actually only acknowledges the significant role played by the non-state sector in the Chinese economy after 14 years of economic reforms. By 1992, the non-state sector already produced 47% of China's total industrial output.[7] The non-state sector also predominates over Chinese agriculture and commerce. But it is still premature to say that the market economy has replaced central planning. Central planning still predominates in many interior provinces, in the financial and banking system, and in most of the state sector. Conservative forces against market-oriented reforms still interpret the concept of 'socialist market economy' as something stressing socialism, rather than the market. This is because they hold that 'socialist'

[6]*Renmin Ribao*, 21 October 1993.
[7]*Liaowang*, No. 48, 30 November 1992, pp. 22–24.

defines the nature of 'market economy' as something different from capitalist market economy. The Chinese media has revealed confusion in the mind of the population about the seemingly increasing polarization and inflation, which the market economy is generating and there is still a lingering fear of the market economy for many people.[8] But it seems that market-oriented economic reforms have created a sustainable momentum and are increasingly embraced by the general public. Rural reform, rapid growth of the SMEs and the coastal development strategy have created China's largest pro-reform constituency. An ideological climate generally favourable to, or at least more tolerant of, market forces has taken shape.

Deng's view – that the most important features of socialism are the predominance of public ownership and an ultimate common prosperity – was reaffirmed at the Congress, but as the fourteen years of economic reforms have already diversified China's ownership system, the definition of 'public ownership' has become far more elastic than ever before. Jiang Zemin's report interpreted Deng's argument that public ownership not only includes the state enterprises but also the rising collectives and the 'township and village enterprises' that are responsive to market signals and have been largely responsible for the relative success of China's economic reforms. Most economists also consider stockholding companies as publicly owned if the state has a larger share. On common prosperity, 'simultaneous prosperity for everyone is impossible,' Jiang claimed. 'We should thus widen the differences in personal income to a reasonable degree' in order to achieve higher efficiency and the ultimate goals of common prosperity, a sharp contrast to the more conservative tone of his 1989 article.

Deng's discourse on socialism breaks with the orthodox communist convention, which defines socialism as the reverse of capitalist market economy, substituting the administrative plan for competitive markets and abolishing class inequality by nationalization of the means of production. It also moves away from Chen Yun's moderate Leninist approach, which holds an expanded role for the market as a temporary expedient of undeveloped socialism. Deng's socialist market economy disputes

[8]Dong Ruishen, Guanyu fazhan shichang jingji zhong de jige wenti (On a Number of Questions in Developing Market Economy – an Interview with Economist Wang Yu), *Liaowang*, No. 32, 10 August 1992, pp. 16–17.

the Marxist proposition that socialism and capitalism inherently contradict each other. Deng's theory, in fact, regards market regulation as a permanent feature of a developing socialist country like China.

The effort at doctrinal building at the 14th Congress was aimed at establishing Deng's full theoretical authority in the CPC, just as in 1945 in Yanan an effort was made to establish Mao Zedong thought as the authority in the Chinese communist movement. Deng's doctrine was now elevated to the status of Mao Zedong Thought. Deng's doctrine was officially called the 'developmental theory of Marxism' applicable for a large and populous developing country like China. Deng's achievement in economic reforms was compared to Mao's in the war period in the sense that Deng was claimed to have found a right path for China, combining the universal truth of Marxism with the actual conditions of China.

A more cautious attitude towards political reform was adopted. The 14th CPC Congress did not advocate a radical separation of functions between the Party and the government. Qiao Shi and Li Ruihuan, both members of the Politburo Standing Committee, were made the heads of the National People's Congress and the CPPCC. This seemed to suggest Deng's rethinking of the political structure in China. Rather than separating the Party from top-level government, Deng indicated that he preferred a more solid Party control. At the same time, placing members of the Politburo Standing Committee in charge of the two previously less important institutions seemed to strengthen the two bodies and facilitated more fruitful consultations with people's deputies and experts.

This cautious attitude also reflected the lessons Deng and other leaders have drawn from the Tiananmen Crisis and the disintegration of the Soviet Union. Deng's authoritarian theme on the need of Party's unity and control has been reemphasized since 1989. At the 13th Congress, Zhao claimed that 'it was high time to put political structural reform on the agenda for the whole Party.' But at the 14th Congress, Jiang's report only called for streamlining the size of China's bureaucracy and overcoming the overlap between the functions of the Party and the government. The previous decision on abolishing Party cells in government organizations was dropped. The disintegration of the Soviet Union and its subsequent political and economic disorder seem to have strengthened Deng's belief about authoritarianism. In the tradition of a Confucian elitist ruler, Deng noted, 'If he (Gorbachev) loses his party, how can he organize socialist economic development?'[9] Any general assumption about Deng's insistence on the 'socialist' attribute is mainly political, as it attests to Deng's political concern for the legitimizing power of the Party's continued existence. But at the level of political culture, it also reflects Deng's affinity with the Confucian cultural inclination towards elite rule and state intervention in the name of maintaining stability and national interests.

Tony Saich's claim that 'with the Party bankrupt in terms of ideological leadership, Deng and his supporters know that its legitimacy to rule will be dependent on its capacity to deliver the economic goods'[10] does not seem to be accurate because Chinese reformers led by Deng have been trying to establish a coherent doctrine to facilitate delivery of the economic goods, and the 14th Congress saw the culmination of such efforts. Deng proved to be able to produce ideas which induce actions, and his doctrine, though lacking sophisticated intellectual structure and Western liberal values, has already given strong impetus to economic reforms by legitimizing market-oriented actions and exploring new reform options.

Furthermore, in the process of reforms, the authoritative centre of ideological interpretation, the Party leadership, is constantly in dispute over the discursive framework and orientation of reforms. Deng's views largely prevailed despite many challenges from both inside and outside the Party thanks to the power of some of his ideas, such as 'seeking truth from facts' and 'one country, two systems,' as well as sensible tactics, such as avoiding direct ideological confrontation with reform opponents when conditions were not ripe and managing to encourage reform experiments under reformist ideology.

The fact that Chinese reformers embrace Deng's ideas is the major reason why the reformers gave such wide publicity to Deng's theory even to the degree of a personality cult. Ding Guangen, a member of the Politburo, stated on 19 June 1993 that Deng's theory is

[9]*Mirror*, September 1992, pp. 11.
[10]Tony Saich, 'The Fourteenth Party Congress: A Programme for Authoritarian Rule,' *China Quarterly*, No. 132, December 1992, p. 1139.

> a source of strength to encourage the Party and the Chinese people to strive unremittingly for the realization of socialist modernization. . . . It is crucial to arm the Party cadres at all levels, particularly senior ones, with the theory. Only by mastering the theory and applying it can leaders at all levels calmly observe and deal with the changeable and complicated situation in the reform, opening up and modernization drive.[11]

Jiang's report referred to Deng as 'the chief architect of our socialist reform, of the open policy and of the modernization programme' and compared the reforms under Deng to 'another great revolution' like Mao's 'New Democratic Revolution.' The message is similar to what Deng Liqun had attributed to Chen Yun in 1981. While Mao discovered the law of Chinese revolution before 1949, Deng knows how to modernize China. This unprecedented eulogy of Deng also indicated the continued need for personalization and ideology in Chinese politics to establish political authority and pursue desired policy alternatives, especially at a time of transition into the post-Deng era.

Intentionally or not, Deng and his followers seem to be building a bridge between Chinese-style socialism and East Asian authoritarianism. Like in the NIEs, where a hard Confucian state has played an important role in coordinating a modernization programme based on the logic of market competition and ensuring social justice, Chinese reformers led by Deng are also attempting to create conditions in which the state promotes and coordinates a market-oriented modernization programme, while managing to solve problems arising from unfettered market competition. In this context, one noteworthy event was that the Chinese government even agreed in 1993 to set up a zone in Suzhou to allow Singaporean investors to build a 'mini-Singapore,' which will not only adopt Singaporian 'hard ware,' but also its 'soft ware;' i.e., the zone will completely model Singaporean management, an indication of Deng's determination to learn from the Singaporean experience in economic development and 'good governance.'

The Chinese constitution was also amended to facilitate economic reforms and reflect the new conventions. A *Beijing Review* article claimed, 'the planned economy, once regarded as the

[11]*Beijing Review*, 5–11 July 1993, pp. 4–5.

cornerstone of socialism, has finally lost its dominance in China after four decades'[12] and amendments were made to the 1982 Constitution at the first session of the Eighth National People's Congress held in March 1993.

The major revisions were: first, the concept of the primary stage of socialism was incorporated into the preamble of the Constitution; second, the concept of a state-owned economy was introduced to replace the old ambiguous concept of state economy, which actually means state-run economy; third, the stipulation in the 1982 Constitution that 'China practices a planned economy on the basis of socialist public ownership and that she ensures the growth of the national economy through overall economic planning with a supplementary role for market regulation' was dropped. Instead, the concept of 'socialist market economy' was incorporated. Fourth, the 1982 Constitution states that 'state enterprises have decision-making power with regard to operation and management within the limits prescribed by law, on the condition that they submit to the state's unified leadership and fulfil all their obligations under the state plan.' Now it becomes simply 'state-owned enterprises have decision-making power in operation and management within the limits prescribed by law.' Fifth, the wording of 'the responsibility system, the main form of which is household contracts linking remuneration to output' has replaced that of 'rural people's communes and agricultural producers' cooperatives.'[13]

These revisions, on the one hand, reflect the Dengist discursive conventions and the significant gains that reformers have made in the course of economic reforms; on the other hand, they reveal the political and ideological sensitivity of constitutional changes. Reformers do not attempt constitutional change until they have achieved significant victory in economic reforms and a new institutional framework is established, as in the case of replacing 'communes' with the old administrative structure. But they also show a lack of legal tradition in Chinese political culture in which pragmatism and Party policies may transcend the rule of law and the Constitution.

[12]'Constitution Amended to Advance Market Economy,' *Beijing Review*, April 26–May 2, 1993.
[13]*ibid*. pp. 14–15.

CONCLUSIONS

Since 1978, China has undergone a dramatic process of economic and social transformation, during which the country has experienced and is still experiencing an outpouring of competing ideologies aimed at inducing, justifying or resisting economic and social changes. Different political actors have articulated their diverse beliefs, goals and means to influence policy options. In this context, the doctrinal failure of Maoism and the primacy of the modernization goal have compelled the Chinese communist reformers to initiate the theoretical and operational reformulation of socialism.

From the very outset of reform, Chinese political elites with divergent views have taken the issue of doctrines very seriously. Consequently, there has been a dynamic process of ideological controversy and ideology-policy interactions. Ideological controversy has taken place mainly between pro-market reformers and more conservative central planners. The former tends to be more liberal politically while the latter generally endorses greater ideological control. Deng Xiaoping, as China's paramount leader, plays the role of the arbitrator, who has demonstrated a clear preference for a controlled political reform and a market-oriented economy.

The competing ideologies have striven to establish certain overarching conventions that can influence policy options by increasing or reducing the political cost of compliance or non-compliance. The competing ideologies generally operate either as a stimulus to reform policies or as a constraint on them, and they have thus affected the pace, scope and content of China's economic reforms. For instance, the truth debate quickened the pace of rural reform, and the primary stage of socialism dramatically expanded the scope of China's tolerance of private business and of her opening to the outside world. Likewise, the campaigns against bourgeois liberalism effectively halted experiment in the stockholding system and deferred other experiments, as well as precluded any attempt at privatization.

The major conservative ideological trends have deep-rooted causes, such as personalities trained and brought up under Maoism; an institutional bias against market forces and new values; vested interests in maintaining central planning and bureaucratic power; and an entrenched leftist political culture, which gives ideological righteousness a higher place than ideological innovation. Under these conditions, Chinese reformers have needed to adopt a gradual approach in their ideological renovation and must rely more on pragmatically induced doctrinal changes, as shown in the case of the rural responsibility system and its ideological implications. The system, a peasant invention that was encouraged by reformist policies, has induced an ideological reinterpretation of how socialism should operate in China. With the success of rural reforms, the early discourse on the responsibility system as a necessary concession to capitalism is gradually replaced by the perception of it as a long-term feature of socialism.

Parallel to this dynamic process are the discursive interactions between Chinese intellectuals and political elites. China's dramatic social changes and doctrinal renovation have provided unprecedented opportunities for intellectuals, especially economists, to engage in the interpretation and the transcendence of the official discourse so as to reflect their beliefs and influence policy options. While the two extremes of such interpretation and transcendence are frequently identified respectively by the political elite as leftism and bourgeois liberalism, much of the rational intellectual discourse with a facade of value neutrality has been incorporated into the official doctrine, such as the concept of guidance planning, the coastal development strategy and the neo-authoritarianism.

Ideological controversy, a constraint on reform, is not always necessarily a disservice to reform. A moderate degree of ideological adversary is occasionally complementary to reform in the absence of institutionalized democracy because it generates pressure on reformers to act with prudence for tangible results, and it guards against any simplistic approach to China's complicated economic problems, as shown in the revision of the development strategy for the SEZs. In fact, China's much praised gradual approach to reform is to a certain extent attributable to the ideological and political compromises reached between reformers and conservatives.

Since 1978, Chinese reformers have made conscious efforts to gradually transform the orthodox doctrine into a more elastic and pro-business ideology. Deng Xiaoping, as China's paramount leader, has in many ways pioneered this effort. He has questioned many tenets of Marxism, Leninism and Maoism that stand in the way of economic development and returned to what he calls Marxist methodology: historical materialism, which stresses economics over politics; and dialectic materialism, which gives him a perspective that constantly balances the Right and the Left, the elite and the masses, tactics and strategies, and short-term goals and long-term objectives.

Furthermore, under the Chinese circumstances, no independent social force is in a position to produce a comprehensive theoretical framework to rationalize and legitimize the tremendous social transformation since 1978. Deng's doctrine, to a great extent, fills this gap by providing an ideology of economic, social and political development through synthesizing orthodox Marxism, early Maoism, East Asian authoritarianism, Western market capitalism and other sources.

This effort culminates in what is officially called 'Deng Xiaoping's theory of socialism with Chinese characteristics,' which has at least five major themes: First, it gives primary weight to development. By neutralizing competing objectives, Deng has reduced the goal of socialism in China into that of economic development, and everything else should serve this purpose. Based on his perception of Marxism as a philosophy of economic primacy and of China's post-1949 political and economic upheavals as the failure of the Soviet and Maoist models, Deng advocates market-oriented economic reforms and an open-door policy. While enhancing the Party's legitimacy and establishing Deng's own authority in the Party, this developmental rationale has also become a nationalist call for united efforts of all Chinese to modernize the country and a rallying point for the increasingly diversified Chinese society.

Second, Deng's doctrine is based on pragmatism. Deng does not believe that answers to the questions posed by realities could be read mechanically out of Marxist writings or Western classics. He has a strong faith in experience and experiment over any 'grand theory.' As an advocate of the overarching ideology of 'seeking truth from facts,' Deng often reacts to situations as they arise and develops new ideas and modifies or abandons old ones. In the fifteen years of economic reform, many practical measures and pragmatically induced ideas, which were deemed unacceptable in the prevailing ideological conventions were gradually tolerated and justified by Deng and his followers and even incorporated into the official doctrine.

Third, Deng's doctrine stresses incremental and persistent change. Political consideration is predominant in conceiving incrementalism. By gradually reducing the apparent marginal benefit to reform opponents or sceptics, Deng's incrementalism has facilitated a relatively smooth reform by increasing the political cost of non-compliance and encouraging the gradual acceptance of pro-reform policies. Dengism perceives reform as something with priorities and the old structure as something with at least transitional values. Reforms are generally guided in such a way that they entail the lowest political, ideological and economic costs and produce the highest political, ideological and economic payoffs in order to ensure that reform policies enjoy broad support.

Fourth, Deng's doctrine is nationalistic. Like the previous generations of modernizers, drawing on China's past humiliating experience with the West, Deng deems it his mission to make the country strong and powerful so as to regain China's past glory. He constantly places China's development in an international context and endeavours to build an efficient and competitive economy, as well as an economic and political model as an alternative to Western capitalism and Soviet-style socialism. The nationalist theme is also to enable the Chinese population to develop a stronger identity with the central authority.

Fifth, Deng believes in an authoritarian hard state and an elitist party to push reforms. To Deng, the state should be hard enough to single-mindedly promote modernization and resist pressures from social groups and partisan interests, and the Party should be powerful and efficient enough to ensure the modernization of this large and populous country in peace and stability. By advocating the four cardinal principles, which have evolved and contained elements different from Stalinism, and by resisting Western liberal values, Deng has demonstrated perhaps more of the Confucian tradition of authoritarian governance than that of Stalinism.

But the reform process also suggests that Deng's doctrinal innovations, innovative as they are in many aspects, are still insufficient for China's dramatic economic and social changes. His developmentalism has created an imbalance between economic and social goals such as education and environment; his pragmatism does not provide a new coherent value system expected for a country whose cultural traditions favour moral standards; Nor does it offer an adequate solution to the increasingly wide-spread corruption; his incrementalism has lost some good opportunities for reforms; and his authoritarianism reveals China's institutional weakness, the lack of rule of law, and the necessity of certain political reforms.

However, compared with the late 1970s (when he returned to power without absolute authority, especially in the economic field), Deng is now able to provide an authoritative interpretation of Chinese style socialism based on relatively successful economic reform. Despite its lack of an elaborate intellectual structure and its evolving and formative nature, Dengism has dramatically expanded the official doctrine's elasticity and relevance to Chinese reality. Deng's doctrine has proved successful in decisively influencing China's economic and political developments. It has thus acquired a certain credibility as a guiding philosophy for China's economic reforms.

As discussed in this study, the past fifteen years have witnessed a number of cycles of policy oscillation. The disputed issues and their impact on economic reforms apparently suggest a pattern of repetition with variations and a curve indicating that the ideas in favour of market-oriented economic reform have gradually gained the upper-hand over the conservative discourse. The latter is clearly in decline, although the interactions between the various schools of thought are continuing. The conservatives lost to reformers largely due to their inability to offer inspiring ideas or credible policy alternatives, to their increasingly diminishing institutional support as a result of profound economic reforms and institutional changes, and to the very fact that people are simply fed up with and to a certain degree even 'immunized' against ideological onslaught. Consequently, each ideological campaign since 1978 has been followed by a more vigorous reform drive.

The ideological rise and fall over the past fifteen years also demonstrates several significant changes: doctrine is no longer regarded as a detailed prescription for immediate problems but instead as a broad-range of long-term goals for the future and as a way of theoretical thinking on the general trends of development; doctrine is no longer all-embracing, but parochial, less doctrinaire and more secularized and ready to be internalized; and the mainstream of the Party cares less about securing an active commitment to the official ideology from the people, as it is ready to accept and even encourage a substantial degree of indifference from the majority of the population. The Party does not allow any open challenge to the authority of its doctrine, which is still described as the 'development and enrichment of Marxism,' but the doctrine encourages people to become rich.

It is possible that in the post-Deng era, the basic thrust of Dengism may continue to exert a strong influence on China because (1) its credibility is largely based on China's relatively successful economic performance; (2) there is still no other credible model for a large country like China to move out of Stalinism; Russia's prolonged turbulence has only rendered Deng-style gradualism more appealing; and (3) Dengism has acquired a certain affinity with the Chinese political culture and the East Asian experience, which is still apparently attractive to Chinese, including many intellectuals. But efforts to interpret and transcend Dengism have also started in China. As the country further develops, new ideas and interests emerge, and a political structure to accommodate them must be found.

Deng's economic reforms have so far given the Chinese a tangible sense of achievement, a factor contributing to Deng's doctrinal appeal. But despite such success, China is undergoing tumultuous transformation and faced with many challenges. Continued political shifts and social dislocations will be inevitable. China's first non-governmental development report has forecasted six major areas of possible crises: increasing gaps between regions, unemployment, high inflation, corruption, rising crime and internal migration; and has advised the government to avert the simultaneous eruption of all six.[1] Dengism is apparently unable to cope with all these crises. Any mismanagement of them could be very costly for China's drive towards modernization.

Furthermore, the very breadth of Deng's doctrine and its lack of intellectual elaboration imply that there are still many areas of ambiguities and compromises and that there will be more confusion, debate, interpretation and transcendence in the post-Deng era. The post-Deng leadership has to further define Dengism or develop new ideas and policy alternatives when new situations rise, especially in times of crisis, when the authority of charismatic Deng has disappeared but his authoritarianism is still supposed to hold.

In a broader context of political culture and civilization, the Chinese experience of competing ideologies and economic reforms seems to suggest that Chinese reformers have been trying to bridge the gap between socialism and capitalism, the East and the West, Leninism and East Asian authoritarianism, and the Confucian heritage and certain Western values. Shortcomings, setbacks and even occasional crises notwithstanding, the Chinese ideological renovation and economic reform have gone a long way in transforming the Chinese economy and society, and China has developed a relatively effective way out of the centrally planned economy. As a huge, populous, non-Western and non-Christian country under the rule of a 'communist' party, China has experienced, similar in many ways to the East Asian NIEs, a distinctive cultural and political form of change and modernization with long-term implications for the world at large.

[1]Fudan Development Institute, *China Development Report, 1993*, Shanghai, Fudan Development Institute, 1994.

SELECTED BIBLIOGRAPHY

I Sources

A Official documents

Research Department, CPC Secretariat (ed.),
Jianchi Gaige Kaifang Gaohuo (Adhere to Reform, Opening and Reinvigorating the Economy – a Collection of Important Documents Since the Third Plenum), Beijing, People's Press, 1987.
Jianchi Sixiang Jiben Yuanze Fandui Zichanjieji Ziyouhua (Adhere to the Four Cardinal Principles and Oppose Bourgeois Liberalization – a Collection of Important Documents Since the Third Plenum), Beijing, People's Press, 1987.
Shierda Yilai Zhongyao Wenjian Xuanbian (Selected Important Documents since the 12th CPC National Congress), Beijing, People's Press, 1986.
Shisanda Yilai Zhongyao Wenjian Xuanbian (Selected Important Documents since the 13th CPC National Congress, 3 Vols.), Beijing, People's Press, 1991.
Zhongguo Gongchandang Zhangcheng (1982) (The Constitution of the Communist Party of China, 1982).
Zhonghua Renmin Gongheguo Xianfa (1982) (The Constitution of the People's Republic of China, 1982).

B Writings of Chinese leaders pertaining to reform and ideology

Chen Yun, *Chen Yun Tongzhi Wengao Xuanbian 1956–1962* (Selected Articles by Comrade Chen Yun, 1956–1962), Beijing, People's Press, 1980.
Deng Liqun, *Xiang Chenyun Tongzhi Xuexi Zuo Jingji Gongzuo* (Learning from Comrade Chen Yun in Doing Economic Work), Beijing, CPC Party School Press, 1981, (Internal Circulation).
——*Jiaqiang Makesizhuyi Lilun Xuexi* (Enhancing the study of Marxist theory), *Remin Ribao*, 21–3–1991.

Deng Xiaoping, *Fundamental Issues in Present-Day China*, Beijing, Foreign Languages Press, 1987.

——*Selected Works of Deng Xiaoping (1938–1965*), Beijing, Foreign Languages Press, 1992.

——*Selected Works of Deng Xiaoping (1975–1982*), Beijing, Foreign Languages Press, 1984.

——*Selected Works of Deng Xiaoping (1982–1993), Vol.III*, Beijing, Foreign Languages Press, 1994.

Hu Yaobang, Quanmian Kaichuang Shehuizhuyi Xiandaihua Jianshe De Xinjumian, (Creating a New Situation in Socialist Modernization), *Renmin Ribao*, 2–9–1982.

——*Makesizhuyi Weida Zhenli De Guangmang Zhaoyao Women Qianjin* (The Brilliance of the Great Truth of Marxism Guides Us Marching Forward), Beijing, People's Press, 1983.

Jiang Zemin, Aiguozhuyi He Woguo Zhishifenzi De Shiming (Patriotism and the Mission of the Chinese Intellectuals), *Guangming Ribao*, 22–4–1990.

——Qingzhu Zhongguogongchandang Dansheng Qishi Zhounian De Jianghua (Speech Marking the 70th anniversary of the CPC), *Renmin Ribao*, 2–7–1991.

——Jinyibu Xuexi He Fayang Lu Xun Jingshen (Further Studying and Displaying the Spirit of Lu Xun), *Renmin Ribao*, 25–9–1991.

——Zai Xuexi Deng Xiaoping Wenxuan Disanjuan Baogaohui Shang De Jianghua (Speech at the Symposium on Studying the Third Volume of 'Selected Works of Deng Xiaoping'), *Renmin Ribao*, 4–11–1993.

Li Peng, Tan Duiwai Guanxi He Guonei Xingshi (On China's Domestic Situation and External Relations), *Renmin Ribao*, 13–9–1991.

——*Bawu Jihua Gangyao Baogao* (Report on the Outline of the 8th Five-Year Plan), Beijing, People's Press, 1991.

——Zai Quanguo Qiye Gongzuo Huiyi Shangde Jianghua (Speech at the National Conference on the Work of Enterprises), *Renmin Ribao*, 13–2–1991.

Yang Shangkun, Jinian Xinhaigeming Bashi Zhounian De Jianghua (Speech Marking the 80th anniversary of the 1911 Revolution), *Renmin Ribao*, 9–10–1991.

Zhao Ziyang, Various Reports on the Work of the Government.

——Zhao Ziyang Yanhaidiqu Jingji Fazhan Zhanlue (Zhao Ziyang on Strategy of Coastal Economic Development), *Renmin Ribao*, 23–1–1988.

——Ba Xiangzhen Qiye Guanli Jizhi Yinru Guoying Qiye (Introducing the Managerial Mechanism of Township Enterprise into State Enterprise), *Renmin Ribao*, 22–8–1988.

——Report at the 13th CPC National Congress, *Beijing Review*, No.45, 9–15 November 1987.

——Huijian Yahang Daibiao De Jianghua (Talks with the Representatives of the Asian Bank). *Renmin Ribao*, 5–5–1989.

C Writings of Chinese dissidents

Fang Lizhi Liu Bingyan Wang Ruowang Yanlun Zhaibian (Selected Speeches of Fang Lizhi, Liu Bingyan and Wang Ruowang), Hong Kong, Shuguang Publishing House, 1988.

Documents of Dissent: Chinese Political Thought since Mao, Stanford, Calif., Hoover Institute Press, 1980.

D Unofficial and semi-official publications

Bartke, W. and Schier, P., *China's New Party Leadership: Biographies and Analysis of the 12th Central Committee of the CPC*, Armonk, N.Y.: M. E. Sharpe, Inc. 1985.

Chi Hsin, *The Case of the Gang of Four*, Hong Kong, Cosmos Books, 1977.

——*Teng Hsiao-ping: A Political Biography*, Hong Kong, Cosmos Books, 1978.

Department of Ideology and Theory (the China Youth Daily), Sulian Jubian Zhihou Zhongguo De Xianshi Yingdui Yu Zhanlue Xuanze (China's Realistic Response and Strategic Choices after the Dramatic Changes in the USSR), *China Spring*, January 1992.

Lieberthal, K. G. and Dickson, B., *A Research Guide to Central Party and Government Meetings in China*, Armonk, N.Y.: M. E. Sharpe, 1989.

Renmin Buhui Wangji (People Will Not Forget – Reports and documents concerning the 1989 Democracy Movements), Hong Kong, Press Association, 1989.

E Biographies and autobiographies

Chen Yun Yu Xinzhongguo Jingji Jianshe (Chen Yun and the Economic Construction in the New China), Beijing, Central Archives Press, 1991.

Liu Jintian, *Deng Xiaoping De Licheng* (Deng Xiaoping's Journey), Beijing, PLA Cultural Press, 1994.

Mao Mao, *Wode Fuqin Deng Xiaoping* (My Father Deng Xiaoping), Hong Kong, Joint Publishing (H.K.) Co. Ltd., 1993.

Ruan Ming, *Lishi Zhuanzhe Dianshang De Hu Yaobang* (Hu Yaobang at the Turning-Point of History), Hong Kong, Global Publishing Co. Inc.,1991.

Wang Ting, *Chairman Hua: Leader of the Chinese Communists*, London, C. Hurst, 1980.

Zhao Wei, *Zhao Ziyang Zhuan* (Biography of Zhao Ziyang), Hong Kong, Wenhua Jiaoyu Chuban Ltd., 1988.

Xu Jiatun, *Xu Jiatun Xianggang Huiyilu* (Memoir of Xu Jiatun on Hong Kong), Taibei, Lianhebao Ltd. 1993.

II Studies

A General studies pertaining to Chinese politics

Barnett, A. D., *Cadres, Bureaucracy, and Political Power in Communist China*, New York, Columbia University Press, 1967.

Chevrier, Y., *La Chine moderne*, Paris, Presses universitaires de France, 1983.

Chi Wen-shun, *Ideological Conflicts in Modern China: Democracy and Authoritarianism*, New Brunswick, N.J., Transaction Books, 1986.

China's Socialist Economy: An Outline History (1949–1984), Beijing: Beijing Review, 1986.

Cohen, L. J., *Communist System in Comparative Perspective*, New York, Anchor Books, 1974.

CPC Beijing Municipal Committee, *Jianchi Sixiang Jiben Yuanze Fandui Zichanjieji Ziyouhua Ganbu Duben* (Adhere to the Four Cardinal Principles and Oppose Bourgeois Liberalization – a Reader for Cadres), Beijing, Beijing Press, 1990.

Harding, H. Jr., *China's Second Revolution: Reform after Mao*, Washington, D.C., the Brookings Institute, 1987.

Hu Shen (ed.), *Zhongguo Gongchandang De Qishinian* (The 70 Years of the Chinese Communist Party), Beijing, CPC History Press, 1991.

Jin Yu (ed.), *Deng Xiaoping Sixiang Baoku* (Deng Xiaoping Thought Treasury, 2 Vols.), Beijing, Red Flag Press, 1992.

Kapur, H., *The End of an Isolation – China after Mao*, London, Sijthoff & Noordhoff, 1985.

Li Gucheng, *Zhonggong Dangzhengjun Jiegou* (The Party-Government-Military Structure of Communist China), Hong Kong, Ming Pao Press, 1990.

Li Zehou, *Zhongguo Jindai Sixiang Shilun* (Essays on History of China's Modern Political Thought), Beijing, People's Press, 1986.

——*Makesizhuyi Zai Zhongguo* (Marxism in China), Beijing, San Lian Press, 1988.

Lin Yusheng, *Zhongguo Chuantong de Chuangzaoxing Zhuanhua* (Creative Transformation of Chinese Tradition), Beijing, San Lian Press, 1988.

Nathan, A. J., *Chinese Democracy*, London, I. B. Tauris & Co. Ltd, 1986.

Nee, V., *State And Society in Contemporary China*, Ithaca, N.Y., Cornell University Press, 1983.

Pye, L. W., *Political Culture and Political Development*, Princeton, Princeton University Press, 1969.

——*The Mandarin and the Cadre: China's Political Culture*, Ann Arbor, University of Michigan, 1988.

Research Bureau, Chinese Academy of Social Sciences, *Zhongguo Gongchandang Yu Zhongguo Shehuikexue* (The Chinese Communist Party and China's Social Sciences), Beijing, Shehui Kexue Wenxian Press, 1991.

Riskin C., *China's Political Economy – The Quest for Development since 1949*, Oxford, Oxford University Press, 1988.

Schram, S. (ed.), *Authority, Participation and Cultural Change in China*, Cambridge, Cambridge University Press, 1973.

——*The Scope of State Power in China*, London, SOAS, University of London and the Chinese University Press, 1985.

——*Ideology and Policy in China since the Third Plenum, 1978–1984*, (Research Notes and Studies No.6), London, SOAS, University of London, 1984.

Schurmann, F., *Ideology and Organization in Communist China*, Berkeley, University of California Press, 1968.

Schwartz, B. I., *Communism and China: Ideology in Flux*, Cambridge, Mass., Harvard University Press, 1968.

Spence, J. D., *The Gate of Heavenly Peace: the Chinese and their Revolution*, London, Faber and Faber, 1982.

——*The Search for Modern China*, London, Hutchinson, 1990.

Walder, A. G., *Communist Neo-Traditionalism – Work and Authority in Chinese Industry*, Berkeley, University of California Press, 1988.

Wilson, D., *Mao Tse-tung in the Scale of History*, Cambridge, Cambridge University Press, 1977.

Wu Jie, *Deng Xiaoping Sixiang Lun* (On Deng Xiaoping's Thought), Taiyuan, Shanxi People's Press, 1992.

Xiang Meiqing and Wang Furu, *Deng Xiaoping Jianshe You Zhongguo Tese Shehuizhuyi Lilun Yanjiu* (Study on Deng Xiaoping's Theory of Building Socialism with Chinese Characteristics), Shenyang, Liaoning People's Press, 1992.

Yu Guangyuan, *China's Socialist Modernization*, Beijing, Foreign Languages Press, 1984.

B General studies pertaining to ideology

Almond, A. G. & Powell, Jr. B. (ed.), *Comparative Politics Today – A World View*, Boston, Little, Brown and Company, 1984.

Arendt, H., *The Origins of Totalitarianism*, London, George Allen & Unwin Ltd., 1967.

Brzezinski, Z., *Ideology and Power in Soviet Politics*, Cambridge, Mass., Harvard University Press, 1975.

——*Out of Control*, New York, Charles Scribner's Sons, 1992.

Chen Yixin, *Zouxiang Xiandaihua Zhilu* (Road to Modernization), Chendu, Sichuan People's Press, 1987.

Cranston, M. and Mair, P. (eds.), *Ideology and Politics/Ideologie et Politique*, Firenze,Italy, European University Institute, 1980.

De Kadt, E. and Williams, G. (eds.), *Sociology and Development*, Tavistock Publications, 1972.

Deutsch, C. W., *The Nerves of Government: Models of Political Communication and Control*, New York, Free Press of Glenol, 1963.

Djilas, M., *The New Class: an Analysis of the Communist System*, New York, Frederick A. Praeger, 1957.

Drucker, H. M., *The Political Use of Ideology*, London, Macmillan Press Ltd., 1974.

Eagleton, T., *Ideology – an Introduction*, London, Verso, 1991.
Hayek, F. A., *The Road to Serfdom*, London, Routledge & Kegan Paul, 1976.
Huang Shunji and Li Qinzhen, *Daganggan – Zhenhan Shijie De Xinjishu Geming* (Big Lever – the New Technological Revolution that is Shaking the World), Jinan, Shandong University Press, 1986.
Huntington, S. P., *Authoritarian Politics in Modern Society*, New York, Basic Books, Inc., 1970.
——*Political Order in Changing Societies*, New Haven, Yale University Press, 1968.
Konrad, G. and Szelenyi, Y., *The Intellectuals on the Road to Class Power*, Brighton: Harvester Press, 1979.
Li Shenping, *Zhengzhi Tizhi Gaige De Lilun Yu Shijian* (Theory and Practice of Political Restructuring), Beijing, Guangming Daily Press, 1989.
Liu Jun and Li Lin, *Xinquanweizhuyi* (Neo-Authoritarianism – Dispute over the Programme of Reform), Beijing, Jingji Xueyuan Publishing House, 1989.
Liu Xiaobo, *Xuanze De Pipan* (Selective Criticism – Dialogue with Li Zehou), Shanghai, People's Press, 1988.
Mannheim, K., *Ideology and Utopia*, New York, Harcourt, Brace and World, 1955.
Moore, B., *Soviet Politics – the Dilemma of Power, the Role of Ideas in Social Change*, Cambridge, Mass., Harvard University Press, 1950.
Naisbitt, J., *Megatrends – Ten New Directions Transforming Our Lives*, New York, Warner Books., inc., 1982.
Parsons, T., *The Social System*, New York, The Free Press, 1964.
Seliger, M., *Ideology and Politics*, New York, The Free Press, 1976.
Wang Huning, *Bijiao Zhengzhi Fenxi* (Comparative Political Analysis), Shanghai, People's Press, 1987.
Weber, M., *On Charisma and Institution Building*, Chicago, the University of Chicago Press, 1968.
——*Economy and Society*, Berkeley, University of California Press, 1969.
Yan Jiaqi, *Quanli Yu Zhenli* (Power and Truth), Beijing, Guangming Daily Press, 1987.

C Studies pertaining to China's economic and political reforms

(In Chinese)

Board of Editors, China Economics Yearbook, *Jingji Gaige Xinshiwu* (New Things in Economic Reform), Beijing, Economic Management Press, 1985.
Chi Fulin, *Deng Xiaoping Zhengzhi Tizhi Gaige Sixiang Yanjiu* (On Deng

Xiaoping's Thinking of Political Restructuring), Beijing, Chunqiu Press, 1987.

Chen Hanwen, *Jingzheng Zhong De Hezuo* (Cooperation in Competition), Chendu, Sichuan People's Press, 1987.

Fudan Development Institute, *China Development Report (1993)*, Shanghai, Fudan Development Institute, 1994.

Gao Shangquan, *Jiunian Lai De Zhongguo Jingji Tizi Gaige* (Nine Years' Reform of China's Economic System), Beijing, People's Press, 1987.

Zhongguo Fazhan Yu Gaige (China: Development and Reform), Beijing, CPC Archives Press, 1987.

Zhongguo De Jingji Tizhi Gaige (China's Economic System Reform), Beijing, People's Press, 1991.

Jiang Hong (ed.), *Zhongguo De Xiandaihua: Gaige Yu Fazhan Zhanlue* (China's Modernization: Reform and Development Strategy), Beijing, China Economics Press, 1986.

Jiang Yiwei, *Jingji Tizhi Gaige Yu Shichang Kaituo* (Economic Restructuring and Market Exploration), Beijing, Economic Management Press, 1986.

Leng Rong, *Weile Shixian Zhonghua Minzu De Xiongxin Zhuangzhi* (To Realize the Lofty Aspirations of the Chinese Nation), Beijing, Central Archives Press, 1992.

Li Ming, *Zhongguo De Weiji Yu Sikao* (Chinese Crises and Reflections), Tianjin, People's Press, 1989.

Li Yining, *Zhongguo Gaige De Silu* (Ideas on China's Economic Reform), Beijing, Zhongguo Zhanwang Press, 1989.

Li Yongchun, *Zhengzhi Gaige Dashiji* (Annals of Political Reform), Beijing, Chunqiu Press, 1987.

Liu Guoguang (ed.), *Zhongguo Shehuizhuyi Jingji De Gaige Kaifang He Fazhan* (The Reform, Opening and Development of China's Socialist Economy), Beijing, Jingji Guanli Press, 1987.

Liu Zhongxiu (ed.), *Baiwei Xuezhe Dui Shenzhen de Sikao* (Reflections on Shenzhen by One Hundred Scholars), Shenzhen, Haitian Publishing House, 1991.

Xu Muqiao, *Zhongguo Shehuizhuyi Jingji Wenti Yanjiu* (On the Question of Chinese Socialist Economy), Beijing, People's Press, 1980.

Xu Xin, *Zhongguo Jingji Gaige De Tansuo* (Probing into China's Economic Reform), Hong Kong, Kaituo Publishing House, 1987.

Wang Huaining (ed.), *2000 Nian Zhongguo De Guoji Huanjing* (China's External Environment in the Year 2000), Beijing, China Social Sciences Press, 1987.

Wei Xinhua, *Jingji Tizhi Gaige Ruogan Lilun Wenti Tantao* (Explorations on Several Theoretical Questions Relating to Economic Restructuring), Beijing, China Economics Press, 1988.

Wu Jincai, *Zhongguo Chensilu* (Reflections on China 1979–1992) Chendu, Sichuan People's Press, 1992.

Wu Jinglian, *Jihua Jingji Haishi Shichang Jingji* (Planned Economy or Market Economy), Beijing, Chinese Economics Press, 1993.

Yuan Shang and Han Zu, *Deng Xiaoping Nanxun Hou De Zhongguo*

(China after Deng Xiaoping's South Inspection Tour), Beijing, Gaige Press, 1992.

Zhou Ming and Liu Yun (eds.), *Zhongguo Dangdai Shehui Wenti Jishi* (Reports on China's Present-day Social Problems), Beijing, Guangming Daily Press, 1989.

(In English)

Barnett, A. D. and Clough, R. N. (eds.), *Modernizing China – Post-Mao Reform and Development*, Boulder, Westview Press, 1986.

Baum, R. (ed.), *Reform and Reactions in Post-Mao China – the Road to Tiananmen,* New York, Rontledge 1991.

Brugger, B. (ed.), *Chinese Marxism in Flux 1978–1984*, London, Croom Helm, 1985.

——*Chinese Marxism in Post-Mao Era*, Stanford, Stanford University Press, 1990.

Crane, G., *The Political Economy of China's Special Economic Zones*, Armonk, M. E. Sharpe, Inc., 1990.

Goldman M. (ed.), *China's Intellectuals and the State: in Search of a New Relationship*, Cambridge, Mass., Council on East Asian Studies, Harvard University, 1987.

Hamrin, C. L., *China and the Challenge of the Future: Changing Political Pattern*, Boulder, San Francisco, 1990.

Harding, H., *China's Second Revolution: Reform after Mao*, Washington D.C., the Brookings Institute, 1987.

Hsu, R., *Economic Theories in China 1979–1988*, Cambridge, Cambridge University Press, 1991.

Hua Sheng, Zhang Xuejun and Luo Xiaopeng, *China: From Revolution to Reform*, London, Macmillan Press Ltd., 1993.

Laaksonen, O., *Management in China during and after Mao in Enterprises, Government and Party,* New York, Walter de Gruyter, 1989.

Ma Hong (ed.), *Modern China's Economy and Management*, Beijing, Foreign Languages Press, 1990.

Moody, P. R., *Chinese Politics after Mao: Development and Liberalization (1976–1983)*, New York, Praeger, 1984.

Nolan, P. and Dong Fureng (eds.), *The Chinese Economy and its Future: Achievements and Problems,* Cambridge, Polity Press, 1990.

Riskin, C., *China's Political Economy – the Quest for Development since 1949*, New York, Oxford University Press, 1988.

Segal G. (ed.), *Chinese Politics and Foreign Policy Reform*, London, Kegan Paul International for the Royal Institute of International Affairs, 1990.

Stavis, B., *China's Political Reforms: An Interim Report*, New York, Praeger, 1988.

Shirk, S., *The Political Logic of Economic Reform in China*, Berkeley, University of California Press, 1993.

Teiwes, F., *Leadership, Legitimacy, and Conflict in China: from a Charismatic Mao to the Politics of Succession*, London, Macmillan Press Ltd., 1984.

Vogel, E. F., *One Step Ahead in China – Guangdong under Reform*, Cambridge, Mass., Harvard University Press, 1989.

Xue Muqiao (ed.), *Almanac of China's Economy*, Cambridge, Mass., Ballinger Publishing, 1982.

Yu Guangyuan, *China's Socialist Modernization*, Beijing, Foreign Languages Press, 1984.

D Articles

(In Chinese)

Chen Yizi, Zhengzhi Tizhi Gaige Shi Jingji Tizhi Gaige De Baozheng (Political Restructuring is the Guarantee of Economic Restructuring), *World Economic Herald*, 13–7–1987.

Fang Sheng, Duiwai Kaifang He Liyong Zibenzhuyi (Opening to the Outside World and Making Use of Capitalism), *Renmin Ribao*, 23–2–92.

Gao Di, Ruhe Kandai Zhongguo De Qiong (How to Perceive China's Poverty), *Renmin Ribao*, 5–1–1990.

Gao Lu, Shehuizhuyi Shichang Jingji Tifa Chutai Shimo (The Origin of the Wording 'Socialist Market Economy'), *Jingji Ribao*, 14–11–1992.

He Ping and Zhao Lanyin, Jianding Buyi Zou Ziji De Lu (Take Our Own Road Firmly), *Renmin Ribao*, 22–6–93.

Hu Jintao, Jinyibu Jiaqiang Jianshe You Zhongguo Tese De Shehui Zhuyi Lilun De Xuexi Yianjiu He Xuanchuan (Further Strengthen the Study, Research and Publicity of the Theory of Building Socialism with Chinese Characteristics), *Renmin Ribao*, 22–12–1994.

Hua Sheng, Zhang Xuejun and Luo Xiaopeng, Zhongguo Gaige Shinian: Huigu Sikao Zhanwang, (China's Decade of Reform: Looking Back, Reflections and Prospect), *Jingji Yanjiu* (Economic Research), Sept. No. 9, 1988.

Huang Puping, Gaige Kaifang Yaoyou Xinsilu, (Reform and Opening Up Requires New Ideas), *Jiefang Ribao*, 2–3–1991.

Red Flag Editor, Jigou Gaige Shi Yichang Geming (Administrative Reform is a Revolution), *Red Flag*, No. 6 1982.

Ren Zhongyi, Guanyu Ganbu zhidu de Gaige (On the Reform of the Cadre System), *Renmin Ribao*, 10–6–1983.

Shen Tongming, Dui Zhengzhi Tizhi Gaige De Yixie Kanfa (Views on the Reform of Political System), *Zhengzhi Yu Falu* (Politics and Law), No. 5, 1986.

Song Ze and Fang Hanting, Shenhua Gaige he Gaige de Shenceng Zhangai (Deepening Reform and Overcoming Entrenched Obstacles), *Zhongguo Jingji Wenti* (China's Economic Problems), No. 3, 1988.

Su Xiaokang, Wang Luxiang, Zhang Gang, Yuan Zhiming, Xie Xuanjun, Heshang (River Elegy), *Xinhua Wenzhai* (Xinhua Abstracts), No. 9, 1988.

Sun Dinglong and Li Shencai, Deng Xiaoping Jiefang Sixiang De Lilun

Chutan (Initial Study on Deng Xiaoping's Concept of 'Emancipating the Mind'), *Kexue Shehuizhuyi* (Scientific Socialism), No. 1, 1992.

Tang Daiwang, Jigou Gaige Ying Cong Queding Zhineng Rushou (Institutional Reform Should Start with Defining the Functions of the Institutions), *Renmin Ribao*, 3–1–1986.

Wang Huning, Jingji Xingwei Yu Zhengzhi Tizhi Gaige (Economic Behaviour and the Reform of the Political System), *Wenhui Bao*, 8–8–1986.

Wu Jinglian, Lun Kongzhi Xuqiu He Gaishan Gongji (On Controling Demand and Improving Supply), *Renmin Ribao*, 10–10–1986.

——Yingdang Queli Shehuizhuyi Shichang Jingji De Tifa (It is Necessary to Establish the Concept of 'Socialist Market Economy'), *Jingji Ribao*, 4–8–1992.

Wu Shuqing, Gaige Kaifang Bixu Jianchi Shehuizhuyi Fangxiang (Reform and Opening Up must Adhere to the Socialist Orientation), *Renmin Ribao*, 17–11–1989.

Xu Chongde, Shilun Woguo Zhengquan Xingzhi De Zhuanbian (On the Change of the Nature of China's Political Power), *Minzhu Yu Fazhi* (Democracy and Law), No. 11, 1981.

Xue Bingwu, Zhengzhi Tizhi Gaige Shi Jingji Tizhi Gaige de Baozheng (Political Reform is the Guarantee of Economic Reform), *Guangming Ribao*, 30–6–1986.

Yan Jiaqi, Tan Zhongguo Zhengzhi Tizhi Gaige (Talk on China's Political System Reform), *Guangming Ribao*, 30–6–1986.

Yu Guangyuan, Jiaqiang dui Zhengfu Jigou Gaige De Yanjiu (Strengthening the Research in the Reform of Government Institutions), *Guangming Ribao*, 28–2–1983.

Zhao Dongwan, Zhao Dongwan Buzhang Tan Renshizhidu De Gaige (Minister Zhao Dongwan on the Reform of Personnel System), *Xingzheng Yu Renshi* (Administration and Personnel), No. 1, 1986.

Zhen Shiping, Lun Zhongguo Zhengzhi Tizhi Jichu De Gaige (On the Reform of the Basis of Chinese Political System), *Zhengzhixue Yanjiu* (Research in Political Science), No. 1, 1986.

Zhou Longbin, Ping Siyouhua Sichao (Comment on the Ideological Trend of Privatization), *Renmin Ribao*, 4–9–1989.

(In English or French)

Amako, S., China's Reform and Open-Door Policies: the Pace Picks Up, *Japanese Review of International Affairs*, Vol. 6, No. 2, Summer 1992.

Burton, C., China's Post-Mao Transition: the Role of the Party and Ideology in the 'New Period,' *Pacific Affairs* 60(3) Fall 1987.

Canter, P., Changing Patterns of Ownership Rights in the PRC, A Legal and Economic Analysis in the Context of Economic Reforms and Social Conditions, *Vanderbilt Journal of Transnational Law*, 23(3), 1990.

Chamberlain, H. B., Party-Management Relations in Chinese Industries: Some Political Dimensions of Economic Reform, *China Quarterly*, No. 112, Dec. 1987.

Deliusin, L. P., Reforms in China: Problems and Prospects, *Asian Survey*, 28(11), Nov., 1988.

Dickson, B., Conflicts and Non-compliance in Chinese Politics: Party Rectification, 1983–87, *Pacific Affairs*, Vol. 63, No. 2, Summer 1990.

Dittmer, L., The 12th Congress of the Communist Party of China, *China Quarterly*, No. 89, March 1983.

Domenach, J.-L., Chine: la crise la plus longue, *Politique internationale*, No 49, automne 1990.

Dong Fureng, Socialist Countries Diversify Ownership, *Beijing Review*, 5 Oct. 1987.

Etienne, G., 40 ans apres: regards sur la voie chinoise et sur la voie indienne, *Histoires de development*, No. 10, Juillet 1990.

Fu Fenggui, Injecting Vigour and Flexibility into Public Enterprises and Invigorating the Chinese Economy, *Public Enterprises*, 7(2) Feb. 1987.

Galeotti, G. and Breton, A., An Economic Theory of Political Parties, *Kyklos*, Vol.39, 1986.

Gold, T., Just in Time – China Battles Spiritual Pollution on the Eve of 1984, *Asian Survey*, No. 9, 1984.

Goldman, M. I., Soviet and Chinese Economic Reform, *Foreign Affairs*, 66(3), 1988.

Hsu, R. C., Changing Conceptions of the Socialist Enterprises in China, 1979–1988, *Modern China*, 15(4), Oct. 1989.

Ishida, H., What Chinese Socialism is Today: Forty Years' Economic Construction, *Review of Economic and Business*, 18(1), Sept. 1989.

Ishihara, K., Inflation and Economic Reform in China, *Developing Economies*, 28(2) June 1990.

Kamath, S. J., Foreign Direct Investment in a Centrally Planned Developing Economy: the Chinese Case, *Economic Development and Cultural Change*, 39(1), Oct. 1990.

Kuo, W. H., Economic Reforms and Urban Development in China, *Pacific Affairs*, 62(2), Summer 1989.

Lee, Keun and Lee, Yong Hong, States, Markets and Economic Development in East Asian Capitalism and Socialism, *Development Policy Review*, Vol. 10, 1992.

Ling L. H. M., Intellectual Responses to China's Economic Reform, *Asian Review*, 27(5), May 1988.

Liu Hongru, Developments in the Reform of China's Banking and Financial Systems, *Journal of International Law*, 2(29), Fall 1988.

Ma Ding, Ten Major Changes in China's Study of Economics, *Beijing Review*, No. 49, 1985.

Maxwell, N. and McFarlane, B., China's Changed Road to Development, *World Development*, 11(8), Aug. 1983. Special Issue.

Naughton, B., Deng Xiaoping: the Economist, *China Quarterly*, No. 135, September 1993.

Prybyla, J. S., China's Economic Experiment: Back from the Market?, *Problems of Communism*, 38(1), Jan./Feb. 1989.

Pye, Lucian, On Chinese Pragmatism, *China Quarterly*, No. 106, June 1986.

Saich, Tony, The Fourteenth Party Congress: A Programme for Authoritarian Rule, *China Quarterly,* No. 132, December 1992.

Shi Hong, China's Political Development after Tiananmen: Tranquil by Default, *Asian Survey,* 30(12), Dec. 1990.

Shi Tianjian, The Democratic Movement in China in 1989: Dynamics and Failure, *Asian Survey,* 30(12), Dec. 1990.

Schram, S. R., China after the 13th Congress, *China Quarterly,* No. 114, June 1988.

Schull, J., What is Ideology? Theoretical Problems and Lessons from Soviet-Type Societies, *Political Studies,* (1992) XI.

Seymour, J. D., China's Satellite Parties Today, *Asian Survey,* 26(9), Sept. 1986.

Sha, Y., The Role of China's Managing Directors in the Current Economic Reform, *International Labour Review,* 126(6), Nov./Dec. 1987.

Skinner, Q., Meaning and Understanding in the History of Ideas, *History and Theory,* 8 (1969).

——Convention and the Understanding of Speech Acts, *Philosophical Quarterly,* 20 (1970).

Swaine, M. D., China Faces the 1990s: A System in Crisis, *Problems of Communism,* 39(3), May/June 1990.

Swamy, S., The Response to Economic Challenge: a Comparative Economic History of China and India, 1870–1952, *Quarterly Journal of Economics,* February 1979.

Thoma, G. S. A., Problems of Collective Enterprises in the PRC, *Public Enterprises,* 8(3), Sept. 1988.

Watson, A., China's Open-Door Policy in Historical Perspective, *Australian Outlook,* 40(2), Aug. 1986.

White, G., Political Aspects of Rural Economic Reform in China, *IDS Bulletin,* 18(3), July 1987.

——The Impact of Economic Reforms in the Chinese Countryside: Towards the Politics of Social Capitalism?, *Modern China,* 13(4), Oct. 1987.

——The Politics of Economic Reform in Chinese Industry: the Introduction of the Labour Contract System, *China Quarterly,* No. 111, Sept. 1987.

Zhang, Wei-Wei, Dengist China after Deng? Not Certain but Likely, *International Herald Tribune,* 9 Dec. 1994.

Zhou Xiaochuan Why China Refuses All-out Privatization?, *Chinese Economic Review,* Vol. 4, No. 1, 1993.

INDEX